# Photorealistic Materials and Textures in Blender Cycles

Create impressive production-ready projects using one of the most powerful rendering engines

**Arijan Belec**

BIRMINGHAM—MUMBAI

# Photorealistic Materials and Textures in Blender Cycles

**Group Product Manager**: Rohit Rajkumar
**Publishing Product Manager**: Kaustubh Manglurkar
**Book Project Manager**: Aishwarya Mohan
**Executive Editor**: David Sugarman
**Technical Editor**: Simran Ali
**Copy Editor**: Safis Editing
**Proofreader**: Safis Editing
**Indexer**: Hemangini Bari
**Production Designer**: Prafulla Nikalje
**Marketing Coordinators**: Namita Velgekar and Nivedita Singh

First edition published: January 2011
Second edition: June 2013
Third edition: February 2015
Fourth edition: November 2023

Production reference: 1061023

Published by Packt Publishing Ltd.
Grosvenor House
11 St Paul's Square
Birmingham
B3 1RB

ISBN 978-1-80512-963-9

www.packtpub.com

*To the almighty, all-seeing, all-knowing, for giving me the gift of passion and sight.*

*– Arijan Belec*

# Contributors

## About the author

**Arijan Belec** is a professional automotive interior designer and 3D modeling teacher with over a decade of experience in various areas of Blender 3D. He has published multiple books and courses, and over 100 online tutorials on his fast-growing YouTube channel dedicated to teaching 3D design. Arijan specializes in modeling, texturing, rendering, and post-processing highly detailed and realistic artwork for digital marketing and product visualization purposes. Having worked with high-end clients on custom, top-quality luxury designs, he is laser-focused on achieving the highest quality models, materials, and renders without sacrificing one skill to strengthen another.

# About the reviewers

**Aditya Pathak** gained a BTech in CSIT from Symbiosis, graduating in 2021. Now, with 5 years of experience at organizations such as Binance, Dell, Byjus, Evofox, and Anivive, his engagements have spanned various sectors, from gaming and hardware to pharma and entertainment, helping him gain a broad perspective on technology.

Aditya's skills include 3D modeling, animation, motion graphics, and commercials. He has focused on ensuring that technical know-how aligns with the specific needs and narratives of his clients.

**Neil Lasrado**, also known online as Rendergene, has a mechanical engineering foundation. Driven by mathematics, physics, and design, Neil sculpts 3D digital landscapes via Blender, catching eyes such as Xoogler, FalconX, Motionvillee, Fruitbowl, and JBL.

Pursuing an MA at MMU, Neil is inspired by Unreal Engine's capabilities. A dancer, gamer, and tech enthusiast, Neil is a multidimensional creative.

**Wilson Guillaume** is a husband and father of four. Originally from the state of Florida in the United States, he has been a 3D/digital artist for the last 20 years and is co-founder of G7 Comics. His career began as a 3D artist and one of his great achievements was his contribution to the major motion picture *Mr. Magorium's Wonder Emporium*. Wilson is one of the creators of *Dark Child*, a supernatural graphic novel thriller based on Haitian folklore. He is currently working on a couple of major animated projects while enjoying time as a family man.

# Table of Contents

# 6

## Creating Bumpy Surfaces with Displacement Maps     159

# Part 3: UV Mapping and Texture Painting

# 7

## UV-Unwrapping 3D Models for Texturing     185

# 8

## Baking Ambient Occlusion Maps     203

# 9

## Introducing Texture Painting     229

## 10

### Creating Photorealistic Textures on a 3D Model    259

# Part 4: Lighting and Rendering

## 11

### Lighting a Scene in Cycles    287

## 12

### Creating Photorealistic Environments with HDRIs    309

## 13

### Preparing the Camera for Rendering    325

# Preface

*Photorealistic Materials and Textures in Blender Cycles* is a guide to creating impressive, high-quality materials, textures, and renders for 3D models and scenes in Blender. This book begins by introducing the fundamental principles behind Blender's material mechanics, before diving further into more advanced methods of texturing. To achieve the most impressive results, this book also focuses on methods and techniques for highly realistic lighting and rendering.

## Who this book is for

This book will benefit beginner, intermediate, and advanced 3D artists from various areas of 3D design who are looking to deepen their understanding of the concepts and methods used by professionals to create top-quality materials, textures, and renders.

*Photorealistic Materials and Textures in Blender Cycles* will be useful for game developers, architectural visualizers, product designers, interior designers, advertisement producers, digital content creators, and any other professions that require the production of high-quality, aesthetically pleasing, realistic 3D objects.

## What this book covers

*Chapter 1, Creating Materials in Blender*, introduces the fundamental principles of materials and material properties in Blender.

*Chapter 2, Introducing Material Nodes*, introduces material nodes, a Blender mechanism used for controlling and tweaking materials and material properties.

*Chapter 3, Mapping Images with Nodes*, covers how to display saved images and textures on 3D models using a special set of material nodes.

*Chapter 4, Achieving Realism with Texture Maps*, explains the functions of special images called texture maps, used for adding details and features to materials to make them more realistic.

*Chapter 5, Generating Texture Maps with Cycles*, discusses the creation of custom texture maps, allowing us to take any image texture and add higher levels of realism and detail to it.

*Chapter 6, Creating Bumpy Surfaces with Displacement Maps*, covers harnessing special texture maps to control the geometry of a 3D model and create unique surface details and imperfections.

*Chapter 7, UV-Unwrapping 3D Models for Texturing*, details unwrapping 3D models to allow for more precise texture mapping and creating custom textures.

*Chapter 8, Baking Ambient Occlusion Maps*, explores using the lighting from a scene to create special images to shade 3D models and make them appear more realistic.

*Chapter 9, Introducing Texture Painting*, covers how to create custom texture details with Blender's special texture painting tools.

*Chapter 10, Creating Photorealistic Textures on a 3D Model*, applies the learned texturing tools and techniques by completing a 3D model with realistic materials and textures.

*Chapter 11, Lighting a Scene in Cycles*, introduces the various forms of lighting in Blender and covers how to use them to create beautiful lighting environments for our scenes.

*Chapter 12, Creating Photorealistic Environments with HDRIs*, explores 360-degree images of real-life environments to create custom world backgrounds and photorealistic lighting and reflections for our 3D projects.

*Chapter 13, Preparing the Camera for Rendering*, explores camera settings and properties and covers how to use them to create perfect angles for our renders.

*Chapter 14, Rendering with Cycles*, covers controlling and optimizing render properties to create the highest quality render results.

## To get the most out of this book

To get the most out of this book, it is best to have some basic previous knowledge of the Blender interface, as well as basic modeling skills. It is assumed that the reader has a beginner-level grasp of fundamental skills, such as orientating in the 3D world, navigating through property menus, and using basic modeling tools, including grabbing, rotation, and scaling.

| Software covered in the book | Operating system requirements |
| --- | --- |
| Blender 3D 3.4 | Windows, macOS, or Linux |
| GIMP | |

**If you are using the digital version of this book, we advise you to type the code yourself or access the code from the book's GitHub repository (a link is available in the next section). Doing so will help you avoid any potential errors related to the copying and pasting of code.**

If you do not have a grasp of the basic functions of Blender required to follow this book, you can easily learn about these by watching any free, online, beginner Blender tutorials.

# Download the exercise files

You can download the exercise files for this book at `https://packt.link/mA1OU`

# Conventions used

There are a number of text conventions used throughout this book.

`Code in text`: Indicates code words in text, database table names, folder names, filenames, file extensions, pathnames, dummy URLs, user input, and Twitter handles. Here is an example: "Ensure that you have access to the `Chapter 2 Camo Texture.png` file from the resource download."

**Bold**: Indicates a new term, an important word, or words that you see onscreen. For instance, words in menus or dialog boxes appear in **bold**. Here is an example: "Click on the plus button in the **Material Properties** tab to add a new material slot."

> **Tips or important notes**
> Appear like this.

# Get in touch

Feedback from our readers is always welcome.

**General feedback**: If you have questions about any aspect of this book, email us at `customercare@packtpub.com` and mention the book title in the subject of your message.

**Errata**: Although we have taken every care to ensure the accuracy of our content, mistakes do happen. If you have found a mistake in this book, we would be grateful if you would report this to us. Please visit `www.packtpub.com/support/errata` and fill in the form.

**Piracy**: If you come across any illegal copies of our works in any form on the internet, we would be grateful if you would provide us with the location address or website name. Please contact us at `copyright@packt.com` with a link to the material.

**If you are interested in becoming an author**: If there is a topic that you have expertise in and you are interested in either writing or contributing to a book, please visit `authors.packtpub.com`.

## Share Your Thoughts

Once you've read *Photorealistic Materials and Textures in Blender Cycles*, we'd love to hear your thoughts! Scan the QR code below to go straight to the Amazon review page for this book and share your feedback.

https://packt.link/r/1-805-12963-5

Your review is important to us and the tech community and will help us make sure we're delivering excellent quality content.

# Download a free PDF copy of this book

Thanks for purchasing this book!

Do you like to read on the go but are unable to carry your print books everywhere? Is your eBook purchase not compatible with the device of your choice?

Don't worry, now with every Packt book you get a DRM-free PDF version of that book at no cost.

Read anywhere, any place, on any device. Search, copy, and paste code from your favorite technical books directly into your application.

The perks don't stop there, you can get exclusive access to discounts, newsletters, and great free content in your inbox daily

Follow these simple steps to get the benefits:

1.  Scan the QR code or visit the link below

https://packt.link/free-ebook/9781805129639

2.  Submit your proof of purchase
3.  That's it! We'll send your free PDF and other benefits to your email directly

# Part 1: Materials in Cycles

*Part 1* focuses on introducing the central principles of creating materials in Blender by teaching the basics of how to create simple materials, how material nodes work to control material properties, and how to apply textures to 3D objects.

This part has the following chapters:

- *Chapter 1, Creating Materials in Blender*
- *Chapter 2, Introducing Material Nodes*
- *Chapter 3, Mapping Images with Nodes*

# 1

# Creating Materials in Blender

Generating high-quality materials and textures is a big and important step in any area of 3D design. With the right skills, tools, and techniques, you can turn your untextured 3D models into beautiful photorealistic scenes and artwork. That is exactly what we are aiming for in this book. Therefore, we will study the underlying mechanics of materials and textures in Blender, and learn how to produce the highest quality results, to teach you how to finish and present your work in the most attractive way possible.

In this chapter, we will learn to create simple materials in Blender. We will first prepare our workspace, optimize it for a material creation workflow, and introduce the interface, before creating our first materials. We will learn to control key material properties including base color, roughness, and specularity, among others.

We will cover the following topics in this chapter:

- Preparing the Shading workspace
- Creating materials
- Adding multiple materials to an object
- Tweaking material properties

## Technical requirements

In this book, we will be using *Blender 3.4.1*. However, the same principles and methods will most likely be applicable in earlier versions of Blender.

The latest version of Blender can be downloaded at the following link:

`https://www.blender.org/download/`

Blender's official website states the following minimum hardware requirements:

- 64-bit quadcore CPU with SSE2 support
- 8 GB RAM

- Full HD display

- Mouse, trackpad, or pen and tablet

- Graphics card with 4 GB RAM and OpenGL 4.3 support

- `Less than 10-year-old system and OS`

These specifications are defined by the official Blender website as the minimal requirements, but higher specifications will obviously lead to better performance.

The prepared resources can be found in the `Chapter01` folder within the book's downloadable resources folder, available here: `https://packt.link/mA1OU`.

## Preparing the Shading workspace

Blender has multiple **workspaces**. A workspace is simply a way of arranging the windows and tools in Blender to make them more convenient for a particular job. For example, the Modeling workspace makes available the most important modeling tools and windows. The **Shading workspace** will do the same but for shading and material creation. We will work in the Shading workspace because it provides us with all the tools we need for now.

By default, Blender displays four separate windows in the workspace, as indicated in *Figure 1.1*.

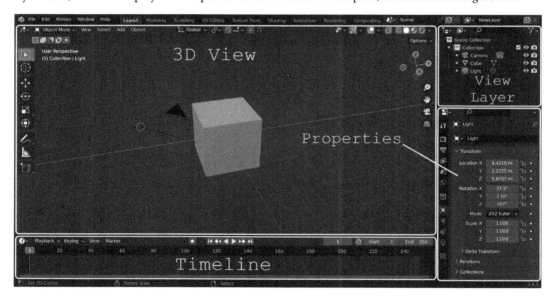

Figure 1.1 – Default Blender workspace

To work with materials, we will need some different windows. To save time, we can avoid having to open these windows manually by clicking on the **Shading** button on the bar at the top of the screen, as shown in *Figure 1.2*.

The Shading workspace has some new useful windows for texturing and creating materials. We now have a **Shader Editor** window, which we will later use for creating and working with material nodes. On the left side of the screen, we have an **Image Editor** window and a **File Browser** window. These windows can help us load and preview images and navigate through our computer to find images and files.

We also have an **HDRI** in the background, and an HDRI previewer. This changes the environment in our scene to give us a better idea of what the object would look like with realistic lighting coming from a particular environment. We will learn more about HDRIs later.

Figure 1.2 – Shading workspace

With just one click, we have prepared our workspace for material creation and texturing. Next, we will start creating some simple materials.

## Creating materials

We will now learn to create new materials and control some of their basic properties. We will also learn to apply multiple materials to a single object, which will be useful for texturing models more complex than the default cube.

In the next few steps, we will create a new material and change some of the properties of that material:

1.  Navigate to the **Material Properties** tab on the right side of the screen and click the **New** button to create a new material.

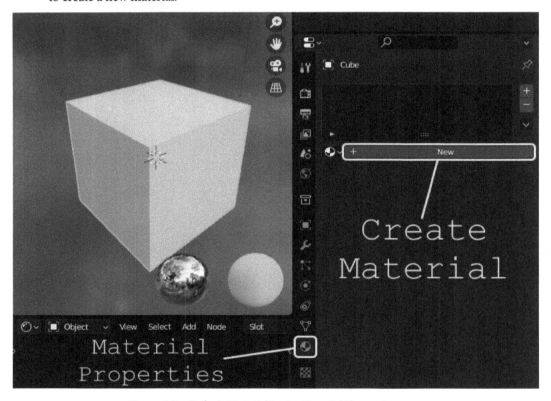

Figure 1.3 – Default Material in the Material Properties men.

2.  In the **Surface** menu below the default material, find the **Base Color** box. Clicking on this box will open the color wheel, where you can choose any color for the material.

    Let's create a military green color to practice some of the color controls. We will click on the green/yellow area in the outermost part of the color wheel, as shown in *Figure 1.4 (bottom)*.

Figure 1.4 – Base Color box (top), opening the color wheel (bottom)

3.  Use the **Value** slider next to the color wheel to reduce the brightness of the color. This brightness is referred to as **Value**.

You can manually type in a value in the slider below the color wheel, marked in *Figure 1.5*.

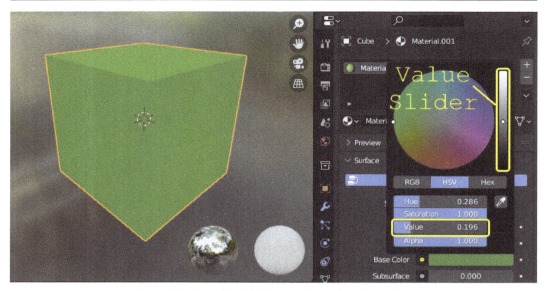

Figure 1.5 – Adjusting the Value setting of the base color

4.  Use the **Saturation** slider to reduce the saturation of the base color.

    This will make the color appear paler, as if the color got washed out. In this case, we need to use the slider to get the color that we want. As you move the slider, the marker moves closer to the center of the color wheel. The closer the marker is to the center of the color wheel, the lower the saturation.

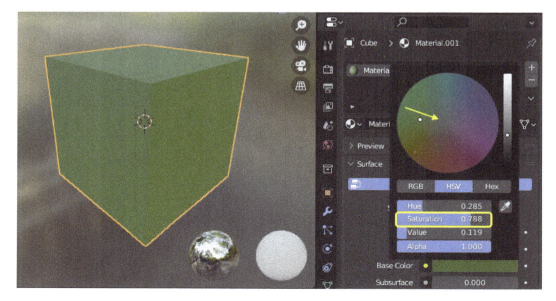

Figure 1.6 – Adjusting the Saturation setting of the base color

We went over some settings in our default material and changed the color of our cube. Next, let's go over how to create a second material so that we can have different materials on different parts of an object.

## Adding multiple materials to an object

We will now learn how to add multiple materials to a single object. In the next few steps, we will split our cube in half and create a separate material for each half:

1.  In Edit Mode, add a loop cut with *Ctrl + R* to cut the cube into two parts.

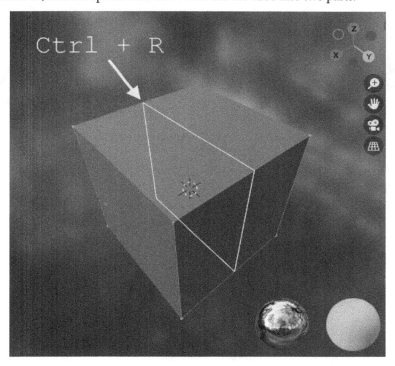

Figure 1.7 – Adding a loop cut to a cube

2.  Click on the plus button in the **Material Properties** tab to add a new material slot.

    This will not create a new material; it will only create a new slot. We can use this slot to either create a new material or load an existing material from another object. This time, we need a new material.

Figure 1.8 – Adding a new material slot

3.    Click on the **New** button to create a new material. The new material will be named **Material.002** by default.

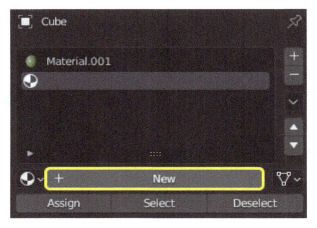

Figure 1.9 – Creating a new material

4.    Switch to **Face Select** mode by pressing *3*, and select one half of the cube in Edit Mode. Then select the new material (**Material.002**) and click the **Assign** button.

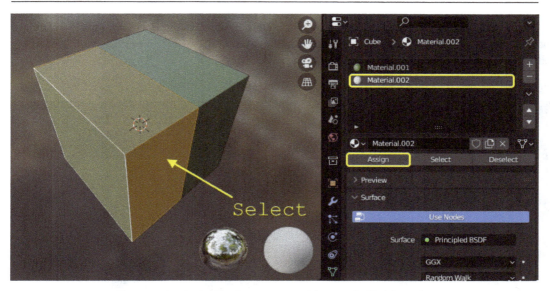

Figure 1.10 – Assigning the new material to one half of the cube

The selected half of the cube now has the new material assigned to it, and our cube has two materials on it.

Figure 1.11 – A cube with two materials

While we are at it, let's add some color to the new material. We will soon start learning about some other material properties, so let's make the other material a similar color but not the same. This will allow us to compare the shading on the two materials.

*Figure 1.12* shows the color properties of the new material.

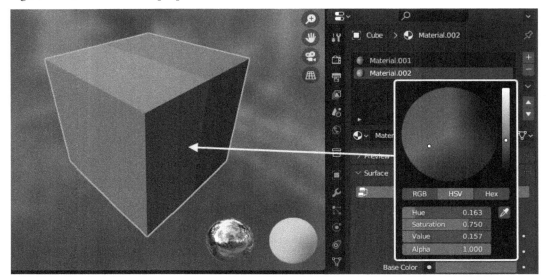

Figure 1.12 – New material color properties

We have now learned to create new materials and assign them to an object so that we can have multiple materials on one object. Next, we will introduce some other important material properties that we need to develop a good understanding of if we want to create realistic, high-quality materials.

## Tweaking material properties

In this section, we will learn about new material properties such as Roughness, Specular, Metallic, and more. This information will help us improve our understanding of how materials work in Blender, which we can then put to good use to create high-quality materials and textures.

## Specular

The **Specular** property is used to determine how much light is reflected by a surface. If you rotate the cube in the 3D viewport, you will notice that the object has a shiny surface, as is visible in *Figure 1.13*. This is because the object is specular.

Figure 1.13 – Specular surface

We can control the specular level using the **Specular** slider in the **Material Properties** tab, as shown in *Figure 1.14*.

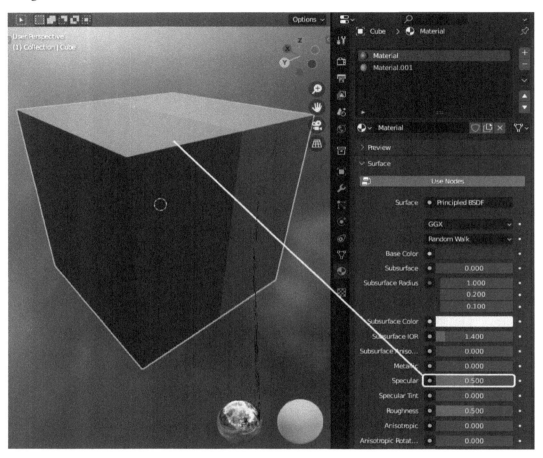

Figure 1.14 – The Specular slider

When we reduce the specular level on one of the materials to **0.000**, light will no longer be reflected by the surface and it will become much darker, as shown in *Figure 1.15*.

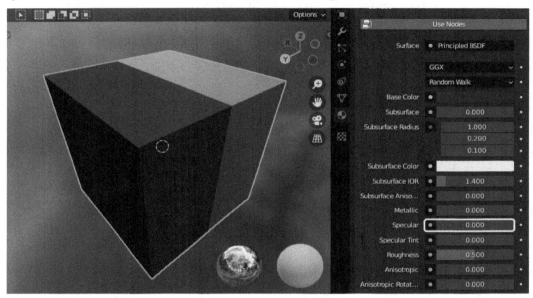

Figure 1.15 – Specular set to zero

Let's bring the specular level of both materials back to the default **0.500** so that we can demonstrate another, perhaps more important material property called **Roughness**.

## Roughness

The **Roughness** property is used to control how clear or rough a reflective surface appears. If we set the **Roughness** level to **0.000**, the reflection of the material becomes clear, as shown in *Figure 1.16*.

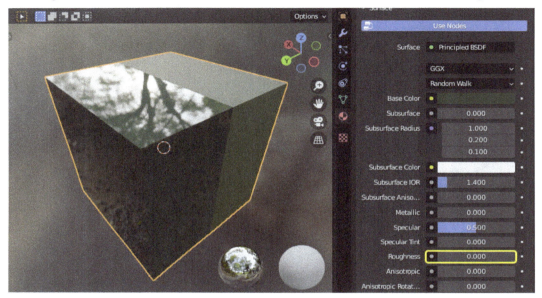

Figure 1.16 – Roughness set to zero

This is because the **Roughness** level determines how much scattering there is in the light reflected by a surface. *Figure 1.17* presents a diagram depicting how light rays are reflected by a surface with high roughness compared to a surface with low roughness.

On a surface with high roughness, light rays are scattered randomly due to (simulated) micro-imperfections on the surface, making the reflected image appear blurry. On a smooth, low-roughness surface, all the light rays are reflected at exactly the same angle, keeping the reflected image sharp and clear.

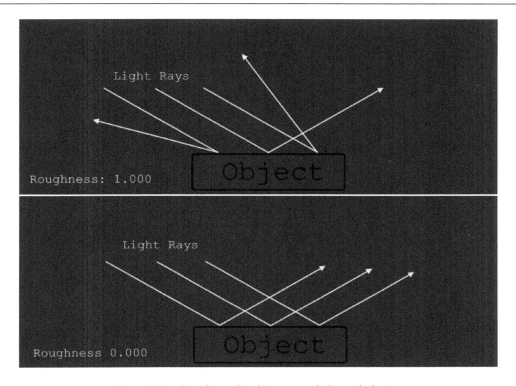

Figure 1.17 – Roughness level impact on light ray behavior

A low roughness value applies to materials such as car paint, polished wood, gold, glass, water, and other materials with smooth surfaces.

A high roughness level still reflects the same amount of light, but the light is scattered so the reflection is not clear at all, instead showing just an even increase in brightness across the entire surface, as in *Figure 1.18*. A high roughness level applies to rough materials such as concrete, rubber, plywood, galvanized metal, skin, and most fabrics.

Figure 1.18 – A material with a roughness value of 1.000

We discussed the three most basic material properties. We will now look at some properties used for more specific situations, starting with the **Metallic** property.

## Metallic

The **Metallic** property is used to make materials look more like they're made from metal. Let's introduce how the **Metallic** property works with the help of some background information.

We can sort all materials into one of two groups: **metals** and **dielectrics**. Iron, gold, silver, aluminum, copper, and all other metals naturally fit into the group of metals. Every other material, including stone, dirt, wood, plastic, rubber, and virtually everything else, is dielectric. These two groups are defined in physics by their electroconductive properties, but they are relevant to us because they reflect light in a distinctly different way.

*Figure 1.19* shows two spheres with almost the same material. They have the same base color, specular, and roughness properties. The difference in their reflectiveness is caused by the different metallic values. We can put this difference into words by saying the reflection in the left material is as if we are looking through red-tinted glasses, while the right reflection looks like an image with a red overlay. Regardless, the difference is obvious and important to keep under consideration.

Figure 1.19 – Metallic versus non-metallic shaders

To make a material metallic, simply turn the **Metallic** value all the way up in the **Material Properties** tab.

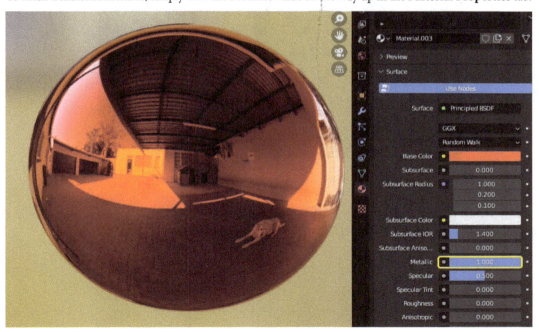

Figure 1.20 – Metallic slider

We will use this property later to create some more realistic materials. Next, let's talk about the **Clearcoat** property.

## Clearcoat

The **Clearcoat** property can be used for simulating a layer of polish on a material. As an example, let's look at a material such as carbon fiber. In *Figure 1.21*, we can see the bumpy fibers that we need for the material (which we will learn to create with normal maps), but something is still missing.

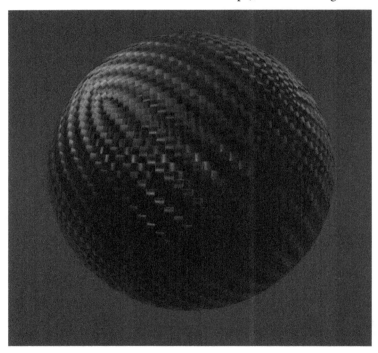

Figure 1.21 – Carbon fiber material before Clearcoat

To complete the material, we will increase the **Clearcoat** level in the material properties, as shown in *Figure 1.22*. For the best result, also set **Clearcoat Roughness** to **0.000**.

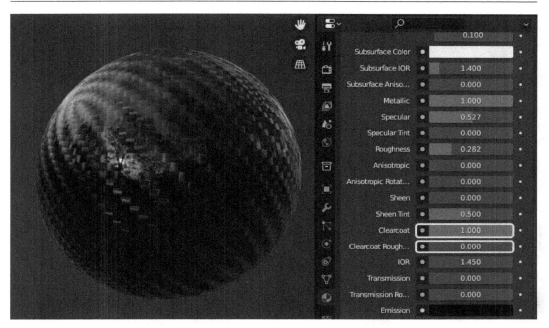

Figure 1.22 – Adding the Clearcoat property

As we can see, there appears to be a transparent layer of coating on the surface of the material, hence the name *clearcoat*.

Figure 1.23 – Carbon fiber after adding the Clearcoat property

This property can be used to finish other materials, such as polished wood. Next, we will introduce one last material property before we move on to studying material nodes.

## Emission

**Emission** is a property that defines how much light a material produces and casts into the environment. The emissive nature of an object is controlled separately by the emission color and strength values. These factors are self-explanatory, and their default values are black and **1.000**, respectively.

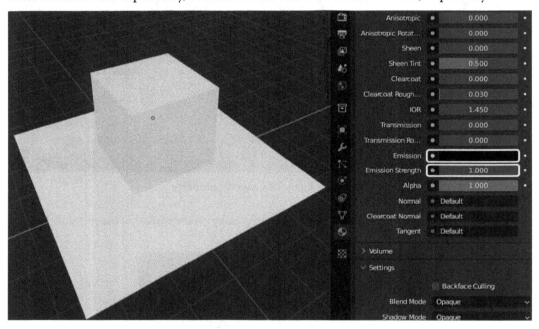

Figure 1.24 – Emission color and strength

If we set the emission color to a bright green, the object will turn slightly green, but the difference is hardly visible, as shown in *Figure 1.25*.

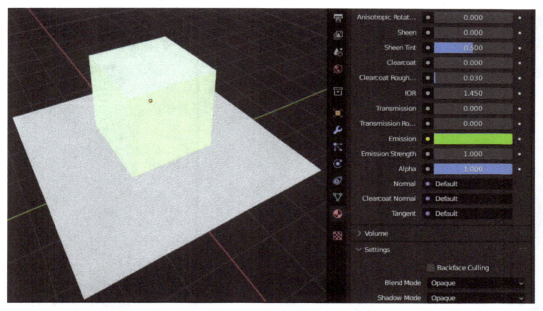

Figure 1.25 – Emission in Material Preview

To make this difference more visible, we need to render the light in our scene. This means that we will no longer use the temporary environmental lighting that we have employed until now. Rather, we will tell Blender to render the light as it is emitted from real light sources in the scene.

In the following steps, we will render the light and make our emission effect more visible:

1.  In the **Render Properties** menu, set **Render Engine** to **Cycles**.

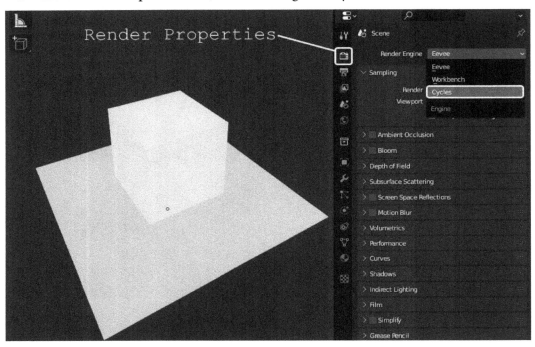

Figure 1.26 – Render Properties tab

2.   In the top-right corner of the screen, switch to **Rendered View.**

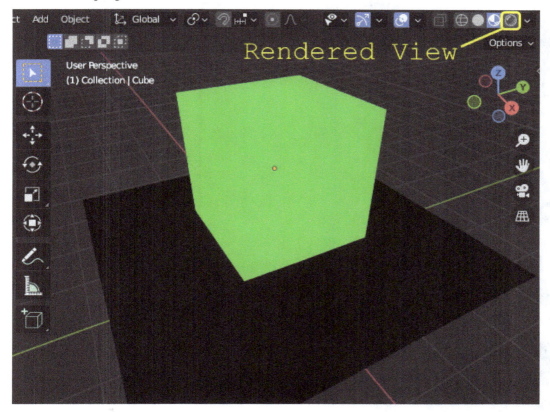

Figure 1.27 – Rendered View

Now, in **Rendered View**, the scene looks more realistic and the cube appears to be emitting light.

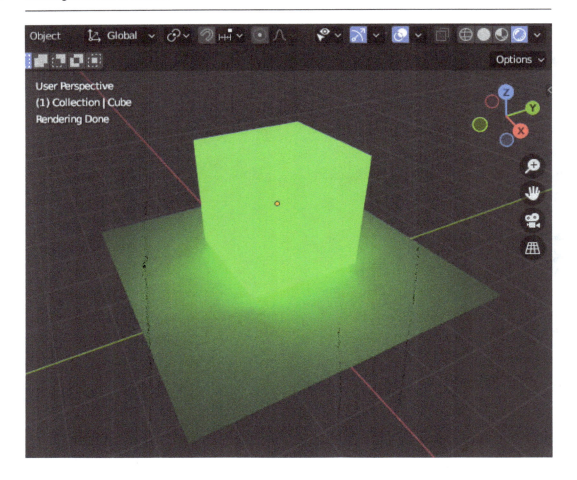

Figure 1.28 – Scene in Rendered View

We now have an idea of what the **Emission** property does. Later, we will learn to use the emission property to our advantage when creating beautiful materials and rendering environments.

## Summary

In this chapter, we went over some of the basic and common material properties. We learned about the base color, specular, roughness, metallic, and emission properties and we gained an understanding of the different factors that need to be considered to create high-quality materials.

In *Chapter 2, Understanding Material Nodes*, we will introduce material nodes and learn to use their powers to gain greater control over material properties, which will allow us to create much more sophisticated and realistic materials and textures.

# 2

# Introducing Material Nodes

In this chapter, we will begin to explore Blender's powerful material generation system known as **Material Nodes**. We will learn what they are, why they are so important, and how we can use them to create photorealistic materials. Starting with the basics, we will go over the most important nodes and then progress to creating some more sophisticated node combinations. By the end of the chapter, you will be ready to create some basic materials and textures and will feel comfortable exploring all the other material nodes and combinations.

The following topics will be covered in this chapter:

- Understanding the default nodes

- Creating textures with the Image Texture node

- Exploring powerful nodes

- Generating a camouflage texture

## Technical requirements

Ensure you have access to the 'Chapter 2 Camo Texture.png' file in the 'Chapter02' folder within the book's downloadable resources available here: `https://packt.link/mA1OU`.

# Understanding the default nodes

Let's begin by studying the default nodes. In the **Shader Editor** window, we will find two nodes, as shown in *Figure 2.1*.

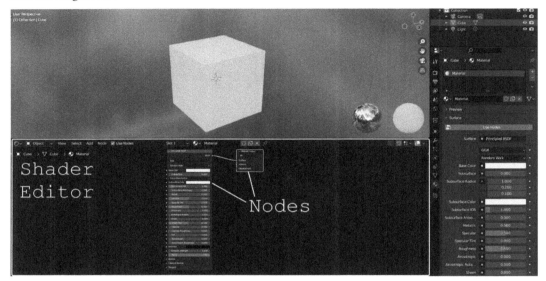

Figure 2.1 – Default nodes in the Shader Editor

We will learn what these nodes are, what they can do, and how they work together to create materials.

The big node from *Figure 2.1*, with lots of sliders and buttons, is called the **Principled BSDF** node. You probably noticed that this node has almost all the sliders and properties from the **Material Properties** tab on the right side of the screen, as shown in *Figure 2.2*.

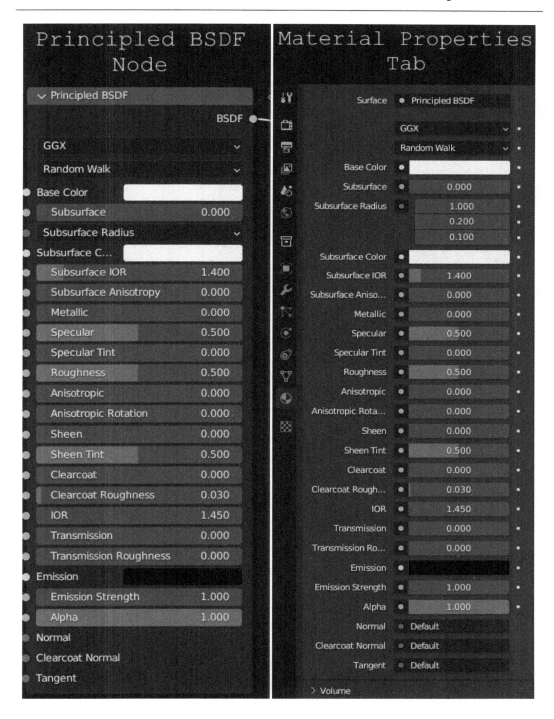

Figure 2.2 – The Principled BSDF node versus the **Material Properties** tab

The reason that this node is the same as the **Material Properties** tab is because they serve the same purpose: to gather all the most important material properties and make them easy to control. This set of properties makes up the **Principled BSDF** shader.

The reason we have the **Principled BSDF** shader in the form of a node is so that we can control the material properties (such as base color, roughness, and so on) with more advanced functions than just a number determined by the slider. For example, instead of just setting a base color for the entire material, we can use material nodes to replace the base color with an image, as in *Figure 2.3*.

At the end of the node chain, we have the **Material Output** node. This node simply takes the material created by the other nodes and displays it on the surface of an object.

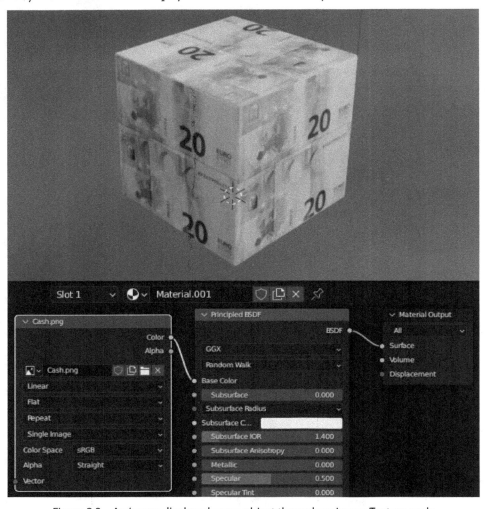

Figure 2.3 – An image displayed on an object through an Image Texture node

There are a lot of different nodes in Blender, and we will learn how to use them to create advanced and realistic materials by combining their powers and abilities. Now that we have a grasp of what nodes are and how they work, we will learn how to create our first node-based materials.

# Creating textures with the Image Texture node

We are now going to start exploring some fundamental nodes by creating some basic textures. First, we will learn about the **Image Texture** node, which is one of the most important nodes within the Shader Editor, along with the **Principled BSDF** node and a few others.

## Loading images into materials

The **Image Texture** node is used to load images into our materials. In the next few steps, we will learn how to add an **Image Texture** node, load an image, and connect it to other material nodes:

1.  In the **Shader Editor** window, press *Shift + A* to open the **Add** menu. From the **Texture** section, click on **Image Texture**.

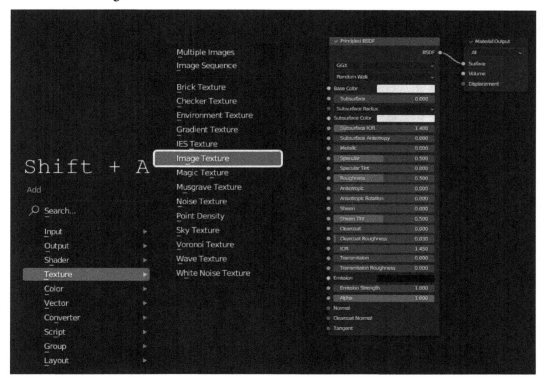

Figure 2.4 – Adding an Image Texture node

Alternatively, click on the **search...** box and search `image texture`.

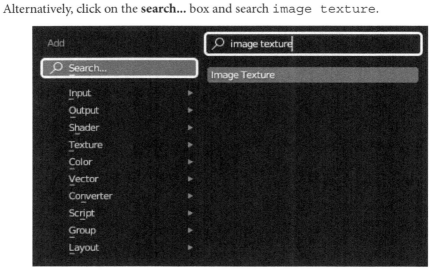

Figure 2.5 – Using the search box to add a node

2.  When the **Image Texture** node is selected, click the *left mouse button* to place it into the Shader Editor.

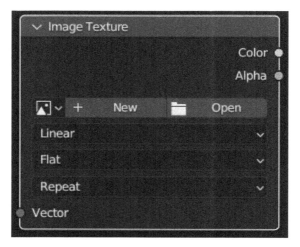

Figure 2.6 – Placing an Image Texture node

3.   Click and drag on the **Color** output on the right side of the **Image Texture** node and connect it with the **Base Color** input of the **Principled BSDF** node.

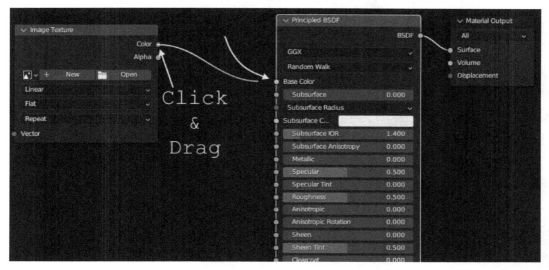

Figure 2.7 – Connecting two nodes

This will display the color produced by the **Image Texture** node as the base color. Since there is no image loaded in the node, the material will appear black, as in *Figure 2.8*.

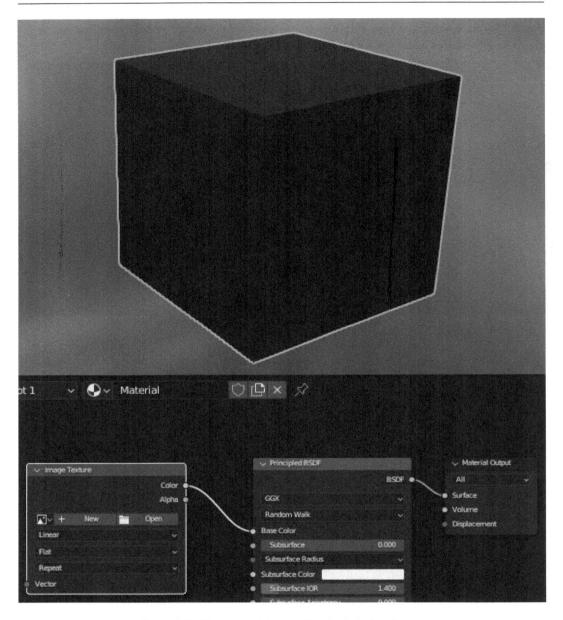

Figure 2.8 – Black material caused by the lack of an image

We now have two options. Either we will generate an image inside Blender or we will load an image from our computer. Let's try loading an image first.

4.  Click on the **Open** button in the **Image Texture** node.

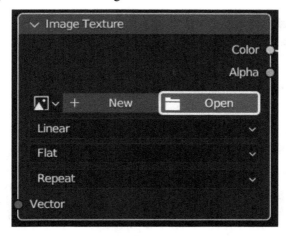

Figure 2.9 – The Open button in an Image Texture node

5.  Locate an image and click on **Open Image**.

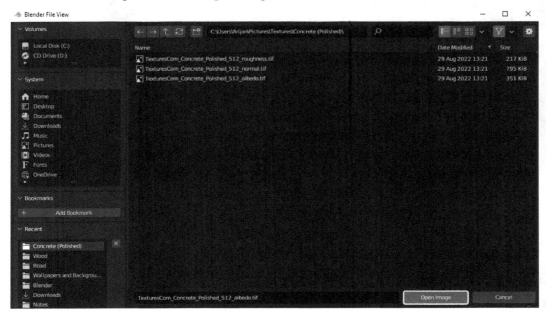

Figure 2.10 – Loading an image into Blender via the file browser

The image will now be displayed on the surface of the object.

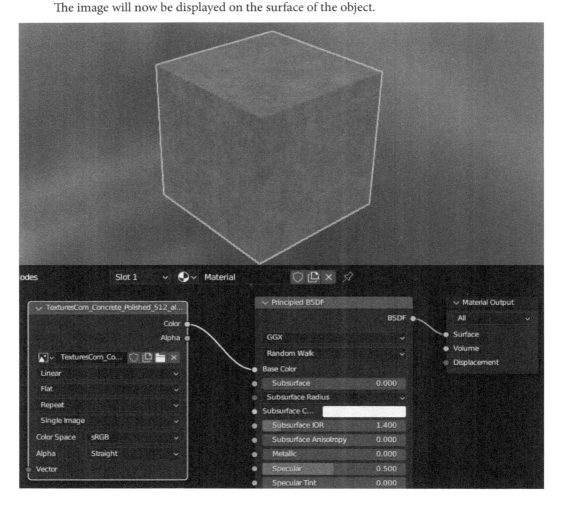

Figure 2.11 – An image displayed on an object through an Image Texture node

Next, we'll use nodes to generate images.

## Generating images with nodes

We can also use the **Image Texture** node to generate simple images. Here is how:

1.  Click on the **X** button in the **Image Texture** node to remove the current image.

Figure 2.12 – Removing an image from the Image Texture node

2.  Click on the **New** button to create a new image. This will open a menu with some properties for the new image.

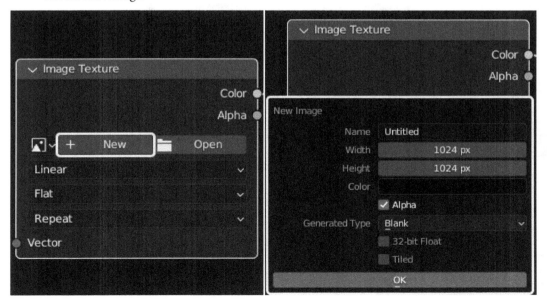

Figure 2.13 – Creating a new image

Here, we can name the image and set the resolution and the color, as shown in *Figure 2.14 (left)*. To make things more interesting, we will set **Generated Type** to **Color Grid**.

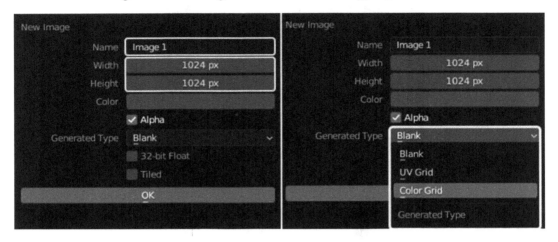

Figure 2.14 – Adjusting the settings of the new image

3.  Click on the **OK** button to generate the image.

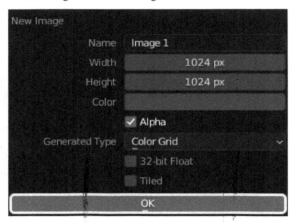

Figure 2.15 – Generating the image

This will create a **Color Grid** texture and apply it to our cube since this node is already plugged into the base color of the **Principled BSDF** node, as shown in *Figure 2.16*.

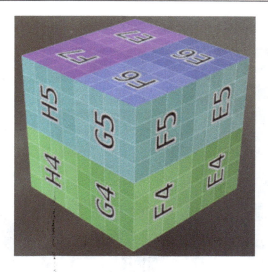

Figure 2.16 – Color grid texture on a cube

We can view all generated and loaded images in 2D in the **Image Editorwindow**, in the bottom-left corner of the shading workspace.

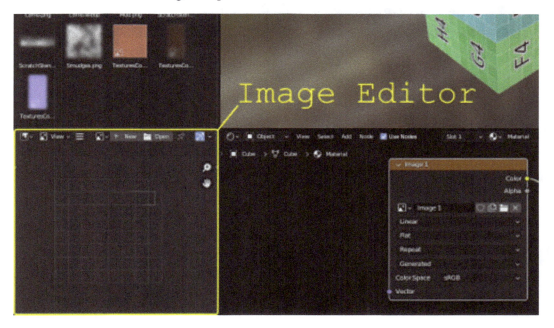

Figure 2.17 – Image Editor window

To view an image, click on the **Image Browser** icon and select the image.

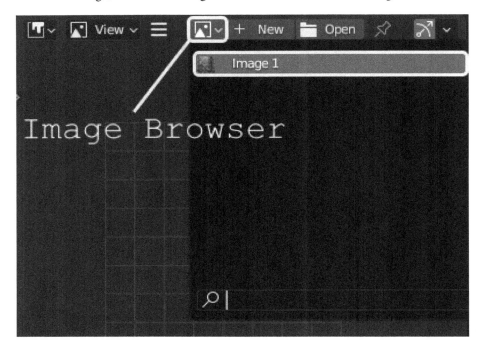

Figure 2.18 – Viewing an image from the Image Browser

We can now view our generated or loaded image in its full glory.

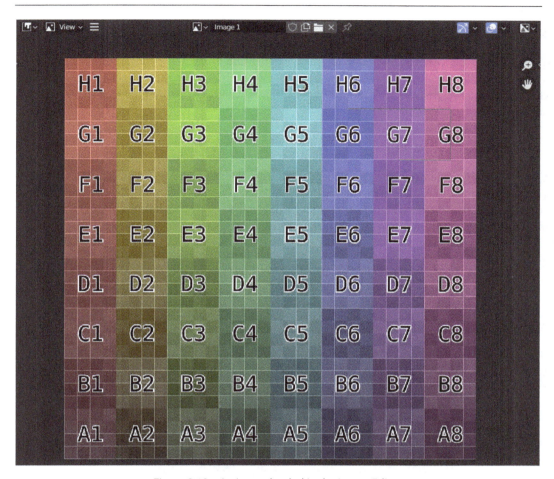

Figure 2.19 – An image loaded in the Image Editor

We have now learned what nodes are and how they can work together to create more complex results. We also learned how to use the **Image Texture** node to load images into our materials. Next, we will explore some other useful material nodes.

# Exploring powerful nodes

We will now introduce some new nodes to give us a better idea of just how powerful and versatile the node system is. This will give us a good foundation for creating high-quality materials by showing us which tools we have available to us. We will use the color grid image that we generated previously to demonstrate how other nodes work.

## Color control nodes

We can use nodes to adjust the colors of image textures in Blender. To do this, we will learn about the **Hue Saturation Value** node and the **Bright/Contrast** node. These two nodes will help us to quickly adjust the brightness, contrast, hue, saturation, and value properties of an image without using an external image editing program. In the next few steps, we will learn to use the **Hue Saturation Value** node:

1.  With *Shift + A*, add a **Hue Saturation Value** node from the **Color** section.

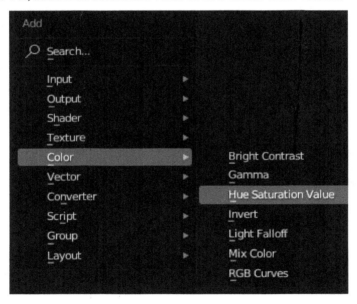

Figure 2.20 – Adding a Hue Saturation Value node

2.  Drag this node and hover it between the **Image Texture** node and the **Principled BSDF** node. Before confirming the placement, make sure that the **Color** input of the **Hue Saturation Value** node is next to the **Color** output of the **Image Texture** node, as shown in *Figure 2.21*.

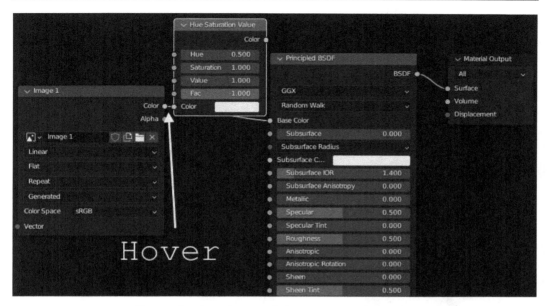

Figure 2.21 – Inserting a node between two other nodes

This will ensure that the node is connected correctly. If the node is not connected correctly, you can always manually reconnect the node to set it up, as in *Figure 2.22*.

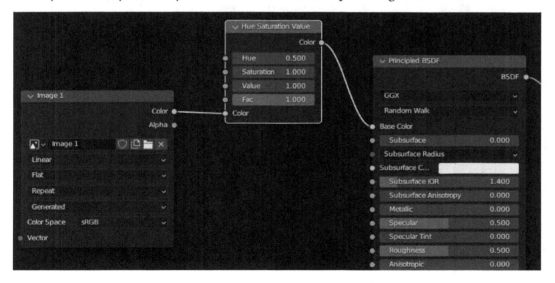

Figure 2.22 – A node placed between two other nodes

We can now adjust the **Hue**, **Saturation**, and **Value** properties of our image texture. If we set **Saturation** to 0.500 instead of 1.000, the colors of the image will be half as intense, as in *Figure 2.23*. Decreasing this value further, to 0.000, would make the texture black and white.

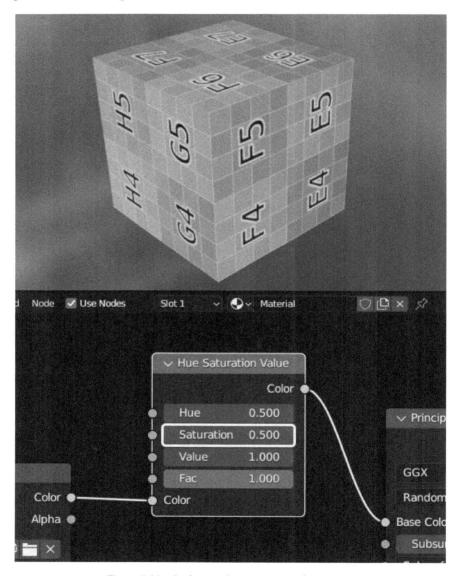

Figure 2.23 – Reducing the saturation of an image

Adjusting **Hue** will change the colors of the texture, and adjusting **Value** will change the brightness, as shown in *Figure 2.24*.

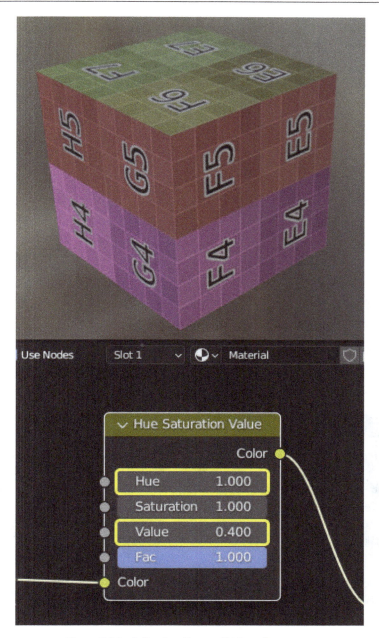

Figure 2.24 – Adjusting Hue and Value of a texture

These are the same properties that we learned to use in the *Creating materials* section of *Chapter 1, Creating Materials in Blender*, using the color wheel. Next, let's discuss the **Bright/Contrast** node.

3.  The **Bright/Contrast** node, as the name suggests, is used to adjust the brightness or contrast of an image. The node can be added from the same place as the **Hue Saturation Value** node, as shown in *Figure 2.25*.

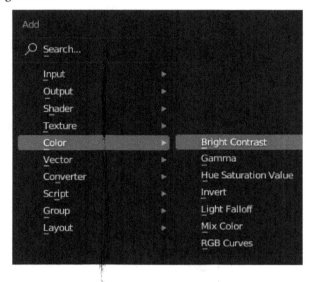

Figure 2.25 – Adding a Bright/Contrast node from the Color menu

4.  Place this node between the **Hue Saturation Value** node and the **Principled BSDF** node.

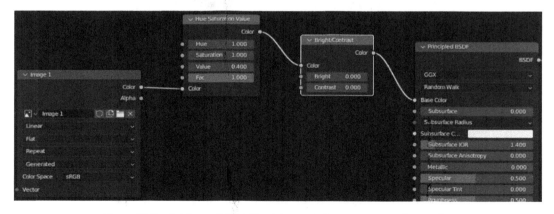

Figure 2.26 – Adding a Bright/Contrast node between two other nodes

The **Bright** slider does the same thing as the **Value** slider in the **Hue Saturation Value** node. The only difference is that it starts from `0.000` instead of `1.000`. The **Contrast** slider will increase the range of brightness in an image, meaning that the darkest colors will become darker, while the lighter colors will become brighter.

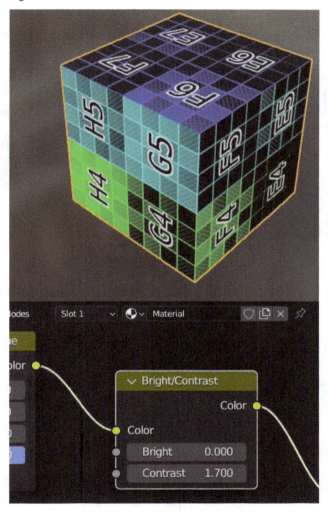

Figure 2.27 – Increasing the contrast of a texture

Notice that, regardless of how you modify the material with nodes, the changes are only visible in the 3D Viewport, while the image in the Image Editor is unchanged. This is because we are not changing the generated image texture; we are only changing how Blender displays it in the material. There are many more useful and fun nodes to explore. Next, let's talk about the **Mix** node.

## The Mix node

The **Mix node** is a powerful and versatile tool that can be used to perform various calculations. One of the elements it can mix is color, and we will learn how to do that. In the next few steps, we will learn how to combine colors and textures using the **Mix** node:

1.  First, delete the **Hue Saturation Value** and **Bright/Contrast** nodes. This is not necessary, but it will clear up our workspace and give us some more space.

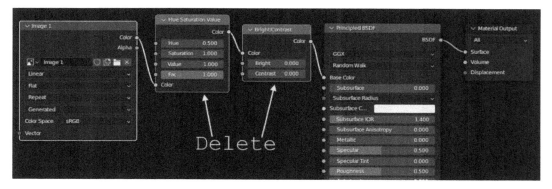

Figure 2.28 – Deleting two nodes

2.  Add a **Mix** node between the **Image Texture** node and the **Principled BSDF** node. Don't connect it yet.

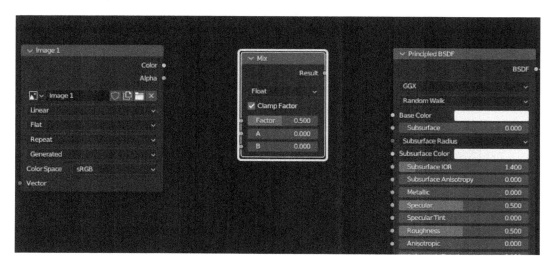

Figure 2.29 – Adding a Mix node

3.  Set **Data Type** to **Color**.

Figure 2.30 – Setting Data Type to Color

4.  Set **Color A** to any color and connect the **Result** output of the **Mix** node to the **Base Color** input of the **Principled BSDF** node.

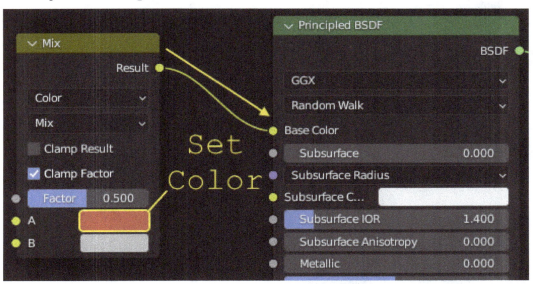

Figure 2.31 – Connecting the Mix and Principled BSDF nodes

Now, the material color is a mix between **A** and **B**. There is an equal mix of red and white because **Factor** is set to `0.500`, causing the base color to appear pink.

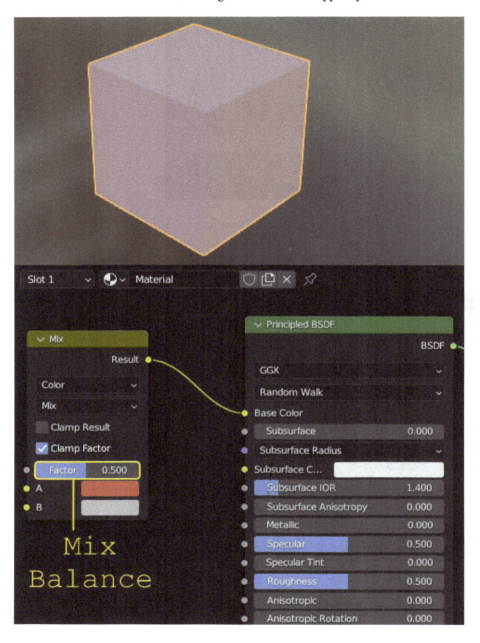

Factor 2.32 – A pink material created by mixing red and white

Reducing the **Factor** value will adjust the color balance to favor **A**, making the base color appear more red.

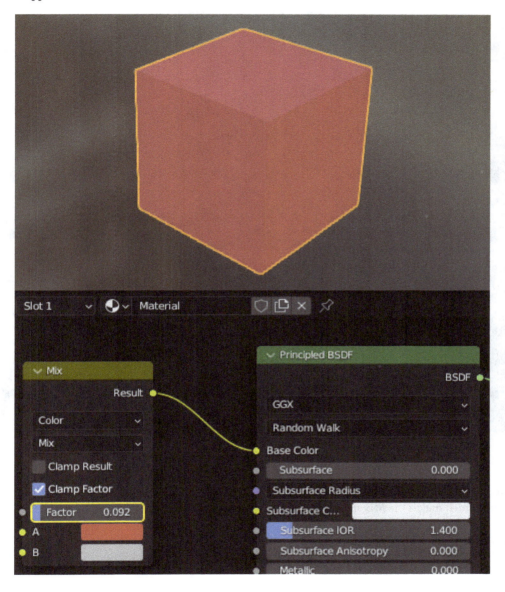

Figure 2.33 – Adjusting the color balance with the Factor slider

5.  Plug the **Image Texture** node into the **B** input of the **Mix** node. We have now created a mix between the image texture and the color red. This is a good way to add overlays.

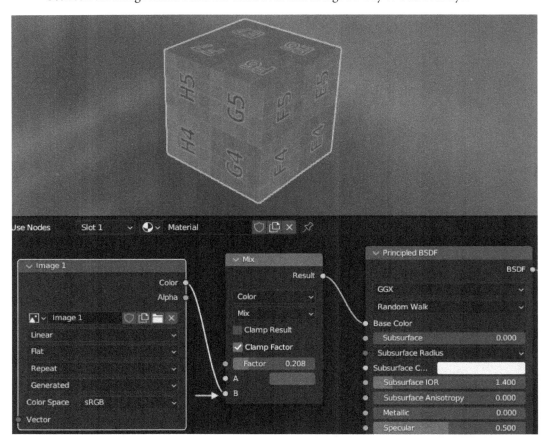

Figure 2.34 – Adding a red overlay to an image texture with the Mix node

The technique that we just used for mixing images and colors can be used for blending textures together, which makes the **Mix** node a very powerful node.

# The Noise Texture node

The **Noise Texture** node is another versatile node that is used to generate randomly colored and shaped patterns. By default, it creates the result in *Figure 2.35*.

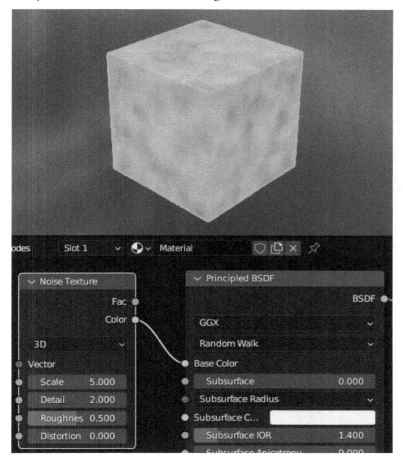

Figure 2.35 – Default Noise Texture output

Increasing the **Scale**, **Detail**, and **Roughness** properties in the **Noise Texture** node will make the pattern look a lot finer, as in *Figure 2.36*.

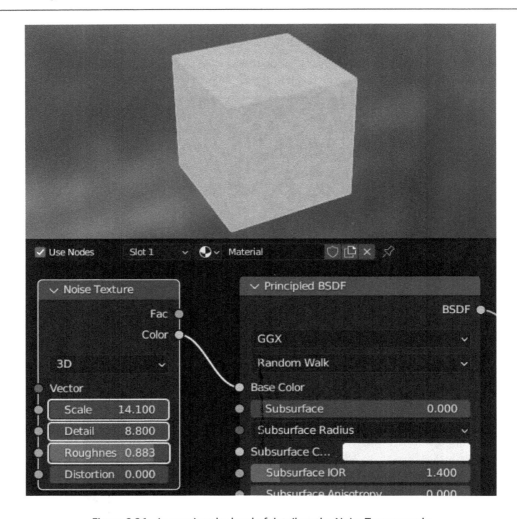

Figure 2.36 – Increasing the level of detail on the Noise Texture node

This node is often used to generate random information that can be converted either into bumps, edgewear, or just a general imperfect appearance for models and textures. We will learn how to generate more advanced patterns with this node in the *Generating procedural camouflage* section. Next, we will introduce the **Voronoi Texture** node, which can also help us generate random patterns and shapes.

# The Voronoi Texture node

The **Voronoi Texture** node is similar to the **Noise Texture** node but generates a randomly colored pixelated pattern on a surface, as shown in *Figure 2.37 (left)*. The shapes on the pattern can be randomized using the **Randomness** slider, as shown in *Figure 2.37 (right)*.

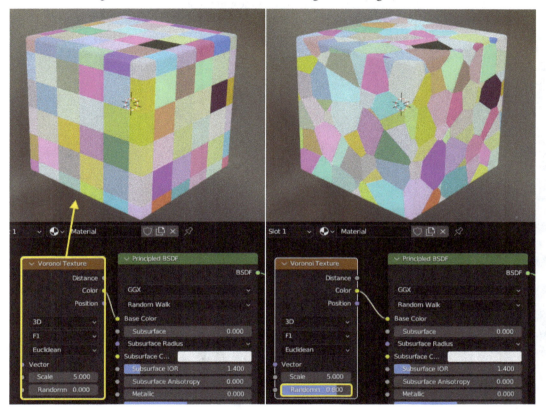

Figure 2.37 – A default Voronoi texture (left) and a randomized Voronoi texture (right)

We will learn how to combine this node with the **ColorRamp** node to create a useful tile texture in the next section.

## The ColorRamp node

The **ColorRamp** node is used for controlling the gradients between the colors of an image of a texture. To demonstrate what it does and how it works, let's combine it with the **Noise Texture** node in a few steps:

1.  Add a **ColorRamp** between the **Noise Texture** node and the **Principled BSDF** node. This will instantly turn the noise texture black and white.

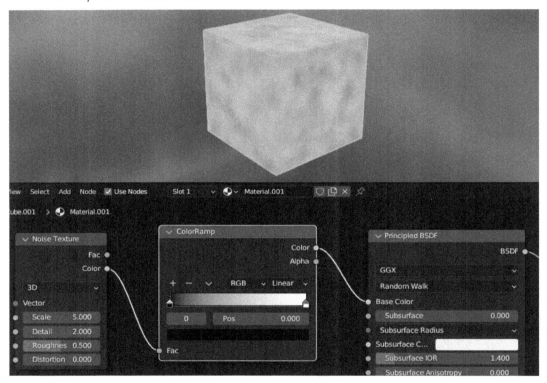

Figure 2.38 – Adding a ColorRamp node

2.  Drag the two color markers and bring them closer to the middle, as in *Figure 2.39*.

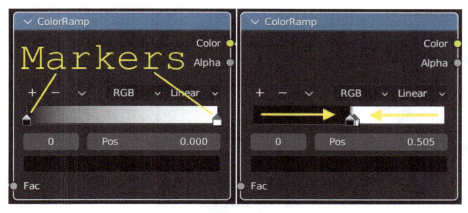

Figure 2.39 – Bringing the markers together in the ColorRamp node

This will drastically change the pattern generated by the **Noise Texture** node. There are now only two colors and the borders between them are sharp. The reason they are sharp is that the markers in the **ColorRamp** node are close together, making the gradient between the two colors very short, as in *Figure 2.40*.

Figure 2.40 – Sharp border between colors caused by the ColorRamp node

3.   Click on one of the markers to change its color.

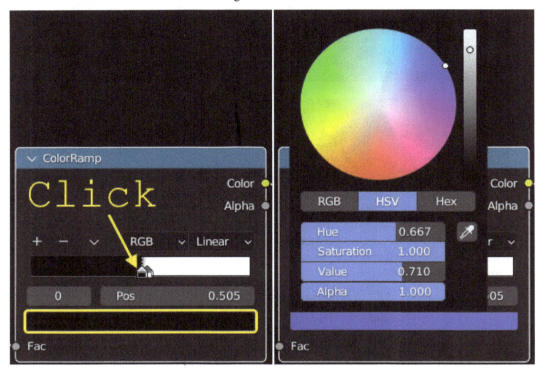

Figure 2.41 – Changing the marker color in the ColorRamp node

We can now freely change the colors in the **ColorRamp** node to create beautiful patterns.

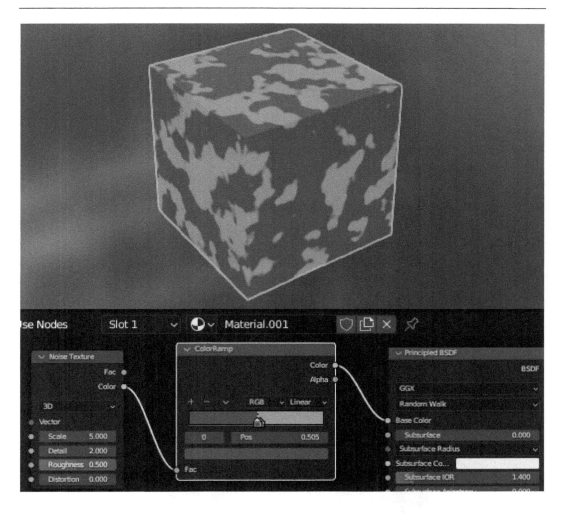

Figure 2.42 – A colorful pattern created with the ColorRamp node

4. Next, click on the plus button in the node to add a new marker.

Figure 2.43 – Adding a new color marker

5. Bring this marker close to the two markers in the middle and set its color to anything you like.

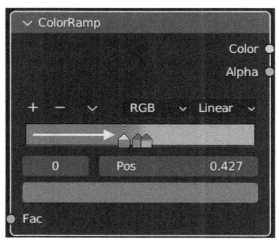

Figure 2.44 – Setting a new color for the marker

This creates a pattern comparable to marble, as shown in *Figure 2.45*.

Figure 2.45 – A noise texture, modified by a ColorRamp node with three colors

6.  You can add as many markers as you like. It is also possible to change the gradient type with the box marked in *Figure 2.46*. Try to copy the settings from *Figure 2.46*.

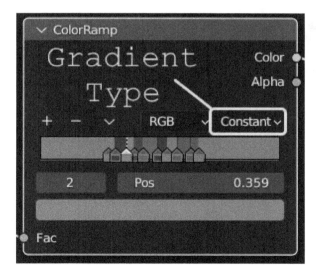

Figure 2.46 – Changing the gradient type in the ColorRamp node

This creates a fascinating result, as shown in *Figure 2.47*.

Figure 2.47 – A colorful pattern generated by combining a Noise Texture node and a ColorRamp node

We can also use the **ColorRamp** node together with a **Voronoi Texture** node to create various textures and patterns. We will now combine the two nodes to create a cartoonish tile texture:

1.    Add a **Voronoi Texture** node and a **ColorRamp** node and connect them to the **Base Color** input of the **Principled BSDF** node.

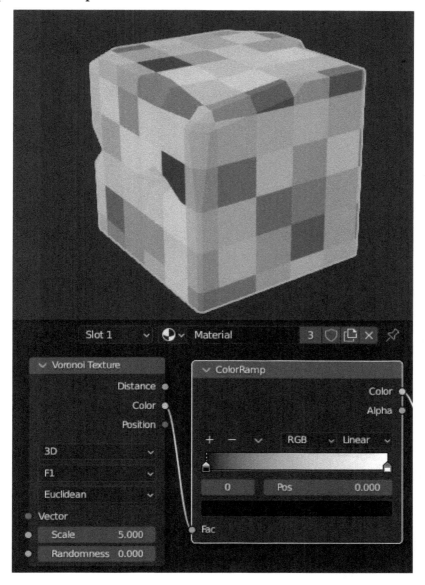

Figure 2.48 – Combining a Voronoi Texture node with a ColorRamp node

2. Set **Scale** to 4.000 and **Randomness** to 0.200, then change the colors in the **ColorRamp** node to brown, beige, and sand, as shown in *Figure 2.49*.

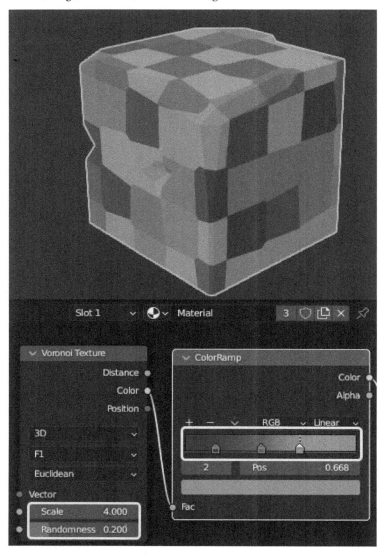

Figure 2.49 – Adjusting the scale, randomness, and colors

We can also use these two nodes to create a height difference for the individual tiles using a **Bump** node, as shown in *Figure 2.50*. This is just a small teaser for bump maps and normal maps, and we will learn more about simulating bumpy surfaces with special nodes and textures in *Chapter 5, Generating Texture Maps with Cycles*.

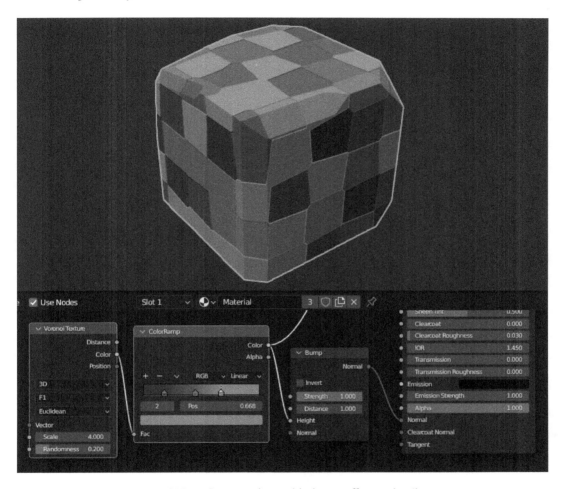

Figure 2.50 – Using a Bump node to add a bump effect to the tile texture

We can use this technique to create tile textures in various shapes, sizes, and colors. Next, let's learn how to create a camouflage texture by layering patterns using the **Mix Color** node.

# Generating a camouflage texture

We will now learn how to combine the **Noise Texture**, **ColorRamp**, and **Mix Color** nodes to create a camouflage texture. This technique will allow us to create various kinds of camouflage. In the following steps, we will create a three-color camouflage pattern:

1.  Add a **Noise Texture** node and a **ColorRamp** node and set **Interpolation** to **Constant** in the **ColorRamp** node.

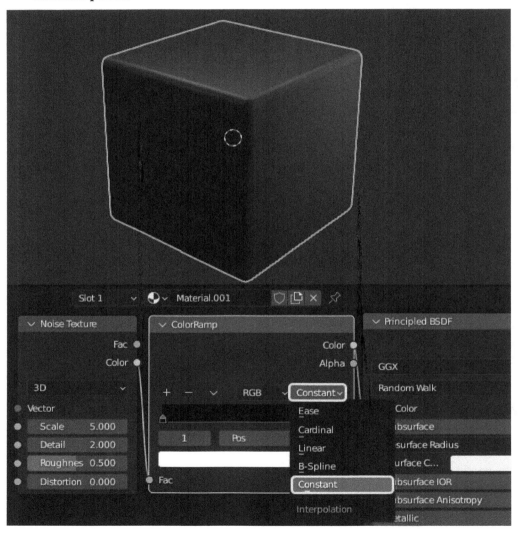

Figure 2.51 – Adding a Noise Texture node and a ColorRamp node with constant interpolation

2. Set **Scale** to 2.000 and **Roughness** to 0.000 in the **Noise Texture** node, and set the white marker position to 0.500 in the **ColorRamp** node.

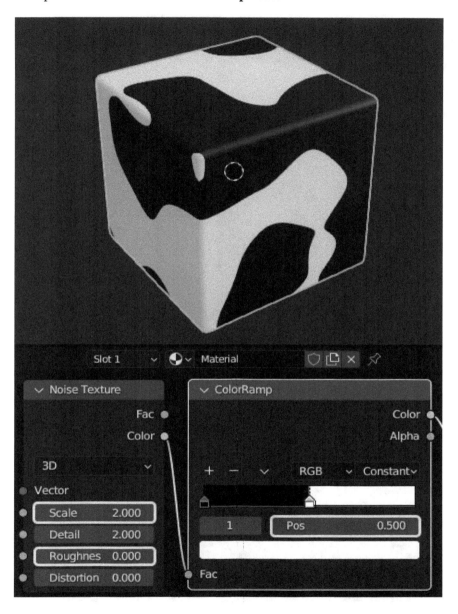

Figure 2.52 – Adjusting the scale, roughness, and marker position

3.    Pick two colors, such as light green and dark green, and set the marker colors to those colors, as shown in *Figure 2.53*.

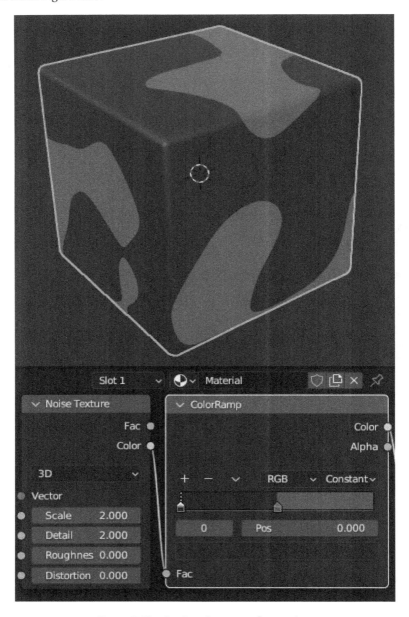

Figure 2.53 – Setting the camouflage colors

4.  In the **Add** menu (*Shift + A*), search for and add a **Mix Color** node and place it as shown in *Figure 2.54*.

Figure 2.54 – Adding a Mix Color node

5.  Select the **Noise Texture** node and the **Color Ramp** node and duplicate them with *Shift + D*. Then, set the colors to black and white, as shown in *Figure 2.55*.

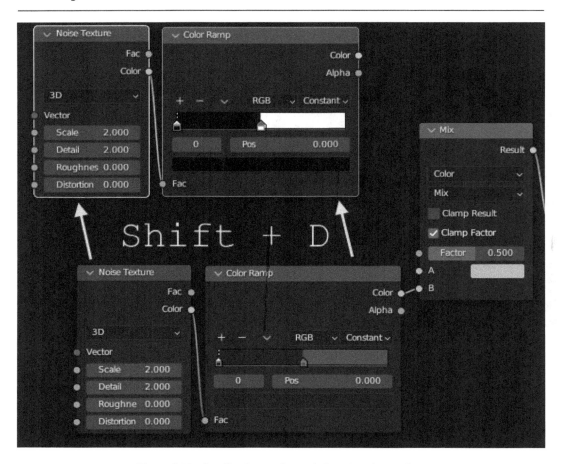

Figure 2.55 – Duplicating nodes and changing their colors

6.  Plug the new **Color Ramp** node into the **Factor** input of the **Mix** node and adjust some settings on the two new nodes.

    For the best results, decrease the white marker value to 0.430 and increase the **Noise Texture** node's **Scale** setting to 2.800.

Figure 2.56 – Adjusting the settings in the new nodes

7.    Finally, set the **A** color in the **Mix** node to whatever you prefer as the third camouflage color, such as a different shade of green, as shown in *Figure 2.57*.

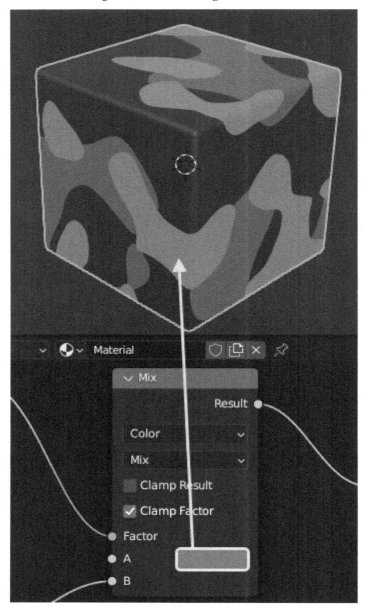

Figure 2.57 – Setting the third camouflage color with the Mix node

We can use this technique to create camouflage textures with various patterns and colors by adjusting some of the settings, such as the **Color Ramp** marker colors and positions, and Noise Texture scale and roughness.

Figure 2.58 – Three different types of camouflage generated with the same node chain

We have now learned how to combine a **Noise Texture** node, a **Color Ramp** node, and a **Mix Color** node to create colorful patterns with an additional, third layer of color. You are encouraged to explore this technique further by using some different nodes, such as a **Voronoi Texture** node instead of a **Noise Texture** node.

## Summary

In this chapter, we learned what nodes are, how they work, and how they can be used to create some simple textures. We also talked about some of the most important nodes to get a feel for what they can do and how they work. We will use this knowledge to create more sophisticated textures later and build high-quality materials.

In *Chapter 3*, *Mapping Images with Nodes*, we will learn how textures are displayed on objects and how we can place textures on more sophisticated objects.

# 3

# Mapping Images with Nodes

In this chapter, we will learn to correctly apply images, textures, and materials to objects. This is an important part of texturing and gives us more control over how a texture appears on a surface, which will allow us to texture more complex objects. By the end of this chapter, you will understand how Blender projects images onto objects, how to control image projection, and how to map textures correctly on some basic shapes.

In this chapter, we will cover the following topics:

- Understanding image mapping
- Using the Node Wrangler add-on
- Mapping textures to 3D models

## Technical requirements

The prepared resources can be found in the Chapter03 folder within the book's downloadable resources folder, available here: `https://packt.link/mA1OU`

## Understanding image mapping

We will first discuss how Blender projects images on 3D models, and how we can control this. Let's look at how a texture appears on a cube by default over the next few steps:

1. Add a new material to the default cube.

Figure 3.1 – Adding a material to the default cube

2.  Using the skills we learned in *Chapter 2, Introducing Material Nodes*, add an **Image Texture** node and load or generate an image for the material.

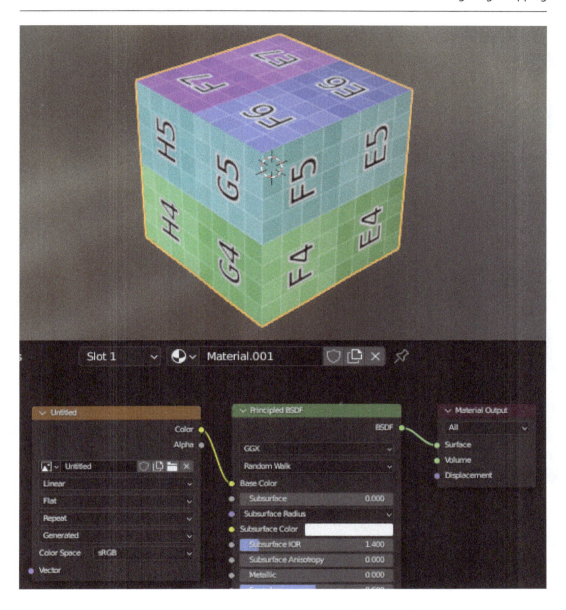

Figure 3.2 – Adding an **image texture** to the material

3.    Open the **UV Editing** workspace from the bar at the top of the screen.

Figure 3.3 – Opening the UV Editing workspace

You have now split the screen into two windows. On the left, we have the UV Editor, and on the right, we have the 3D viewport where we can see the object.

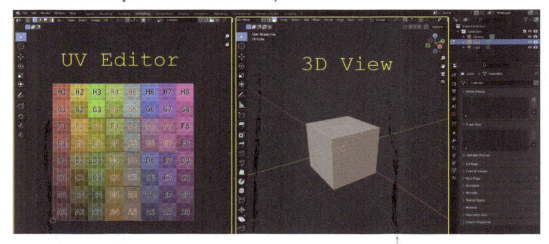

Figure 3.4 – The UV Editing workspace

The UV Editor is a window used for editing how a texture is displayed on a surface. In *Figure 3.5*, you can see the unwrapped 2D version of the cube on top of the texture we generated.

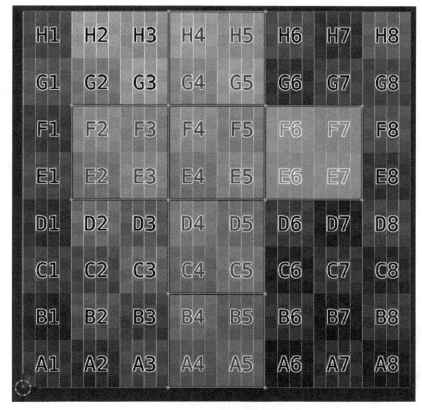

Figure 3.5 – A UV-unwrapped cube

By default, this is how Blender maps an image to the surface of a cube. Each orange square in the UV Editor represents one face of the cube. If you select one face in Edit Mode, you will see only that face in the UV Editor.

Blender also automatically unwraps and textures some other default shapes, as shown in *Figure 3.6*.

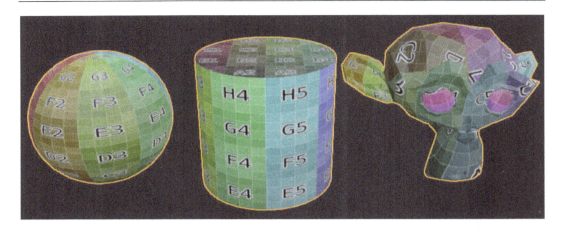

Figure 3.6 – Default objects automatically unwrapped by Blender

The problem with Blender's default texturing method is that there is some stretching and compression in the textures. A good example of that is shown by the default Torus, which can be added from the **Add** menu (*Shift + A*).

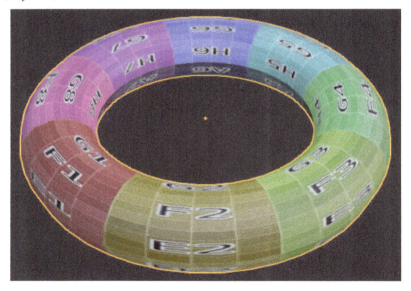

Figure 3.7 – A Torus with visible texture stretching

This compression happens because the image is not mapped correctly. To understand why this is happening, let's look at a simpler UV map by adding a plane. By default, Blender will fit any image that we load into the **Image Texture** node onto the plane, as shown in *Figure 3.8*.

Figure 3.8 – A plane with a texture

This fits perfectly because the plane is a perfect square, and the texture is as well. In the UV Editor, we can see that the face has exactly the same shape as the plane, and it fits the entire image, so no stretching or compression is necessary. But if we select the top edge in the UV Editor and slide it down along the *y*-axis, Blender now has to cover the entire plane with a small part of the texture, which is not large enough, as shown in *Figure 3.9*.

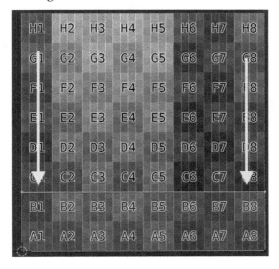

Figure 3.9 – A bad UV map shown in the UV Editor

As a result, the texture gets stretched out heavily in the 3D view, as shown in *Figure 3.10*.

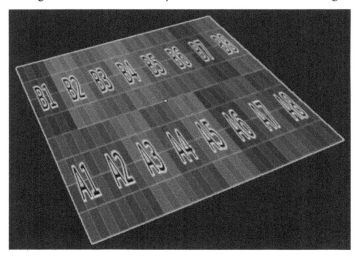

Figure 3.10 – Texture stretching caused by a bad UV map

This can also happen when an image does not have the same proportions as the surface on which it is applied as a texture. For example, this camo texture is much longer than the surface of our plane.

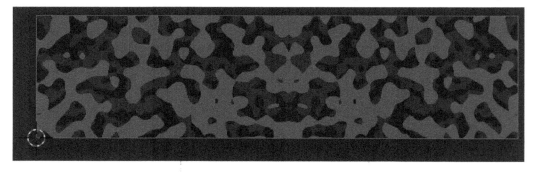

Figure 3.11 – A camouflage texture that is much wider than a plane object

As a result, the image looks compressed in the 3D view, as shown in *Figure 3.12*.

Figure 3.12 – The camouflage texture compressed to fit the plane

To correctly display this image on the surface, we must reshape the UV map in the UV Editor until the shape matches the plane.

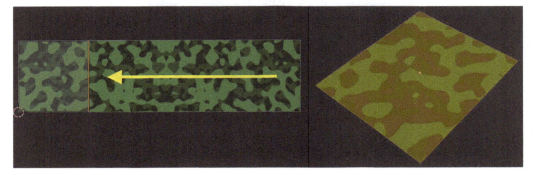

Figure 3.13 – Adjusting the UV map to fit the plane

This is how Blender understands how to correctly display an image on the surface of an object. As you can see, it is manual and quite clunky. There is a way to make this much simpler with nodes, and we will learn to do that next.

## Using the Node Wrangler add-on

We will now learn to use **Node Wrangler**, a simple add-on that will help us quickly map textures onto objects in just a few clicks. First, let's activate the add-on.

Over the next few steps, we will learn to browse and activate add-ons in Blender:

1.   In the top-left corner of the screen, open the **Edit** menu and click on **Preferences...**.

Figure 3.14 – Opening the Preferences menu

2.  On the left side of the menu, click on **Add-ons**. This will open a large list of the add-ons available in Blender by default.

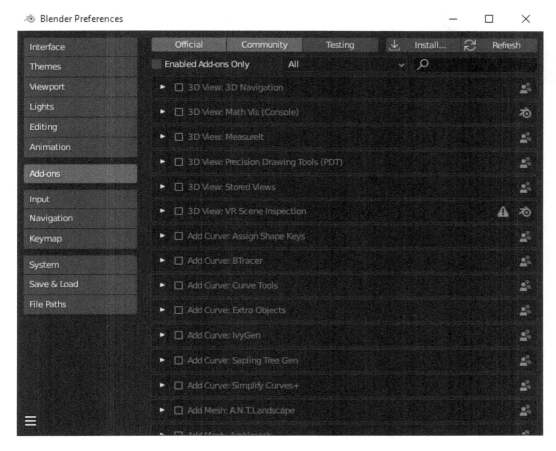

Figure 3.15 – List of add-ons in the Preferences menu

3.    In the search box, type `node wrangler` to find the add-on.

Figure 3.16 – Searching for an add-on

4.    Check the box to the left of the **Node: Node Wrangler** result to activate the add-on, as shown in *Figure 3.17*.

Figure 3.17 – Activating the **Node Wrangler** add-on

The **Node Wrangler** add-on is now active, and we can use it in the Shader Editor to help us with texture mapping. Next, let's learn how to use the add-on correctly.

5.    Create a new material, then select the **Principled BSDF** node and press *Ctrl + T*.

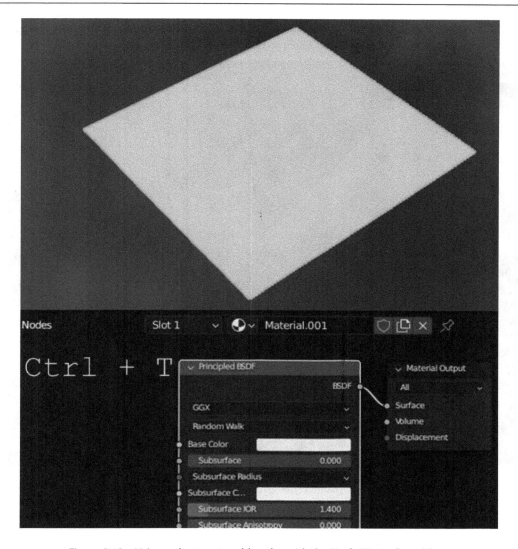

Figure 3.18 – Using a shortcut to add nodes with the **Node Wrangler** add-on

This will create three nodes and plug them into the **Principled BSDF** node. The first is an **Image Texture** node, then a **Mapping** node, and finally a **Texture Coordinate** node.

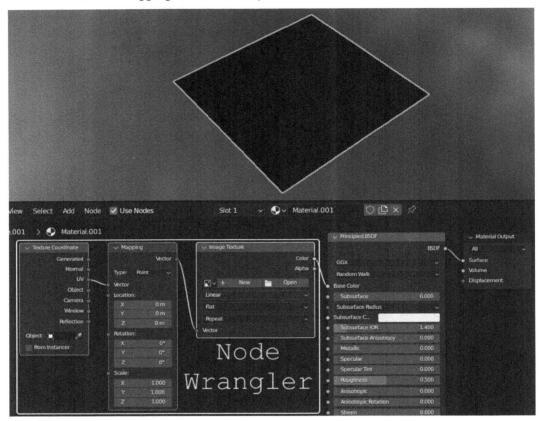

Figure 3.19 – A set of nodes added with the **Node Wrangler** add-on

We are already familiar with the **Image Texture** node, but the other two nodes are key for our UV mapping tasks. We will now learn what they can do and how they work.

## Texture Coordinate node

The **Texture Coordinate** node is used to select how we want to project the image onto our object. By default, it is set to **UV,** so the UV Editor determines how the image appears on the surface. We will also discuss object projection in the following *Mapping textures to 3D models* section.

The **Mapping** node is rather simple – we can use it to adjust the position, rotation, and scale of an image on an object.

For example, try to change the **X-axis Location** value in the **Mapping** node. To do this, you can click and drag either left or right to adjust the value. This will shift the image on the plane.

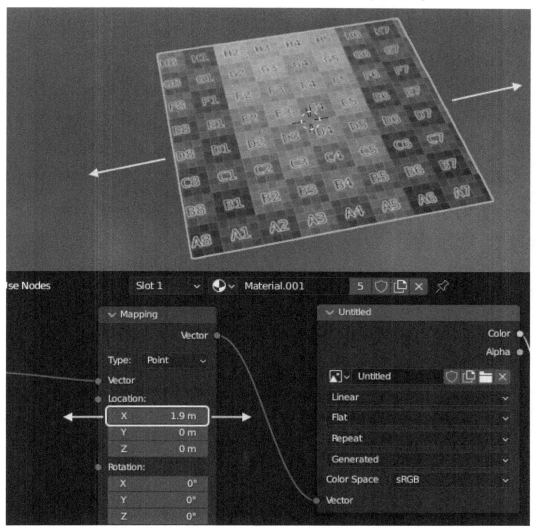

Figure 3.20 – Adjusting the location in the Mapping node causes the image to shift

Setting the **X-axis Location** value in the **Mapping** node is the equivalent of moving the UV map by 1.9 m along the $x$-axis in the UV Editor.

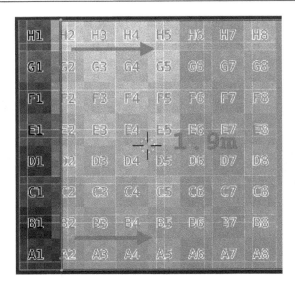

Figure 3.21 – A 1.9 m shift in the Mapping node as depicted in the UV Editor

We can do the same with **Rotation**, and more importantly, **Scale**.

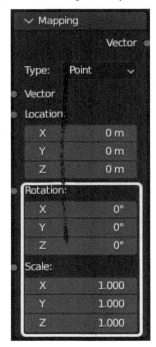

Figure 3.22 – The Rotation and Scale sliders in the Mapping node

Increasing the **X**-axis **Scale** value from the default **1.000** to **2.000** will compress the image on the $x$ -axis so that two image lengths can fit onto the surface of the plane, as shown in *Figure 3.23*.

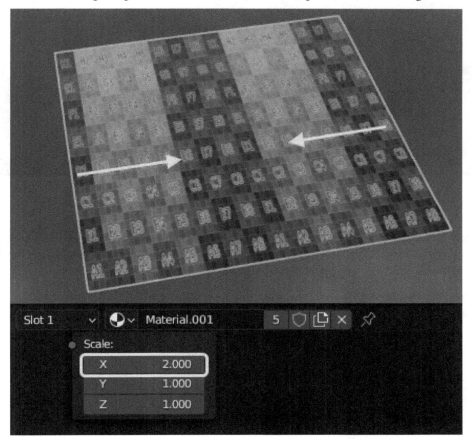

Figure 3.23 – Increasing the scale of a texture in the Mapping node

This has the same effect as scaling the UV map by a factor of 2 on the *x*-axis.

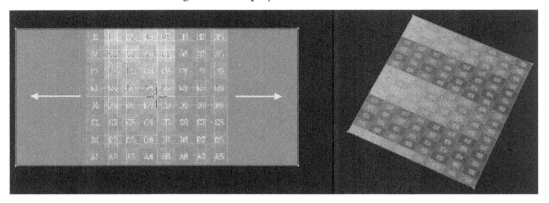

Figure 3.24 – UV map extended as a result of scaling

Note that even though the UV map extends beyond the image in the UV Editor, we do not see any black areas on the texture. This is because the image is tiled automatically when we expand the UV map outside of the limits.

If we increase the scale on all axes by the same value, the texture will simply become tiled on the surface, as shown in *Figure 3.25*.

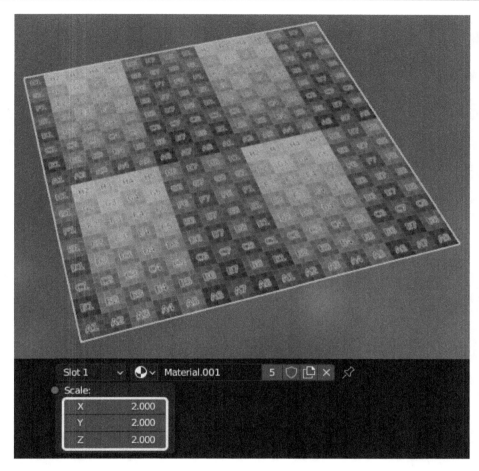

Figure 3.25 – Tiling a texture by increasing the scale

Likewise, if we decrease the scale factor to the same value on all axes, we effectively zoom in on the texture, as shown in *Figure 3.26*.

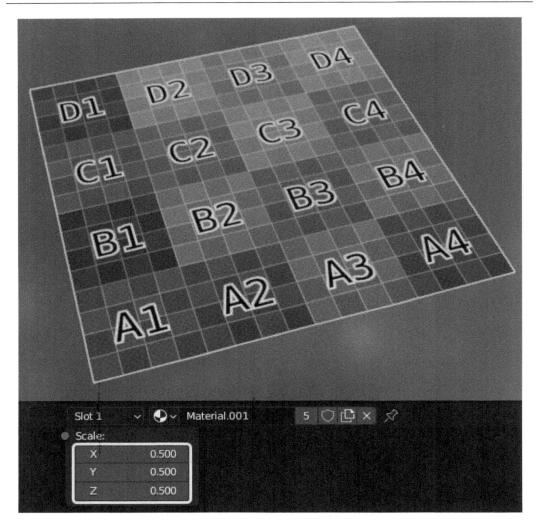

Figure 3.26 – Decreasing the scale of a texture

We have now learned how **Node Wrangler** works, and we will use this feature to our advantage when texturing objects. Next, let's look at how we can use **Node Wrangler** to easily texture more complex 3D models.

# Mapping textures to 3D models

We will now learn to use **Node Wrangler** to quickly map textures onto any 3D model. Typically, it is best to map textures by manually UV-unwrapping the model, but that is a slow and tedious process that can often be avoided simply by using the **Node Wrangler** add-on. We will learn about UV mapping later, as it creates better results than **Node Wrangler**, but is more difficult to learn. So for now, we will learn how to apply a simple texture to a complex object in just a few steps:

1.  Add the **Node Wrangler** nodes to the **Principled BSDF** node in a new material.

Figure 3.27 – Adding the **Node Wrangler** nodes to a new material

2.  Load an image into the **Image Texture** node. By default, the **Texture Coordinate** node is set to **UV**. Since we did not UV-unwrap the model and Blender does not know how to correctly unwrap this model without our help, the result will be a complete mess.

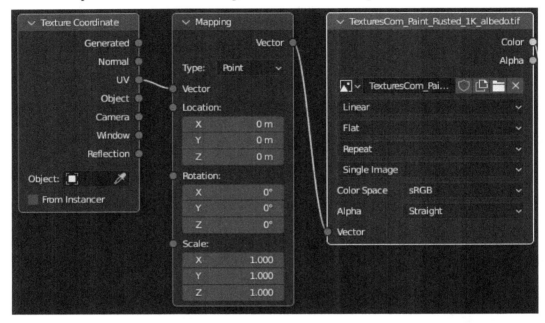

Figure 3.28 – Default settings in **Node Wrangler**

*Figure 3.29* shows the default result.

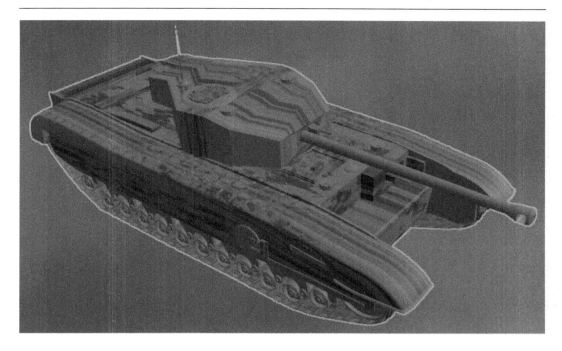

Figure 3.29 – Bad mapping caused by bad UVs

3.   Change the connection between the **Texture Coordinate** node and the **Mapping** node so that the **Object** output is connected to the **Mapping** node, as shown in *Figure 3.30*.

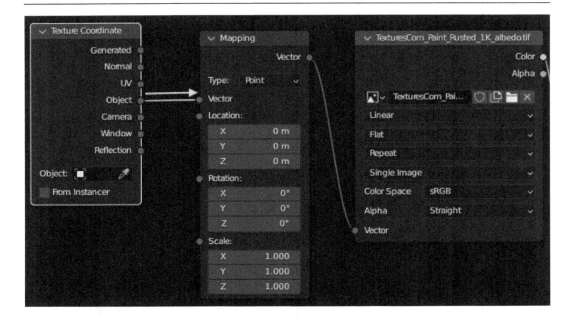

Figure 3.30 – Mapping by object

This will change the way the texture is projected onto the object so that the image will be evenly projected on all sides of the 3D model. This allows us to map a texture to any object instantly, without stretching or deforming the texture on any of the sides as shown in *Figure 3.31*.

Figure 3.31 – Texture mapped by object

Now, the texture is projected from above, which is why it is still stretched on the sides.

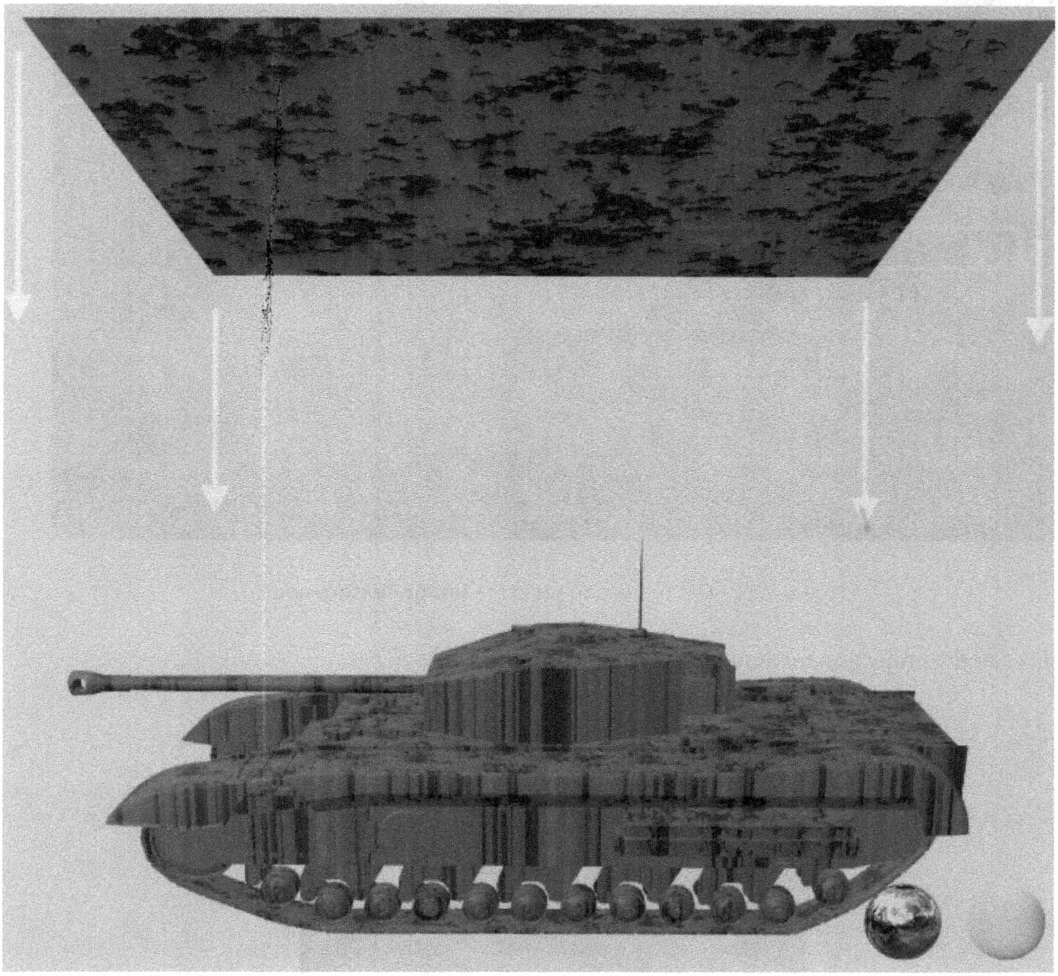

Figure 3.32 – Flat texture projection

The reason it is projected from above is because currently, the projection method is set to **Flat** in the **Image Texture** node, as shown in *Figure 3.33*. If you hover your cursor over the projection method box, Blender will display more information.

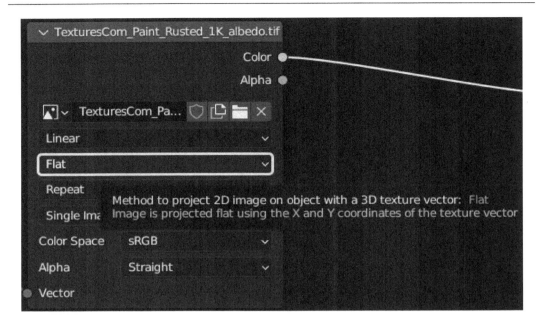

Figure 3.33 – Flat projection set in the **Image Texture** node

4.  Set the projection method to **Box** via the dropdown.

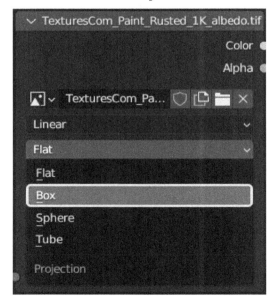

Figure 3.34 – Setting the projection method to Box

This will project the image onto the texture from all directions, making a much more realistic and desirable result. Combining multiple textures and applying them with **Node Wrangler** can create a simple but effective result, as shown in *Figure 3.35*.

Figure 3.35 – Object textured with **Node Wrangler**

We can now easily control the level of texture detail by adjusting the scale in the **Mapping** node. For example, if we set the scale to 4.000 on all axes for a texture, the texture pattern will become much smaller, as shown in the example in *Figure 3.36*.

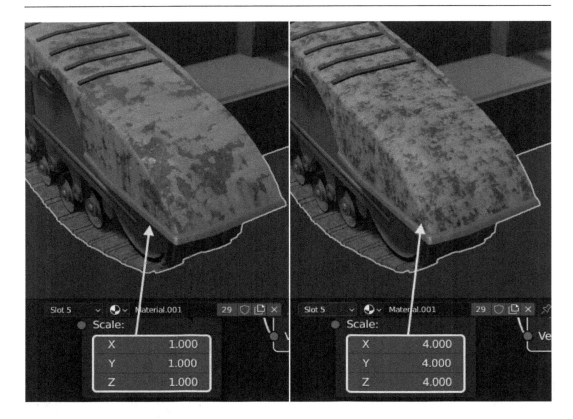

Figure 3.36 – Increasing the scale on a texture in **Node Wrangler**

This method of texturing is usually effective for texturing simple objects, or objects not intended to be observed up close, but rather from a distance. It is not recommended for highly realistic models because mapping imperfections and tiling may be noticeable.

Tiling occurs when a texture is repeated due to its projection being scaled up. An example is shown in *Figure 3.37*, where we can see the same patterns being repeated. It is generally considered an undesirable result but may be useful when creating floor tiles or other pattern textures.

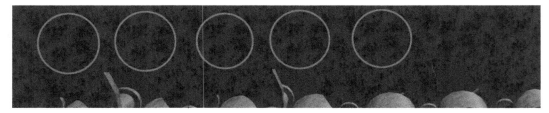

Figure 3.37 – Repetition visible in a highly scaled texture

We now have the tools required to quickly map simple textures onto objects. We will often find ourselves using this feature later to save time.

## Summary

In this chapter, we learned how Blender projects images onto objects via UV mapping and with the help of the **Node Wrangler** add-on. We learned to correctly map textures onto some basic shapes and how to automatically project a texture onto any object. This allows us to map textures quickly and easily onto objects with just a few clicks, saving us time when texturing simpler materials and assets.

In *Chapter 4, Achieving Realism with Texture Maps*, we will learn how we can use albedo maps, roughness maps, and normal maps to improve the quality of our textures.

# Part 2:
# Understanding Realistic Texturing

In *Part 2*, we dive deeper into the more sophisticated texturing techniques that allow us to create realism in Blender. We explore how texture maps can be used to add realistic features to materials, how to acquire and generate custom texture maps, and how to create displacement maps to control surface imperfections on 3D models.

This part has the following chapters:

- *Chapter 4, Achieving Realism with Texture Maps*
- *Chapter 5, Generating Texture Maps with Cycles*
- *Chapter 6, Creating Bumpy Surfaces with Displacement Maps*

# 4

# Achieving Realism with Texture Maps

**Texture maps** are special types of textures used to increase the level of realism of a material. Creating and using texture maps is an important part of the texturing process. These maps are usually created by converting a regular image texture into a texture map using special tools. We will use texture maps in this book to add special effects to our materials, such as surface bumps, patterns, and other details. This is beneficial because we can conveniently apply all the details and properties of real-life materials using just a few separate images.

The level of realism in a 3D artist's work is a key indicator of their skill and professionalism. Being able to create photorealistic works is an important demonstration of an artist's ability, including photorealistic product images and videos, architectural visualization, and interior design. Having the skills to create photorealistic artwork is by far the best way to impress potential clients and employers, and creating high-quality materials is one of the most important factors in achieving photorealism. With just a few simple tricks, we can greatly improve the quality of our work to make it more impressive.

There are many different types of texture maps. Albedo maps determine colors, Roughness maps determine roughness, normal maps simulate bumps and surface details, displacement maps modify geometry to make it bumpy, specular maps control specularity, emission maps control emission colors, metal maps control metalness, and so on. Almost all material properties, such as roughness, metallic, and emission, can be controlled using a texture map, along with other properties that we will learn about later in this book.

In this chapter, we will learn how some of the most important texture maps work to achieve realism in our textures. We will first study what the different types of texture maps can do, before diving into their underlying mechanics, which will help us understand how they work. Since most texture maps work in a similar way, we will only need to cover a few of them to understand them all. We will also learn how to create transparent textures by leveraging Alpha maps.

By the end of this chapter, you will have a clear understanding of how realistic texturing works in Blender, and you will be ready to practice creating high-quality materials with texture maps.

The following topics will be discussed in this chapter:

- Using Albedo maps to create a base texture

- Introducing Roughness maps

- Using Normal maps to detail surfaces

- Creating transparency

## Technical requirements

The prepared resources can be found in the Chapter04 folder within the book's downloadable resources folder, available here: `https://packt.link/mA1OU`

## Using Albedo maps to create a base texture

**Albedo map** is the term used to refer to an image that we apply to an object to create a basic texture. This is also known as a **color map**. We briefly used an Albedo map to create a texture previously in the *Creating textures with the Image Texture node* section of *Chapter 2, Introducing Material Nodes*.

Any image can be used as an Albedo map, such as a picture of a wooden surface, a painting, or a logo. It is thus completely up to you what image you would like to place in a material. For most purposes, you will probably need to use images of materials; we will learn how to acquire these materials later in *Chapter 5, Generating Texture Maps with Cycles*.

*Figure 4.1* shows a simple Albedo map of a brick texture.

Figure 4.1 – Brick Albedo map

As we have learned previously, in the *Creating textures with the Image Texture node* section of *Chapter 2*, albedo maps are loaded into an **Image Texture** node and plugged into the **Base Color** input of a **Principled BSDF** node, as shown in *figure 4.2*.

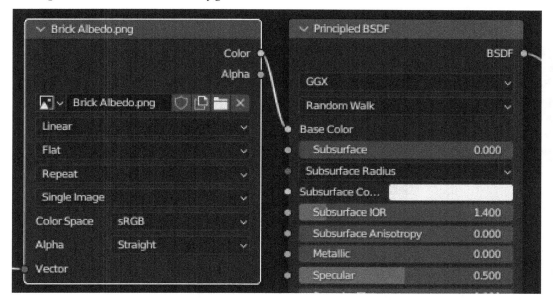

Figure 4.2 – Image Texture node with an Albedo map plugged into a Principled BSDF node

Any image can be an Albedo map, but ideally, it should be a colored, shadeless, and seamless of a material, such as a brick wall or a wooden surface.

A seamless texture is a texture that, when tiled, creates a perfect pattern without any visible separation between individual tiles. *Figure 4.3* shows the brick texture tiled on a plane, without any visible edges between the tiles. Seamless textures can be acquired by searching for `Brick Seamless Texture` in a search engine or using specialized sites, which we will explore in *Chapter 5*.

Figure 4.3 – A tiled, seamless texture on a cube

Albedo maps are the most basic forms of texture maps and they act as a foundation to a realistic material. Acquiring and applying an albedo map is typically the first step in the texturing process. Now that we understand what Albedo maps are and how they work, we can explore some other texture maps and how they will affect our materials to create more detailed and higher-quality results.

## Introducing Roughness maps

**Roughness maps**, as the name suggests, are images used to control the level of roughness on different parts of a texture. Lower levels of roughness will lead to a glossier object. Adjusting this property with a roughness map can have a significant impact on the level of realism of a material, as not all parts of a material always have the same level of roughness. *Figure 4.4* shows the Roughness map corresponding to the Albedo map from *Figure 4.1*.

Figure 4.4 – A Roughness map for a brick texture

As you can see, the Roughness map looks just like the Albedo map, except it is black and white. To understand how a roughness map works, let's view the **Roughness** slider in the **Principled BSDF** node, shown in *Figure 4.5*.

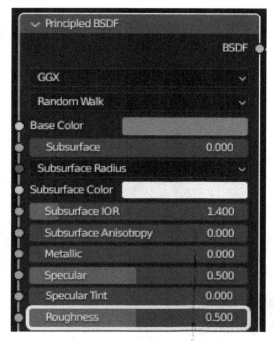

Figure 4.5 – Roughness slider in the Principled BSDF node

To control the roughness of a material, we only need to give Blender a single numerical value between 0.000 and 1.000. Since this is the same type of value used to define the brightness of a color, we can use the brightness of a color to define the roughness of a material. Let's explore how this works.

In the *Creating materials* section of *Chapter 1, Creating Materials in Blender*, we learned that when we switch to the HSV control, we can pick a figure between 0.000 and 1.000 to determine the value or brightness of the color.

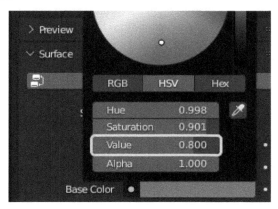

Figure 4.6 – Controlling the value of a color

In the **Roughness** property, a value of 0.000 means no roughness at all, or a completely clear material. In the **Base Color** property, 0.000 means no brightness, or a completely black material. So, to Blender, a black image means the same thing as the number 0.000 in this context. In other words, a black-colored pixel means no roughness at all, while a white-colored pixel means full roughness. We can use this information to create and control roughness maps and make materials appear realistic.

Let's use some basic nodes to create a simple black image, as we learned in the *Generating images with nodes* section of *Chapter 2, Introducing Material Nodes*.

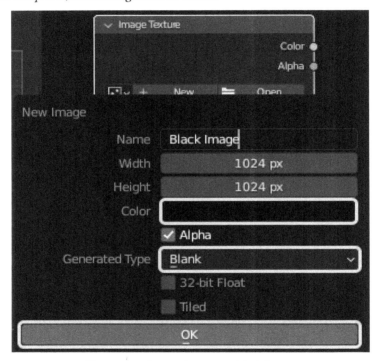

Figure 4.7 – Generating a new black image

Since the image is completely black, Blender reads the value of every pixel as 0.000.

Plugging this image into the **Roughness** input of a **Principled BSDF** node in a material will make Blender use the color of the image as a value for the roughness. Since the color is black, the value is registered as 0.000, making the material completely clear, as shown in *Figure 4.8*.

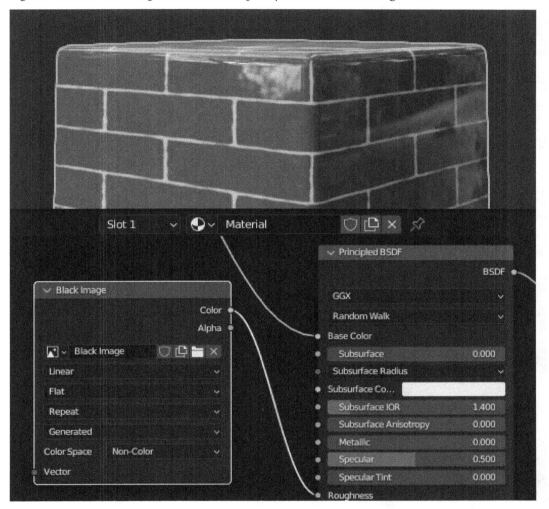

Figure 4.8 – A fully black roughness map creates a completely clear material

As you would imagine, we can use any image to control the level of roughness and get a more detailed result. We will now apply a roughness map to demonstrate how it can control the roughness of a material. Since some pixels of the noise texture are darker than others, the image will cause variations in the roughness of the material when plugged into the **Roughness** input of the **Principled BSDF** node, as shown in *Figure 4.9*.

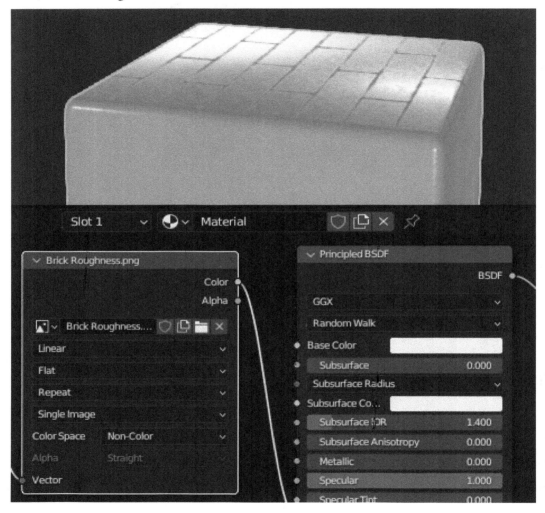

Figure 4.9 – A material with a roughness map but no color map

Combining these two images gives us a better result than just a texture with constant roughness, as shown in *Figure 4.10*.

Figure 4.10 – A material with constant roughness compared to a material with a Roughness map

We have now learned that Roughness maps can be used to control the level of roughness on a texture to create a more realistic material. This is useful in adding a more natural appearance to materials and adding variety to their level of glossiness. For example, it can be used on scratched textures where the scratches are shinier than the rest of the surface, or for making an object appear greasy. Next, let's learn how Normal maps can help us improve this texture further.

# Using Normal maps to detail surfaces

**Normal maps** are special texture maps used to simulate surface details and bumps. Their purpose is to increase the level of apparent detail on a texture or object without adding any new geometry. Normal maps, as with other texture maps, can also be applied through **Image Texture** nodes, but they will require us to change a few extra things to let Blender know that this is a special type of image. *Figure 4.11* shows an example of a Normal map.

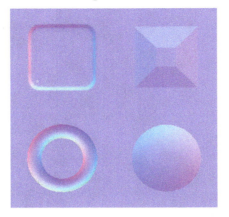

Figure 4.11 – A simple Normal map

To apply this Normal map, we must first set **Color Space** to **Non-Color** in the Image Texture node. Then, we must add a normal map node and plug it into the **Normal** input of the **Principled BSDF** node. Blender will now know how to read this image correctly.

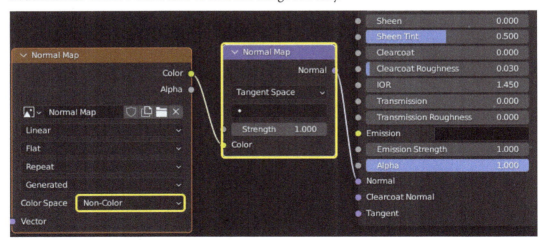

Figure 4.12 – Processing a Normal map

If we apply this Normal map to a material, it will simulate bumps on the surface, as shown in *Figure 4.13*.

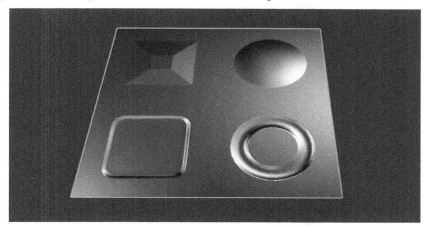

Figure 4.13 – A Normal map applied to a material

Even though this surface appears to have bumps on it in the material view, these bumps are not part of the object's geometry. If we view this object in Edit Mode, we will see that this surface is completely flat, as shown in *Figure 4.14*.

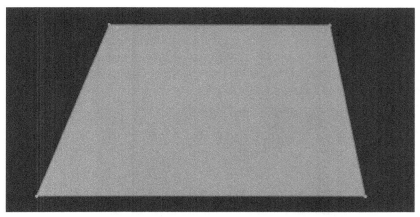

Figure 4.14 – The same surface viewed in Edit Mode

On a Normal map, every angle on a surface is represented by a different color. To understand how this works, look at *Figure 4.15*. As you can see, different parts of the bump have different colors, depending on the direction in which the surface is facing at any point. In this simple diagram, the right direction is defined by pink, up is defined by light blue, left is defined by dark blue, and down is defined by purple.

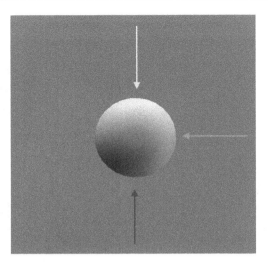

Figure 4.15 – Colors representing different directions

Blender reads the color of each pixel and redirects light rays from a surface depending on the color at a particular part of the Normal map. As a result, this makes the light rays bounce off the surface the same way they would if there were an actual bump.

Normal maps are commonly used to add more realism to textures by making them appear more detailed. For example, they are used for adding bumps and various surface details, such as screws, panel separations, or natural crevices. We will learn two different methods for generating Normal maps in *Chapter 5, Baking Texture Maps with Cycles*. *Figure 4.16* shows a brick texture with a Normal map, which makes it appear as if there are actual bumps on the surface.

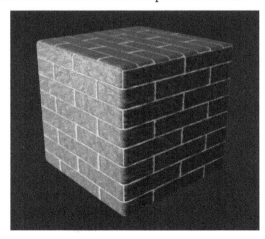

Figure 4.16 – A brick texture with a Normal map

We now have an idea of what Normal maps are, how they work, and what they can be used for. This is important for adding details and increasing the quality of our materials. Next, let's learn how to create transparency on an object using Alpha maps.

# Creating transparency

We will now learn two different ways to create transparency in Blender. First, we will learn how Alpha maps can be used to create transparent areas in a texture, and then we will learn how to create realistic glass in the Cycles render engine. This will allow us to create vegetation, nets, windows, bottles, damaged fabric, and other objects that require some level of transparency.

## Understanding Alpha maps

**Alpha maps** are texture maps used to control the transparency of a material. **Alpha** is a property of color that measures the degree of **opacity**, and opacity is the level of visibility of a texture. If an image is transparent, it means that it has no opacity, or that its alpha value is 0. Alpha maps are useful for textures on which some parts are transparent while other parts are non-transparent, such as vegetation or a fishing net texture.

Much like a roughness map uses the brightness of each pixel to determine the roughness value of a texture, an Alpha map uses the brightness of pixels to determine the alpha value. *Figure 4.17* shows the Alpha map of a simple grass texture.

Figure 4.17 – An Alpha map of a tuft of grass

An Alpha map can be simply plugged into the **Alpha** input of the **Principled BSDF** node, as shown in *Figure 4.18*.

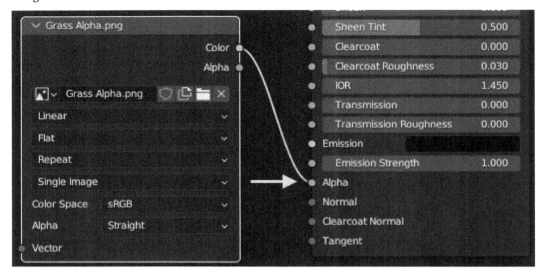

Figure 4.18 – Plugging an Alpha map into a Principled BSDF node

To enable transparency on a material, it is important to adjust one more setting. In the **Material Properties** tab, find the **Settings** menu and set **Blend Mode** to **Alpha Hashed**, as shown in *Figure 4.19*.

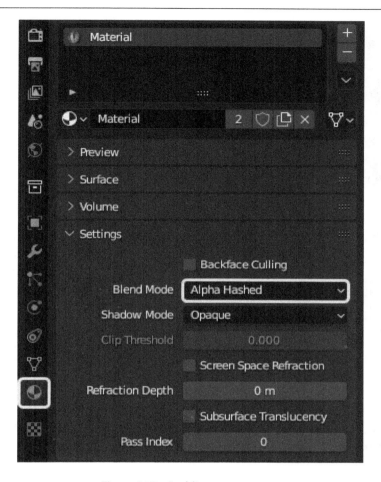

Figure 4.19 – Enabling transparency

We can now observe that the previously black areas on the texture are completely transparent in the 3D view, allowing us to create vegetation and other transparent textures, as shown in *Figure 4.20*.

Figure 4.20 – A plane with a transparent grass texture

We have now learned how Alpha maps can be used to create transparent textures in Blender, which gives us a lot of freedom to create various see-through objects. Next, let's learn how to create a simple but realistic glass material in Blender.

## Creating realistic glass in Cycles

We will now learn how to create glass in Blender. In the following steps, we will create a material and adjust its properties to give us glass:

1.  Set the render engine to Cycles. Since Eevee and Cycles process light differently, this method will not work in Eevee as well as it does in Cycles and the material will not be fully transparent in Eevee.

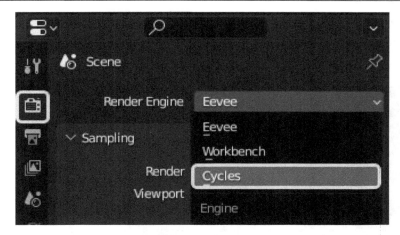

Figure 4.21 – Switching to the Cycles render engine

2.   Add a monkey to the scene.

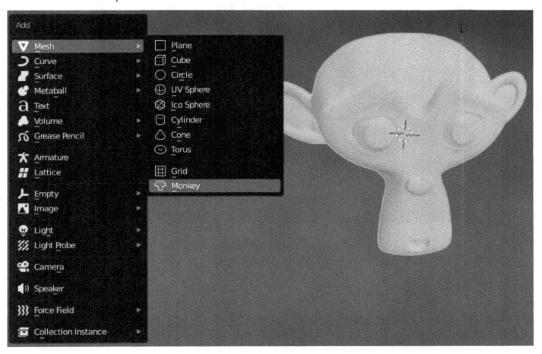

Figure 4.22 – Adding a monkey

3.  In a new material created for this monkey, set **Roughness** to 0.000 and **Transmission** to 1.000, as shown in *Figure 4.23*.

    To improve the shading, press the Right Mouse Button and select Shade Smooth

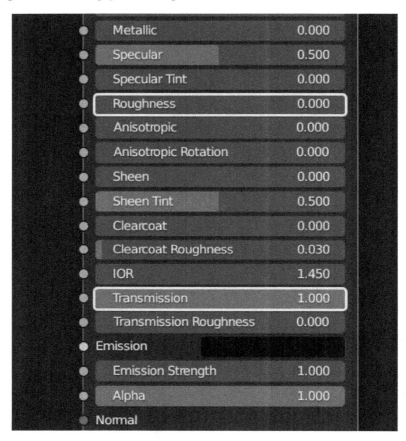

Figure 4.23 – Adjusting the properties for glass

In the rendered view, the monkey now has a perfect glass texture, as shown in *Figure 4.24*. This image uses an HDRI environment image to make the glass more realistic. You will learn how to use HDRIs in *Chapter 12*, *Creating Photorealistic Environments with HDRIs*.

Figure 4.24 – Glass material in rendered view

This method will still work in Eevee, but the glass will not be transparent, as shown in *Figure 4.25*.

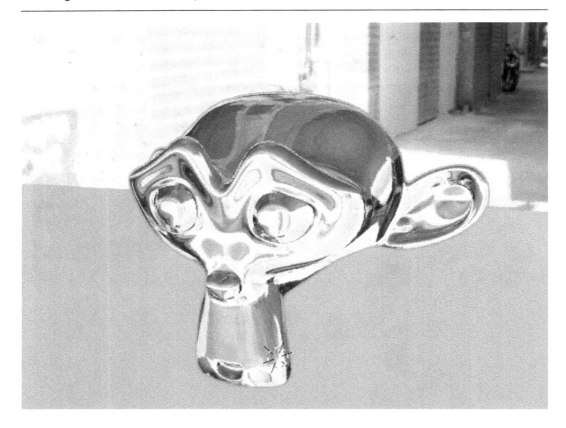

Figure 4.25 – Glass material in Eevee

We can now create transparent materials with two different methods. Alpha maps can be used to create materials and textures with transparent areas, such as plants, fences, or nets. Glass materials can be used to create furniture, windows, jewelry, and various kinds of ornaments.

## Summary

In this chapter, we learned what texture maps are and how they work, and we explored some of the most commonly used texture maps. We also learned how to create transparency with Alpha maps and by creating glass.

In *Chapter 5, Generating Texture Maps with Cycles*, we will learn how to create our own texture maps inside Blender, or with the help of some external tools, and apply them to our materials. This will give us the freedom to download any material from the internet and easily bring it into Blender or create our own custom materials and texture maps.

# 5

# Generating Texture Maps with Cycles

In this chapter, we will learn to acquire or create texture maps both inside Blender and with the help of **GIMP**. GIMP is a popular, free image-editing program that we will use throughout this book to create texture maps and custom decals. We will begin by exploring ways to find textures online, before learning about the different ways to turn textures into texture maps. We will then apply the textures to our materials in Blender.

By the end of this chapter, you will be able to create, download, and apply your own materials and texture maps in Blender.

The following topics will be covered in this chapter:

- Using texture libraries
- Applying texture maps in Blender
- Creating Roughness maps in Blender
- Baking Normal maps in Blender
- Generating Roughness maps in GIMP
- Generating Normal maps in GIMP

## Technical requirements

GIMP will be used in this chapter to create texture maps and modify textures. It can be downloaded for free from https://www.gimp.org/downloads/.

The prepared resources can be found in the Chapter05 folder within the book's downloadable resources folder, available here: https://packt.link/mA1OU

## Using texture libraries

**Texture libraries** are websites from which you can download a variety of high-quality textures and texture maps. Although most texture libraries charge a subscription fee for full access, they still have lots of textures available for free. Here are some popular texture libraries:

- `https://www.textures.com/`
- `https://ambientcg.com/`
- `https://polyhaven.com/`

To find materials and texture maps on `Textures.com`, visit the site and find the **Library** button in the top pane, as marked in *Figure 5.1*.

Figure 5.1 – The Textures.com home page

Then, click on the **PBR Materials** section on the left side of the page, as shown in *Figure 5.2*.

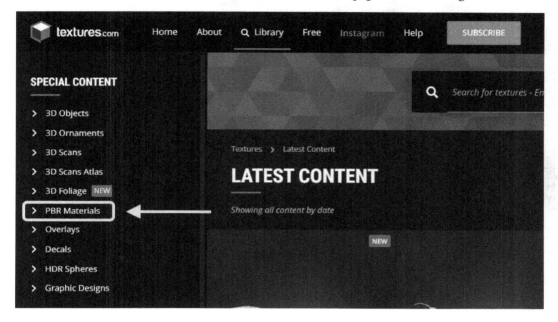

Figure 5.2 – The PBR Materials section

This will open a large library of materials, which include texture maps. You can see this in *Figure 5.3*.

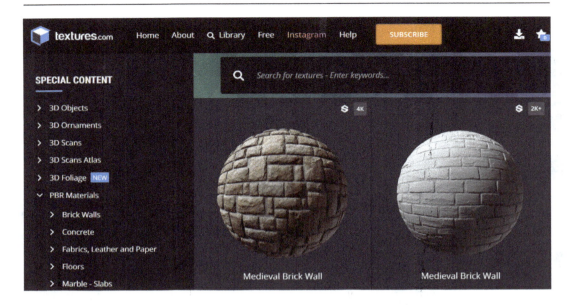

Figure 5.3 – A library of PBR materials

Clicking on a material will reveal download buttons for the texture and its texture maps, as shown in *Figure 5.4*.

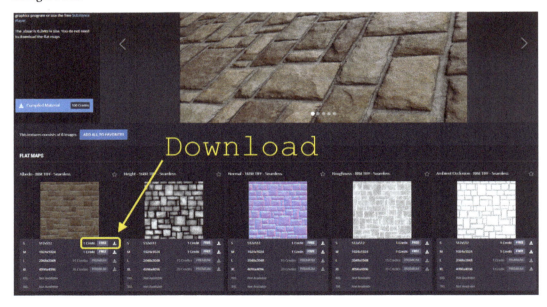

Figure 5.4 – Downloading a texture map

Since all texture libraries work in a similar way, we can now find and download high-quality textures and texture maps from various websites. Here, you will find most of the materials you will ever need. Next, we will learn to correctly apply these texture maps in Blender.

## Applying texture maps in Blender

We will now apply an Albedo map, Roughness map, and Normal map to a material in Blender using nodes. For this exercise, you can use any material from any of these websites, as they all work the same way.

Let us add the texture maps to a material on a cube:

1.  Add a Node Wrangler to a **Principled BSDF** node with *Ctrl + T*, and plug it into the base color.

Figure 5.5 – Adding a Node Wrangler

2.  Click on the **Open** button in the **Image Texture** node, and load the Albedo map. The Albedo map file will most likely have a complex name, but it will end with the word albedo. For example, the file might be named TexturesCom_Wall_BrickPlain3_2.5x2.5_B_1K_albedo.

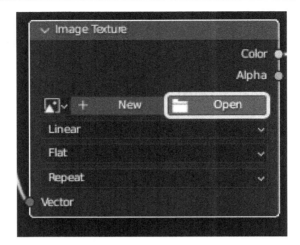

Figure 5.6 – Opening a file

3.    Next, add a second Node Wrangler, and plug it into the **Roughness** input. In this Image Texture node, load the **Roughness** map. This image will have the same name as the Albedo map, except it will end with `Roughness`.

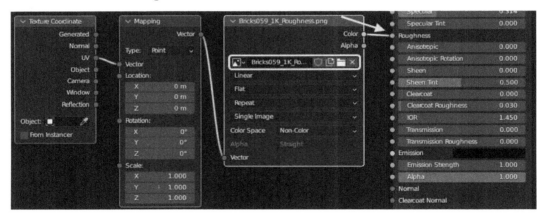

Figure 5.7 – Loading a Roughness map with a second Node Wrangler

4.    Set **Color Space** to **Non-Color** in the Roughness map Image Texture node.

This will tell Blender to read this image not as a color map but as an image containing a different type of information. In this case, we want it to read the value of each pixel.

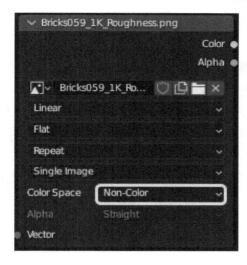

Figure 5.8 – Setting Color Space to Non-Color

5.    Add one last Node Wrangler, and plug it into the **Normal** input. Load the Normal map here, and set **Color Space** to **Non-Color**.

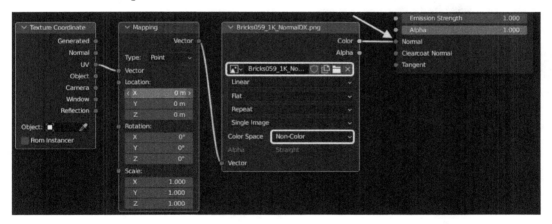

Figure 5.9 – Loading a Normal map with a Node Wrangler

6.    Add a **Normal Map** node, and place it between the Image Texture node and the Principled BSDF node.

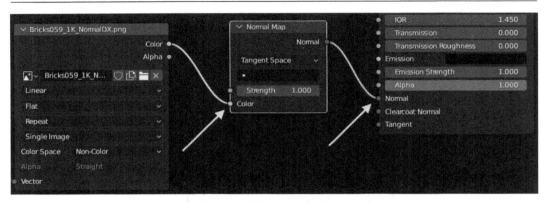

Figure 5.10 – Adding a Normal map node

The material now has all the basic texture maps applied and looks more realistic, as shown in *Figure 5.11*.

Figure 5.11 – A brick texture with texture maps applied

We have now learned how to correctly load texture maps into Blender and apply them to a material. Next, we will learn how to turn an Albedo map into a Roughness map in Blender, using nodes.

# Creating Roughness maps in Blender

We will now learn to use nodes to convert an Albedo map into a Roughness map and apply it to our material. This method is useful because it gives us direct control over the Roughness map, so we can make changes to it without loading it into an external program every time.

In the following steps, we will use nodes to turn an Albedo map into a Roughness map:

1. Load an Albedo map through a Node Wrangler.

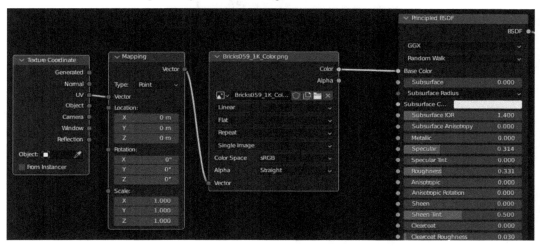

Figure 5.12 – Loading the Albedo map

2. Add a second Node Wrangler, and once again, load the Albedo map into the Image Texture node. These nodes should be plugged into the **Roughness** input, with **Color Space** set to **Non-Color**.

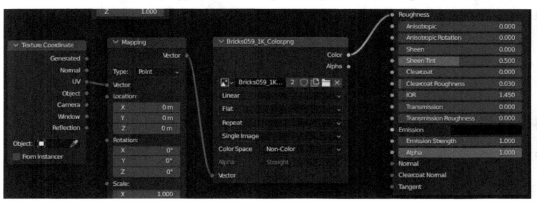

Figure 5.13 – Converting an Albedo map into a Roughness map

3.  In the second Image Texture node, click on the button marked with **2**.

Figure 5.14 – Making a copy of an image

This will make a copy of the same image so that Blender can process the two images separately. One will be used as the Albedo map and the other as the Roughness map.

4.  Add a **Hue Saturation Value** node between the second Image Texture node and the Principled BSDF node. Set the saturation to 0.000.

The Hue Saturation Value node is used to make our texture black and white, as a roughness map should be.

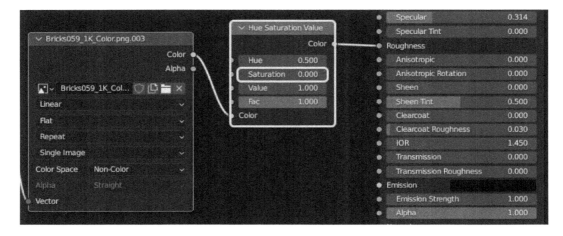

Figure 5.15 – Adding a Hue Saturation Value node

5.    Add a **Bright/Contrast** node. This node is useful to make changes to the roughness map. Increasing or decreasing the brightness will make the roughness greater or smaller, respectively. Changing the contrast will change the difference between the rough and clear parts of the map.

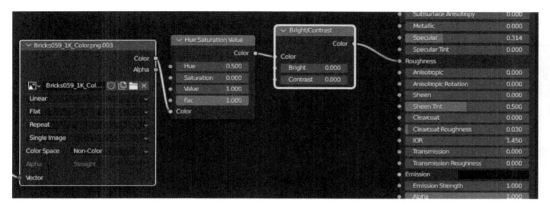

Figure 5.16 – Adding a Bright/Contrast node

We can now turn any texture into a Roughness map with a simple node setup. This method is convenient when you need to adjust a Roughness map because it saves time. Next, we will learn to bake Normal maps in Blender.

# Baking Normal maps in Blender

We will now learn to **bake** normal maps in Blender using the Cycles render engine. **Baking** is the process of saving attributes such as color, roughness, or even bumpiness into an image that can be exported or used elsewhere. The features on the surface in *Figure 5.17* can be baked into a normal map image so that it can be used to simulate the same features, without actually creating them as a 3D surface. This method will allow us to simulate highly detailed surfaces without increasing the polygon count of our scene.

Figure 5.17 – Surface details

These features are easy to replace with a normal map because they are quite close to the surface, and they appear as bumps rather than separate objects. In the following steps, we will turn these surface details into a normal map:

1.  Add a plane right above the surface with the details.

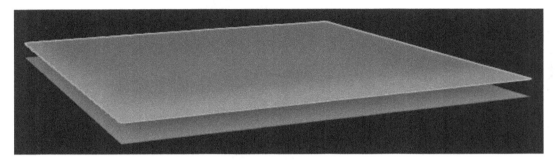

Figure 5.18 – Adding a plane above the surface with details

2.  Create a new material for the new plane, and add an **Image Texture** node.

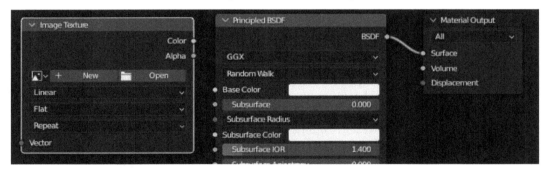

Figure 5.19 – Creating a new material

3.  Create a new image in the Image Texture node, and name it Normal Map.

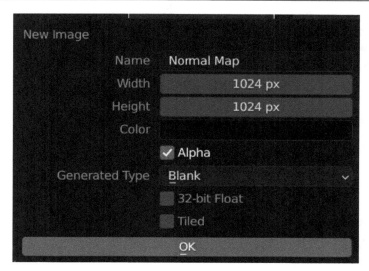

Figure 5.20 – Generating an image for a Normal map

4.  In the **Render Properties** tab on the right side of the screen, set **Render Engine** to **Cycles**.

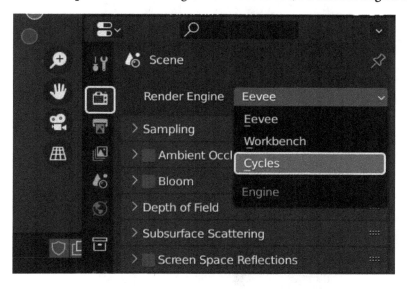

Figure 5.21 – Switching to the Cycles render engine

5.  Select the bottom surface first, and while holding *Shift*, select the top surface.

    The previously selected object(s) now have an orange outline, while the last selected object has a yellow outline. These selection types are referred to as **Selected** and **Active**, respectively.

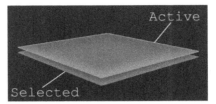

Figure 5.22 – A Selected object and an Active object

6.  Navigate to the **Bake** menu at the bottom of the **Render Properties** tab, and adjust the settings, as shown in *Figure 5.23*.

    In this menu, set **Bake Type** to **Normal**, check **Selected to Active**, and click **Bake**. We now tell Blender that we need a Normal map, generated from the selected object's surface, to be baked into the active object's material.

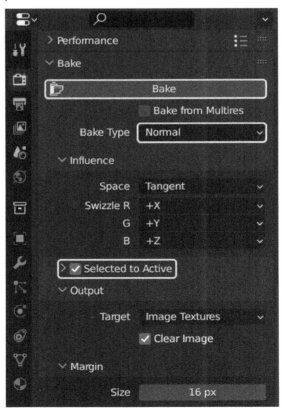

Figure 5.23 – Baking details from the Selected object to the Active object

If baking does not happen, ensure that the Image Texture node from the Active surface is selected in the Shader Editor.

Additionally, if the baked image is a dark yellow color (*Figure 5.24*) instead of purple (*Figure 5.25*), the Normal map is inverted. To fix this, correct the normals on both meshes with *Shift + N* and bake again.

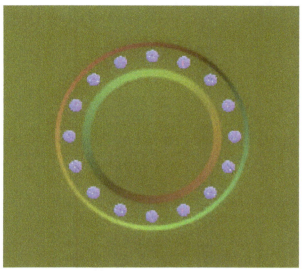

Figure 5.24 – The inverted Normal map

A successfully baked Normal map should look something like *Figure 5.25*.

Figure 5.25 – A baked Normal map

7.    Plug the Image Texture node into the Principled BSDF node and map it as you wish.

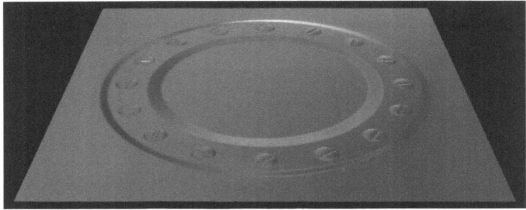

Figure 5.26 – Surface details simulated by a Normal map

We can now bake Normal maps to easily simulate surface details without adding lots of new geometry, which would increase our file size. Next, we will learn to create a roughness and a normal map externally in GIMP.

## Generating Roughness maps in GIMP

We will now learn to use GIMP for generating roughness maps. To do this, we will modify a texture in GIMP to turn it into a roughness map. This will allow us to easily create a roughness map for any existing texture. First, we will install GIMP and then we will quickly start creating texture maps.

GIMP can easily be substituted with other image editing programs such as Photoshop or even Paint.NET. The reason we are using GIMP is because it is completely free, and it has more advanced built-in features than other free image editors.

In the following steps, we will install GIMP and use it to create a Roughness map:

1.    Visit the link provided in the *Technical requirements* section of this chapter. Then, select your operating system and download GIMP directly from the website.

# Downloads
Translations: en

## Current Stable Version
The current stable release of GIMP is **2.10.34** (2023-02-21).

Show downloads for GNU/Linux | macOS | Microsoft Windows | All
(we think your OS is Microsoft Windows)

## GIMP for Windows                    Operating System

Figure 5.27 – Downloading GIMP

2.    Follow the Installation instructions provided by the program.

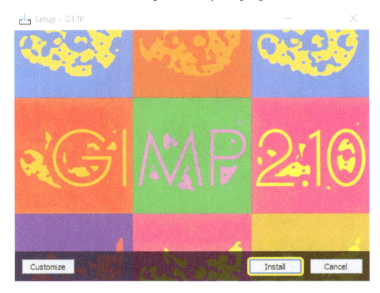

Figure 5.28 – Installing GIMP

3.    Open GIMP, and press *Ctrl + O* to open the file browser.

Figure 5.29 – Opening the file browser

4.    Locate and open an image texture from the file browser.

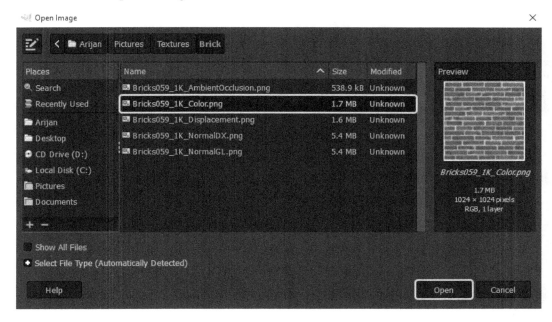

Figure 5.30 – Loading an Albedo map into GIMP

5.    In the top pane of the screen, open the **Colors** menu and select **Hue-Saturation**.

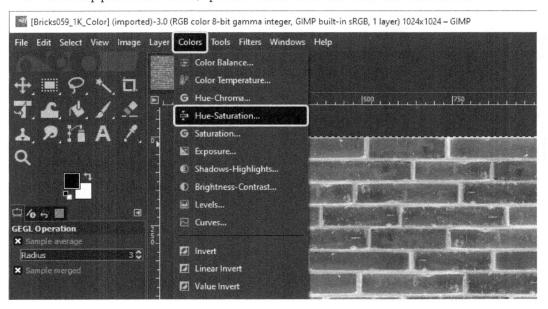

Figure 5.31 – Opening the hue-saturation properties

6.   In the menu, set the **Saturation** slider to its minimum value to make the image black and white.

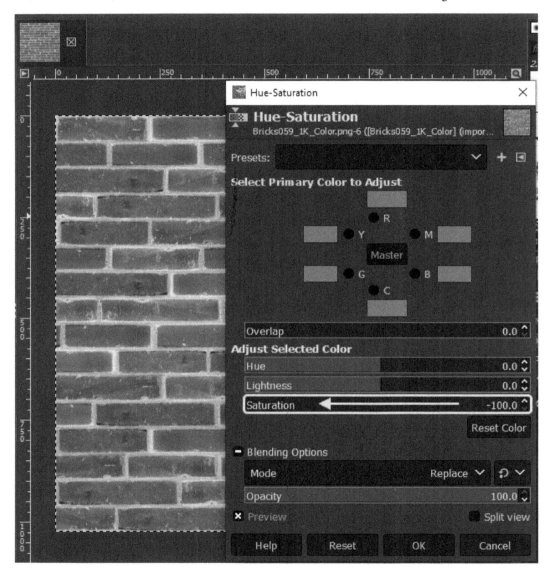

Figure 5.32 – Reducing the saturation of the image

7.    Next, go to the **Colors** menu again and click on **Brightness-Contrast…**.

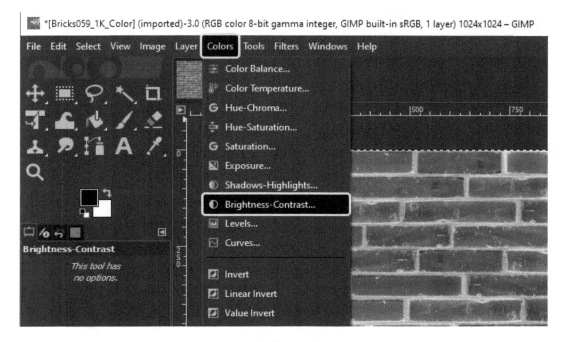

Figure 5.33 – Opening the Brightness-Contrast properties

8.    Optionally, adjust the **Brightness** and **Contrast** settings of the Roughness map using the sliders, as shown in *Figure 5.34*.

Figure 5.34 – Adjusting the brightness and contrast

9.  Open the **File** menu in the top-left corner, and click on **Export As**.

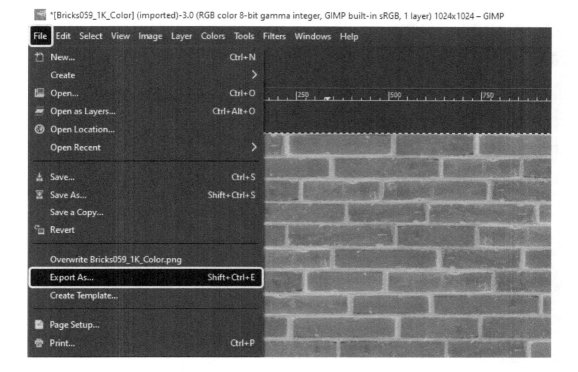

Figure 5.35 – Exporting the file

10. Name the file Roughness_Map.png, and click the **Export** button.

Figure 5.36 – Naming the file

11. Once again, click the **Export** button in the second menu.

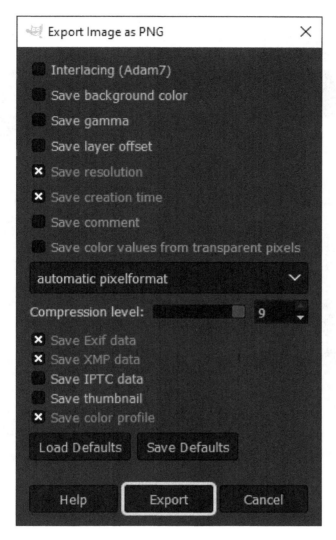

Figure 5.37 – Exporting the file

We now have a new Roughness map saved as an independent image. We can load this image into an Image Texture node to apply it to a material, as we learned previously. *Figure 5.38* shows how you can apply a Roughness map in Blender.

Figure 5.38 – Applying the Roughness map in Blender

> **Tip**
> Keeping a Bright/Contrast node between the Image Texture node and the Principled BSDF node is recommended, as it allows you to adjust the roughness map without opening it in GIMP every time.

Now that we know how to convert Albedo maps into Roughness maps externally, let's learn how to create Normal maps as well.

# Generating Normal maps in GIMP

We will now learn to quickly convert Albedo maps into Normal maps in GIMP. This will allow us to turn any image texture into a Normal map in a few clicks.

In the following steps, we will export a texture as a Normal map:

1.  Open the Albedo map in GIMP.

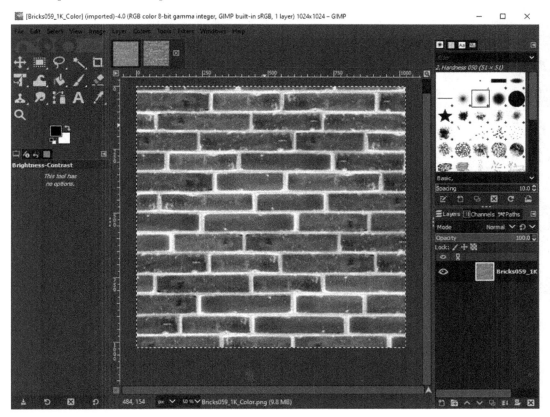

Figure 5.39 – Opening an Albedo map in GIMP

2.   Open the **Filters** menu from the top of the window, find the **Generic** section, and click on **Normal Map**.

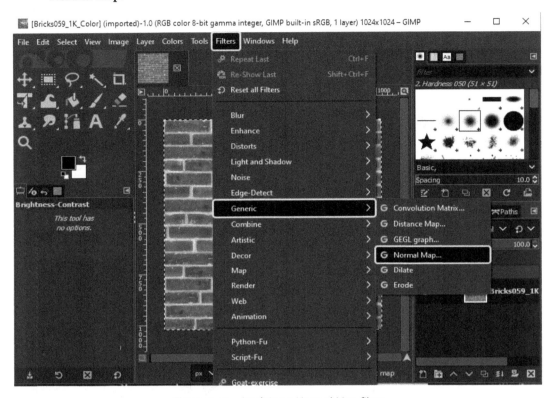

Figure 5.40 – Applying a Normal Map filter

GIMP will instantly turn the image into a Normal map and offer some tools to adjust the image, as shown in *Figure 5.41*. You can tweak the settings, but applying the default settings usually works well.

3.    Click the **OK** button.

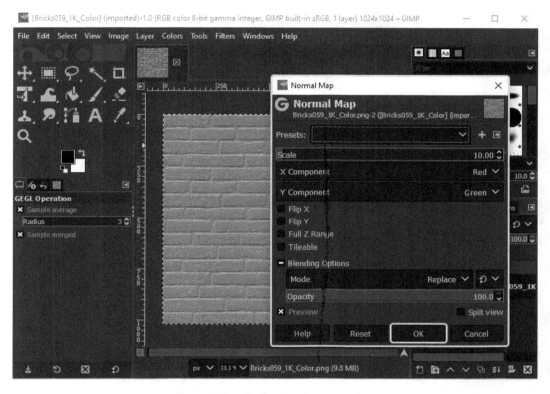

Figure 5.41 – Confirming the conversion

4.    Once again, export the image, and name the file `Normal_Map.png`.

Figure 5.42 – Exporting the Normal map

5.    We can now load this image into an Image Texture node and use it as a Normal map in Blender.

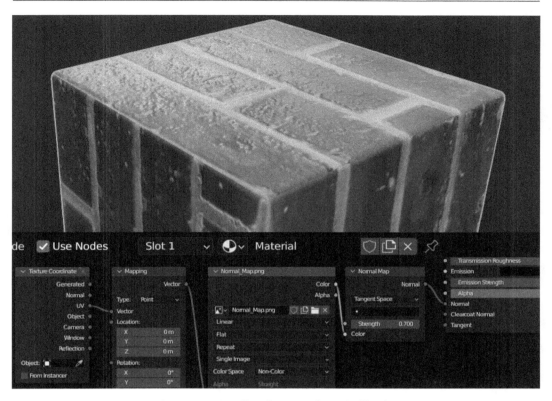

Figure 5.43 – Loading the normal map in Blender

We now know how to turn any texture into a Normal map in a few simple steps in GIMP.

## Summary

In this chapter, we learned how to download textures and texture maps from the internet and apply them in Blender using nodes. We then learned how to create our own Roughness maps and Normal maps in Blender, with the help of GIMP. Having access to an image editing program such as GIMP is important because almost any 3D project will require some external image editing, whether it is for texture maps, custom textures, decals, or post-processing.

We also learned how to bake normal maps. This allows us to easily turn surface details into normal maps that we can apply to any material. Baking can also be used for colors and roughness, and it is a great way to convert procedural materials into savable images.

In the next chapter, we will learn how to create some common materials by using the tools and techniques that we've learned, combining them with some tips and tricks to make them look realistic on a 3D model.

# 6

# Creating Bumpy Surfaces with Displacement Maps

In this chapter, we will learn about Displacement maps. We will first learn about how Displacement maps work and how they can be beneficial, before learning to create and apply them to 3D models in Blender.

Displacement maps will help us improve models and increase the overall level of realism. We will also learn two different ways to create Displacement maps, which will allow us to create them from existing textures, as well as to procedurally generate them inside Blender to create special organic objects and surfaces. This gives us more freedom to create different shapes and meshes with special effects.

By the end of this chapter, you will have a good understanding of how Displacement maps work and how they can be used to create custom, highly realistic surfaces.

The following topics will be covered in this chapter:

- Understanding Displacement maps
- Generating a Displacement map in GIMP
- Applying Displacement maps in Blender
- Generating Displacement maps in Blender

## Understanding displacement maps

**Displacement maps** are special texture maps used to create bumps on surfaces. While Normal maps are used to simulate bumpy surfaces, Displacement maps are used to actually reshape a surface. *Figure 6.1* shows two surfaces. The left surface uses a Displacement map, while the right surface uses a Normal map.

Figure 6.1 – A comparison of a Displacement map with a Normal map

The two surfaces look almost identical from this perspective, but if you look at their geometry, you can see they are very different. *Figure 6.2* shows the geometry of the two surfaces. The left surface has a higher poly count and is filled with bumps, while the right surface is a simple plane consisting of four edges.

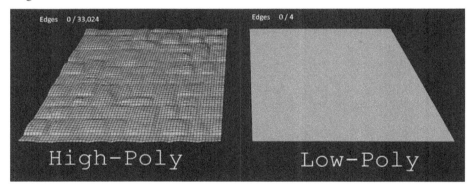

Figure 6.2 – The geometry of a displaced surface and a surface with a Normal map

The Displacement map applied to the high-poly surface causes some of its polygons to move upwards, while others stay low. The higher the number of polygons, the higher the resolution of the bumpy surface. *Figure 6.3* shows a texture-less surface that has a Displacement map affecting its geometry. As you can see, the surface has bumps shaped like the brick texture, and the outline of the surface has changed.

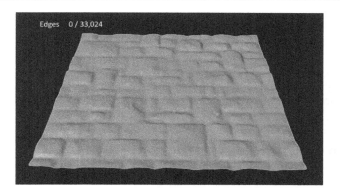

Figure 6.3 – A displaced surface with no texture

*Figure 6.4* shows the Displacement map used to create the surface from *Figure 6.3*. As you can see, the image is black and white, and the spaces between the bricks are completely dark while the bricks are light or dark gray. This map works much like a Roughness map, in that the height of a point on the surface is dictated by the value of the color on that part of the texture.

Figure 6.4 – The Displacement map

Displacement maps can be useful to generate highly realistic surfaces or to randomize shapes to make them appear more natural, which we will explore further in the *Generating displacement maps in Blender* section. There are two ways to generate displacement. One way is using an image editing program such as GIMP to convert a texture into a Displacement map, and another is by generating procedural displacement in Blender using special tools.

Both methods have their own purpose and benefits. Using GIMP allows us to create a specific Displacement map for an existing texture, such as wood or stone, to improve the quality of the textured result. Generating Displacement maps procedurally gives us the freedom to create custom and unique patterns and shapes that can be used to create various types of surfaces and objects.

Now that we understand what Displacement maps are and how they work, let's start creating our own Displacement maps, starting with the first method using GIMP.

## Generating a Displacement map in GIMP

We will now learn how to convert an albedo map into a Displacement map that we can use in Blender. In the following steps, we will use GIMP to turn a simple brick texture into a Displacement map.

This method of creating Displacement maps is beneficial when creating a Displacement map for a specific texture, but it cannot be used to create completely unique surfaces and patterns:

1.    Load an image texture into GIMP with *Ctrl + O*.

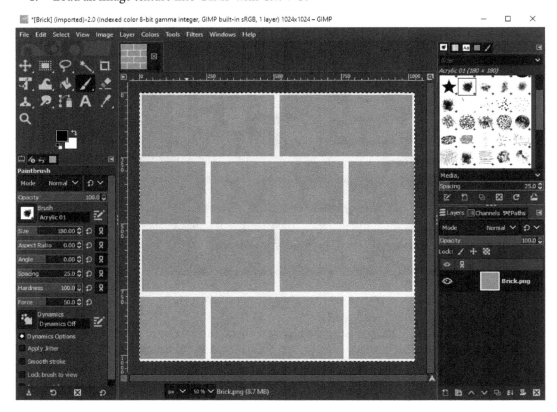

Figure 6.5 – Loading a texture into GIMP

2.  In the top pane, open the **Colors** menu and select **Hue-Saturation**.

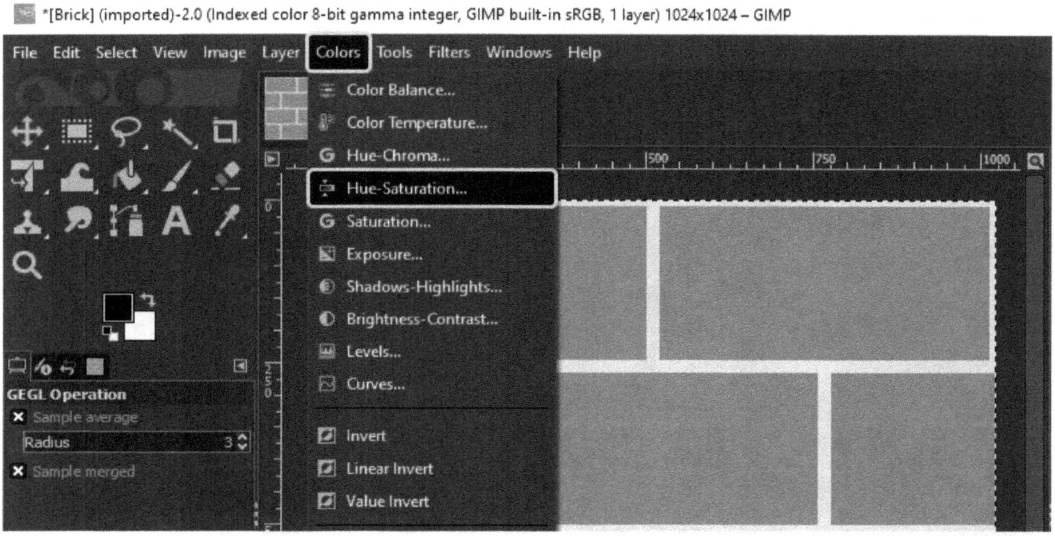

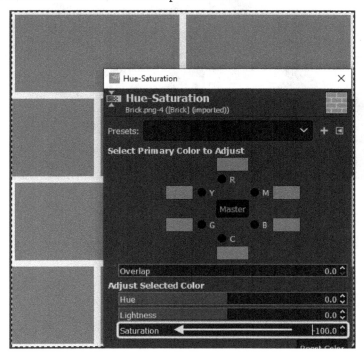

Figure 6.6 – Opening the Hue- Saturation properties

3.  Drag the **Saturation** slider to the lowest possible value.

Figure 6.7 – Reducing the saturation

> **Tip**
>
> The **Hue-Saturation** menu might not work as expected after working with normal maps. To prevent any issues, visit the **Image** menu in the top pane, open the **Mode** section, and select **RGB**.

4.    Now, open the **Filters** menu, and in the **Blur** section, select **Gaussian Blur…**.

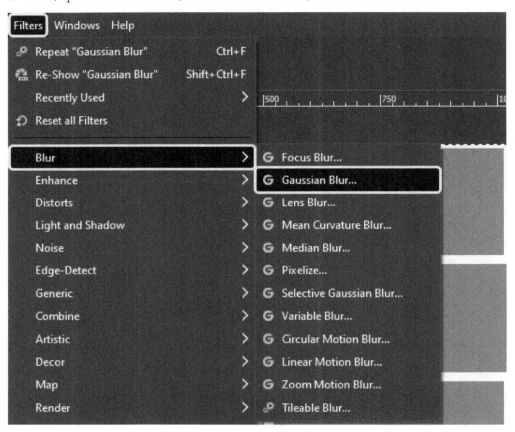

Figure 6.8 – Applying a Gaussian blur

5. Set the **Size** values to 7.

This adds a bit of blur to the image, which will make the Displacement map work better afterward.

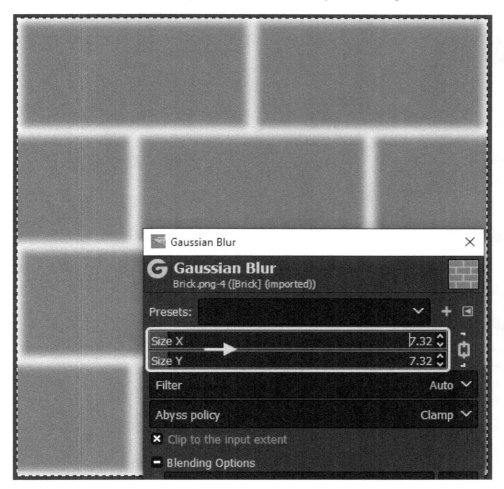

Figure 6.9 – Setting the blur value

6.  In the **Colors** menu, select **Invert**.

This will invert the colors, making the bricks gray and the gaps between them black. On a Displacement map, this means that the gaps are lower than the bricks.

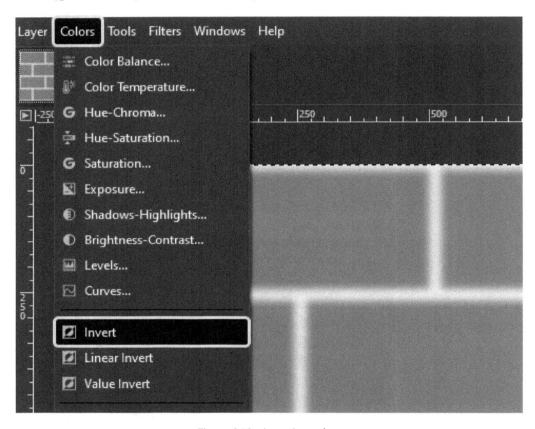

Figure 6.10 – Inverting colors

7.   Export the image with the **Export As…** option.

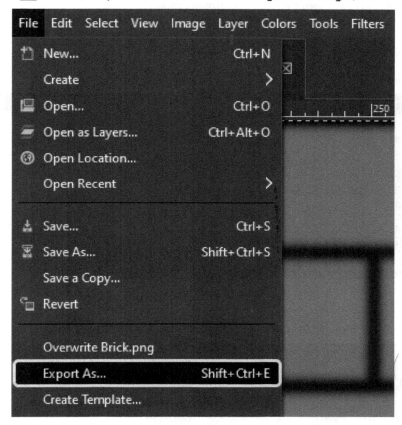

Figure 6.11 – Exporting the file

We now have a simple Displacement map for our brick texture. Now, let's take it into Blender.

## Applying Displacement maps in Blender

We will now learn how to load an image as a Displacement map and tell Blender how to correctly process it with the help of a Displace modifier. A **Displace modifier** is used to deform a mesh according to the value of the colors of a Displacement map.

In the following steps, we will prepare a mesh for displacement:

1.   Add a plane with *Shift + A*.

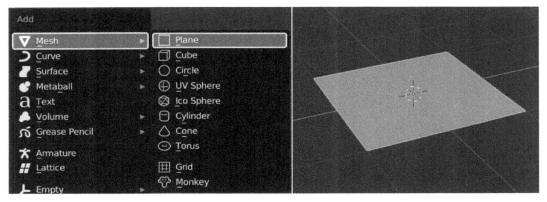

Figure 6.12 – Adding a plane

2.   In **Edit** mode, subdivide the plane by pressing *W* and selecting **Subdivide**.

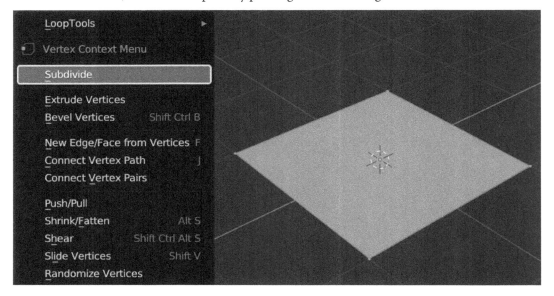

Figure 6.13 – Subdividing the plane

3.  In the **Subdivide** menu that appears in the bottom-left corner of the screen, set the number of cuts to 100.

    This will give us lots of geometry, which in turn will give us a more detailed result.

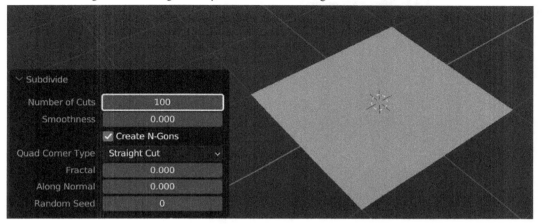

Figure 6.14 – Increasing the number of subdivisions

The plane now has 20,604 edges, which will help achieve a good displacement result. The higher the resolution, the better the result, so feel free to subdivide the surface even further.

Next, we will follow some steps to load our Displacement map and apply it to the surface:

1.  In the **Texture Properties** tab, click the **New** button to add a new image slot.

Figure 6.15 – Adding a new image slot

2. Click **Open** and load the Displacement map that we created earlier.

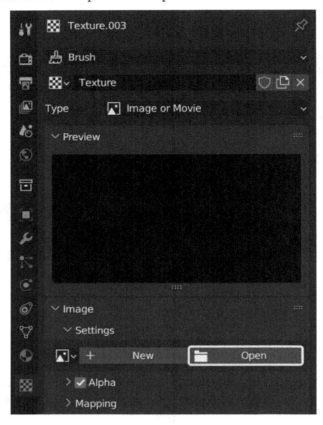

Figure 6.16 – Loading the Displacement map into Blender

3. Rename this image `Displacement Map`.

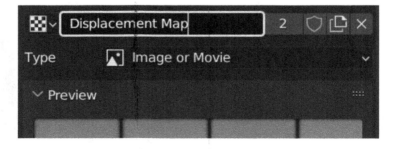

Figure 6.17 – Renaming the image

4.    In the **Modifier Properties** tab, add a **Displace** modifier.

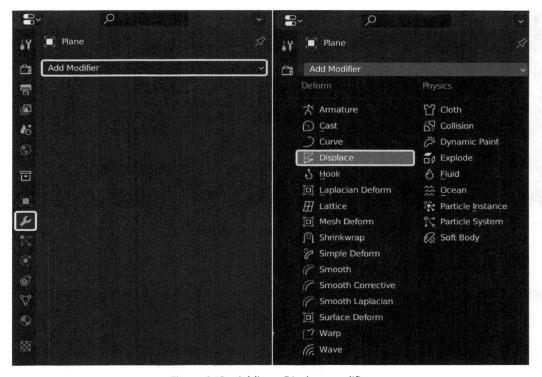

Figure 6.18 – Adding a Displace modifier

5.    In the **Displace** modifier menu, load **Displacement Map**.

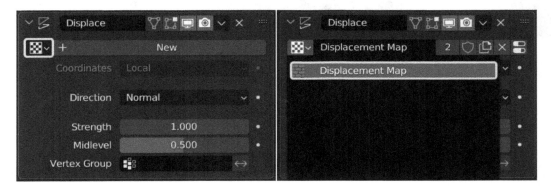

Figure 6.19 – Loading the Displacement map into the Displace modifier

The surface will now have visible bumps created by the Displacement map, as shown in *Figure 6.20*.

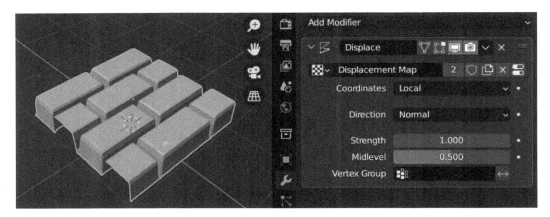

Figure 6.20 – A heavily displaced surface

6.    Adjust the **Strength** value to get a better result.

Figure 6.21 – Adjusting the displacement strength

7.   In the **Object** menu, click on **Shade Smooth** to make the surface appear smoother.

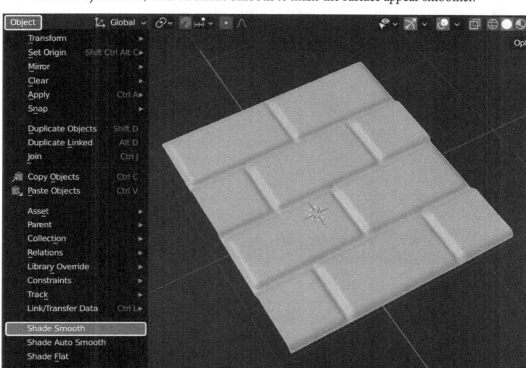

Figure 6.22 – Smooth shading

We now have a Displacement map influencing the mesh and creating a bumpy surface. It will look like *Figure 6.23*.

Figure 6.23 – The effect of a Displacement map on a surface

We can also apply other texture maps to this object to make it more complete, as shown in *Figure 6.24*.

Figure 6.24 – Combining a Displacement map with other texture maps

In this section, we learned how to apply a custom-made Displacement map to a surface, but there are some other interesting results that can be achieved with Displacement maps generated in Blender. Next, let's explore how we can create other types of Displacement maps inside Blender.

# Generating Displacement maps in Blender

We will now learn how to generate Displacement maps inside Blender, without using an image texture or an external image-editing program. In the following steps, we will learn how to make surfaces appear more natural using Blender-generated Displacement maps:

1.  Create a cube, and add a **Subdivision Surface** modifier to it.

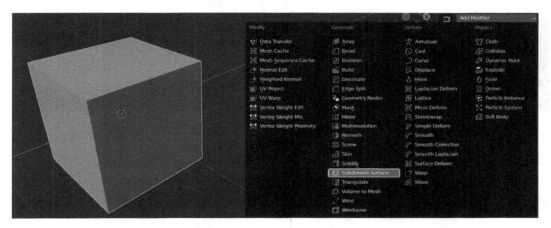

Figure 6.25 – Adding a Subdivision Surface modifier to a cube

2.  Set the **Levels Viewport** value to 5 or 6.

    Keep in mind that subdividing objects to this level may make Blender slower, or even cause crashes.

Figure 6.26 – Increasing the subdivision level

3.  Use the arrow symbol marked in *Figure 6.27* to collapse the **Subdivision Surface** modifier menu, and then add a **Displace** modifier.

Figure 6.27 – Collapsing a modifier (left) and adding a Displace modifier (right)

4.  In the **Texture Properties** tab, create a new texture, and set **Type** to **Clouds**.

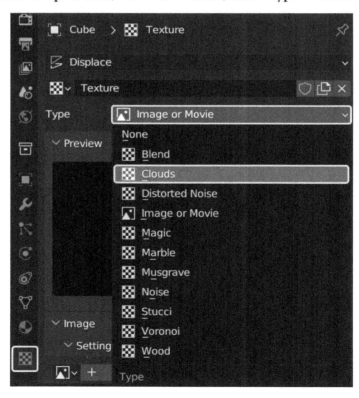

Figure 6.28 – Setting the image type to clouds

The **Clouds** texture, by default, is a mix of randomly scattered noise-like patterns in black and white, as shown in *Figure 6.29*.

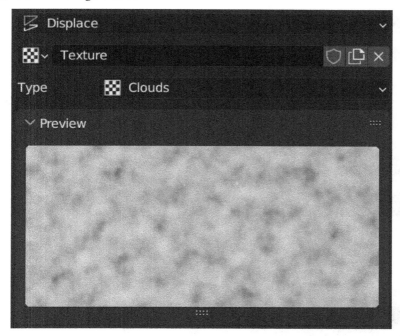

Figure 6.29 – The Clouds texture

As a result, loading this texture into the **Displace** modifier will create randomly distributed bumps of varying heights all over the object, as shown in *Figure 6.30*.

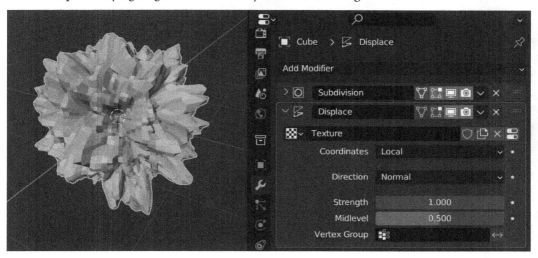

Figure 6.30 – The Cloud texture causing bumps on the surface

5. Reducing the **Strength** value and adding smooth shading will make the object appear as a ball of organic matter.

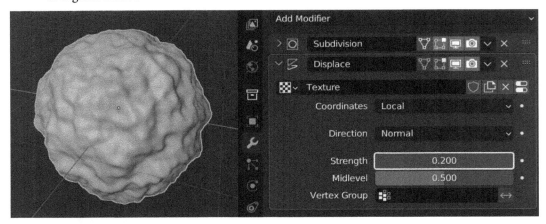

Figure 6.31 – Adjusting the displacement settings

In the **Texture Properties** tab, we can increase the **Size** value to make the texture less detailed, as shown in *Figure 6.32*.

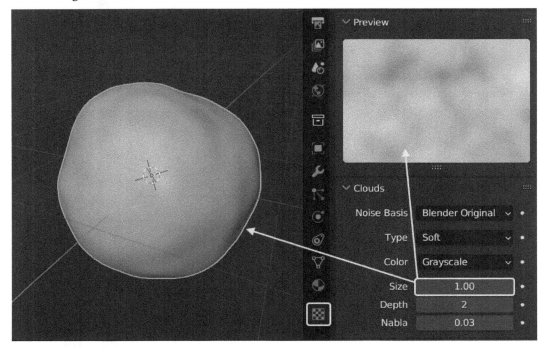

Figure 6.32 – Increasing the Size value

In the **Noise Basis** menu, there are several other options for the type of texture.

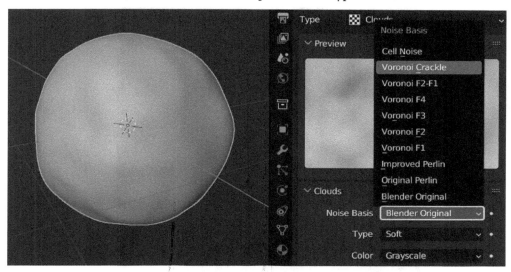

Figure 6.33 – Changing Noise Basis

*Figure 6.34* shows some more variations of the **Clouds** texture, which can easily be created in the **Noise Basis** menu.

Figure 6.34 – Six different shapes created by Blender's built-in textures

By expanding the **Type** menu, we can gain access to even more different patterns.

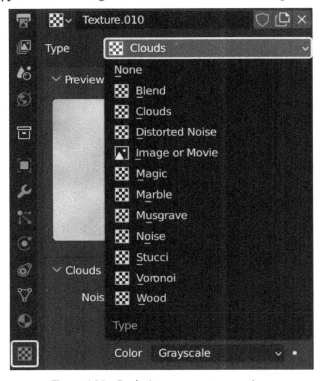

Figure 6.35 – Exploring more texture options

In *Figure 6.36*, we can see some more examples of surfaces that can be generated with this feature.

Figure 6.36 – More shapes created with built-in displacement maps

To prevent performance issues, you can optimize the **Subdivision Surface** modifier by setting a low Levels Viewport value, and a higher level for Render, as shown in *Figure 6.37*. This will allow you to work faster with a less subdivided preview, but the rendered image will still show the model in its full glory.

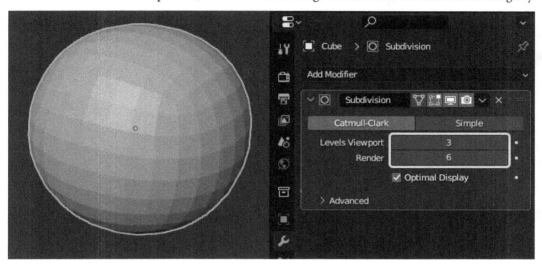

Figure 6.37 – A low viewport subdivision level and a high render subdivision level

We now know how to generate custom and procedural Displacement maps in Blender, in the **Texture Properties** tab. This gives us the freedom to create many different types of surfaces and shapes.

## Summary

In this chapter, we learned that Displacement maps are special texture maps used to create bumpy surfaces in a 3D space. We studied how they work to produce a result and how we can generate custom Displacement maps in GIMP and Blender.

We now have two methods to generate displacement, both externally and internally in Blender. This gives us the possibility to create various types of surfaces, which can contribute significantly to the level of realism of an object or scene.

In the next chapter, we will learn how to unwrap 3D models and gain more control and freedom in the texturing process. This will give us many new possibilities to create custom textures by texture painting.

# Part 3:
# UV Mapping
# and Texture Painting

*Part 3* explores special techniques and workflows that can be used to give us more flexibility for creating authentic, custom textures. Here, we will learn how to unwrap models for custom texturing, bake environmental lighting onto our models to add more detail to the materials, and paint custom details and features onto our textures. We will then put everything into practice by fully texturing a downloadable 3D model.

This part has the following chapters:

- *Chapter 7, UV-Unwrapping 3D Models for Texturing*
- *Chapter 8, Baking Ambient Occlusion Maps*
- *Chapter 9, Introducing Texture Painting*
- *Chapter 10, Creating Photorealistic Textures on a 3D Model*

# 7

# UV-Unwrapping 3D Models for Texturing

In this chapter, we will learn how to UV-unwrap 3D models. This will give us more control over how textures are projected on a surface. We will begin by exploring what UV-unwrapping is and how it works, before learning how to do it correctly and practicing on some models.

We will learn about two methods of UV-unwrapping. First, we will learn how to unwrap objects manually, to give us full control over the result. Then, we will learn an easy method to automatically unwrap objects, which is quicker and easier but often looks less realistic.

By the end of this chapter, you will be ready to UV-unwrap complex 3D models both manually and automatically with Blender's help. This will give us more control over the texture mapping process and allow us to bake custom textures and texture maps.

The following topics will be covered in this chapter:

- Understanding UV mapping
- Unwrapping basic shapes
- Unwrapping a cylinder
- Unwrapping complex shapes

## Technical requirements

This chapter includes an exercise that will require you to download a Tiger Tank 3D model. The model can be found in the Chapter07 folder within the book's downloadable resources folder, available here: https://packt.link/mA1OU

# Understanding UV mapping

UV mapping is the process of applying textures to 3D models by unwrapping them into two-dimensional maps known as UV maps. To understand how UV mapping works, we need to visualize a simple example. *Figure 7.1* illustrates how a cube can be unwrapped into a 2D map.

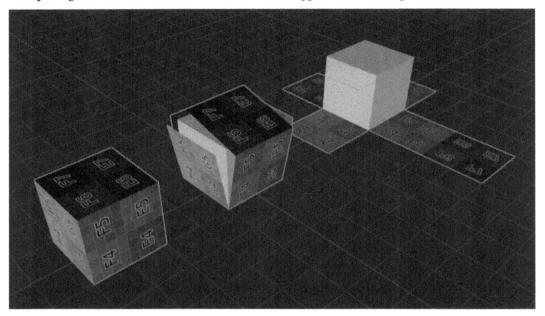

Figure 7.1 – A UV-unwrapped cube

A cube will typically produce a UV map shaped like the surface shown in *Figure 7.2*. As you can see, some of the cube's edges were cut to allow for unwrapping, but some of the edges stayed connected. We will learn which edges to cut shortly.

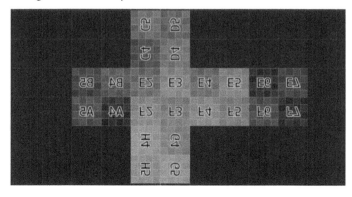

Figure 7.2 – The UV map of a cube

When placed over an image texture, the UV map covers a certain area, as shown in *Figure 7.3*. This covered area is then projected on the surface of the 3D object, as we saw previously in *Figure 7.1*.

| | | | | | | | |
|---|---|---|---|---|---|---|---|
| H1 | H2 | H3 | H4 | H5 | H6 | H7 | H8 |
| G1 | G2 | G3 | G4 | G5 | G6 | G7 | G8 |
| F1 | F2 | F3 | F4 | F5 | F6 | F7 | F8 |
| E1 | E2 | E3 | E4 | E5 | E6 | E7 | E8 |
| D1 | D2 | D3 | D4 | D5 | D6 | D7 | D8 |
| C1 | C2 | C3 | C4 | C5 | C6 | C7 | C8 |
| B1 | B2 | B3 | B4 | B5 | B6 | B7 | B8 |
| A1 | A2 | A3 | A4 | A5 | A6 | A7 | A8 |

UV Map

Figure 7.3 – A UV map placed over a texture

Similarly, a cylinder can be UV-unwrapped by cutting some edges and separating its surfaces, as shown in *Figure 7.4*.

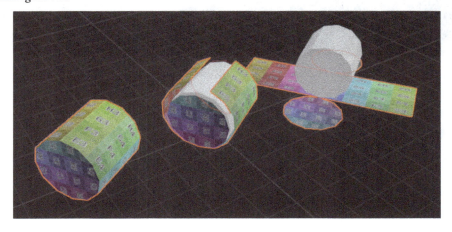

Figure 7.4 – UV-unwrapping a cylinder

This gives us a rough idea of how UV mapping can help us apply 2D images onto 3D objects. Next, let's learn how to unwrap some basic shapes.

## Unwrapping basic shapes

We will now learn how to cut and UV-unwrap 3D shapes to create UV maps. In the following few steps, we will create and unwrap a basic cube. Although Blender typically automatically unwraps a default cube, it is important that we know how to do this manually since lots of 3D objects will need to be manually unwrapped like a cube, and Blender will not be able to do it automatically:

1.  Open the **UV Editing** workspace from the top of the screen.

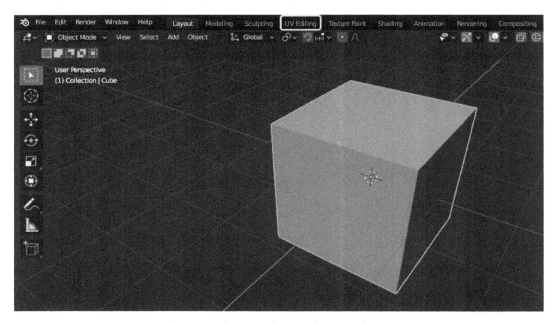

Figure 7.5 – Opening the UV Editing workspace

The screen is now split into two areas: the UV Editor on the left and the 3D View on the right, as shown in *Figure 7.6*. This allows us to see the 3D model and the UV map at the same time, as we are working. In *Figure 7.6*, we can see that the default cube, like all other shapes that can be added from the **Add** menu, is already unwrapped.

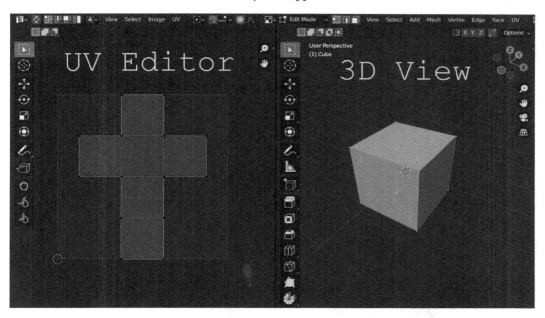

Figure 7.6 – A UV-unwrapped cube in the UV Editing workspace

2.   Delete the default cube and add a plane. Extrude the plane upward by exactly 2 units to create a cube, like in *Figure 7.7*.

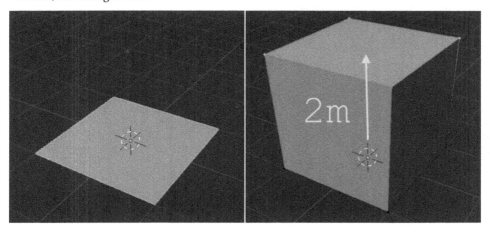

Figure 7.7 – Extruding a plane to create a cube

We are doing this so that Blender does not recognize this shape as a default cube, since it was created from a plane and not by adding a cube. As a result, Blender does not automatically unwrap it as a cube but unwraps it as a plane. This is shown in *Figure 7.8*.

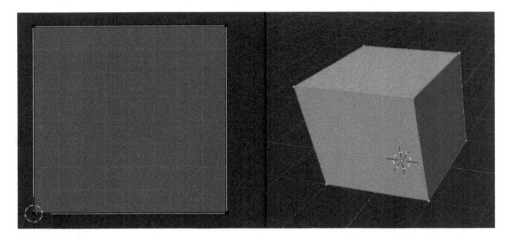

Figure 7.8 – An incorrectly UV-unwrapped cube

We can now use this to demonstrate manual UV-unwrapping.

3.    Select the edges highlighted in *Figure 7.9*.

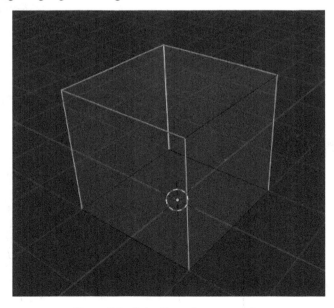

Figure 7.9 – Selecting edges on a cube

We will cut these edges to unwrap the object manually. It is important to remember which edges are selected here because many other objects are unwrapped similarly to a cube, which we will explore in the *Unwrapping complex shapes* section.

4. Open the **Edge** menu at the top of the screen and select **Mark Seam**.

This will mark our edges for cutting when UV-unwrapping.

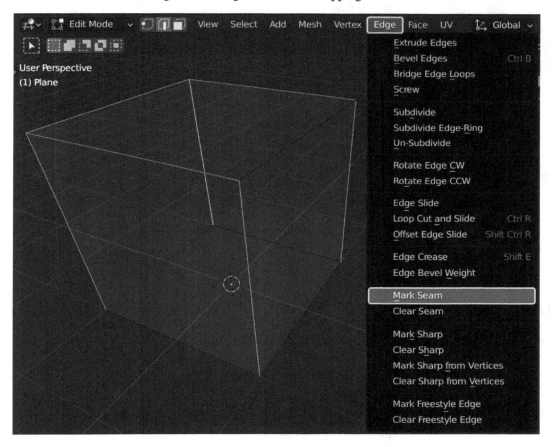

Figure 7.10 – Marking seams on a cube

5.   Press *U* to open the **UV Mapping** menu and click on **Unwrap** (*Figure 7.11*).

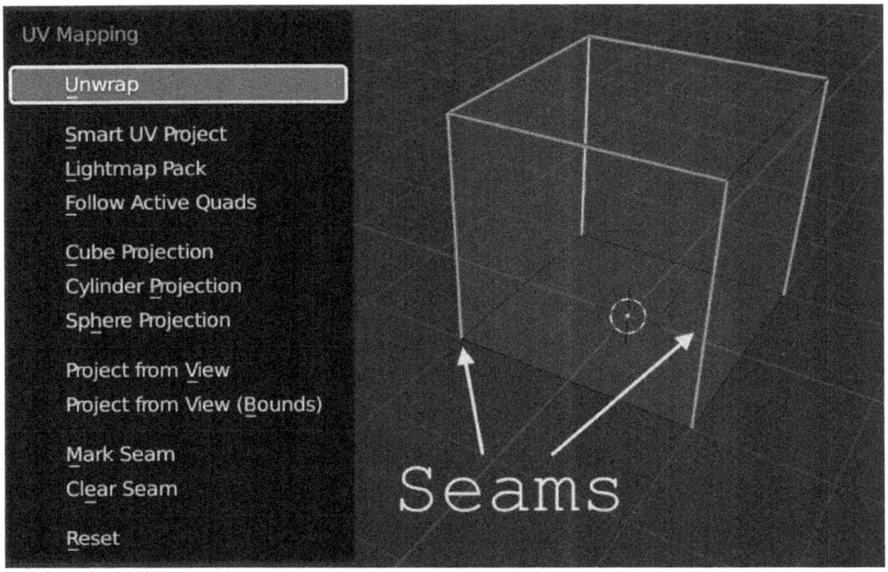

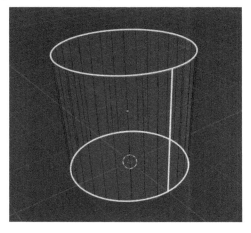

Figure 7.11 – Manually unwrapping a cube

This will create a UV map for the shape, which will appear on the left side of the screen. We saw this previously in *Figure 7.6*.

## Unwrapping a cylinder

We can use a similar technique when unwrapping a cylinder. *Figure 7.12* shows which edges should be marked as seams on a cylinder to correctly UV-unwrap it.

Figure 7.12 – Marking seams on a cylinder

This will create a UV map, as shown in *Figure 7.13*.

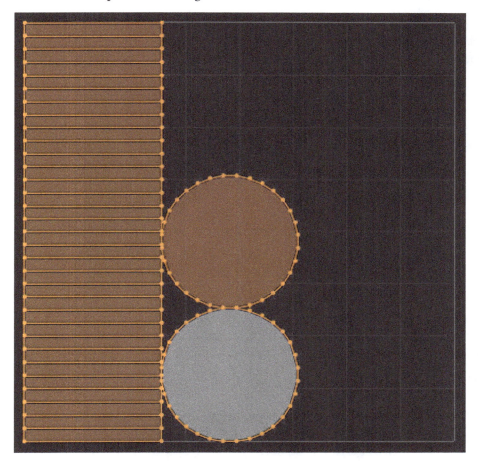

Figure 7.13 – The UV map of a cylinder

As you can see, the UV map shows all the faces of the cylinder, unwrapped and displayed on a 2D surface. This allows us to place a texture onto this object, and the UV map will dictate how the texture is mapped on the surface.

We now know how to unwrap some simple shapes by marking their seams manually. Next, let's look at how to correctly unwrap some more complex objects.

# Unwrapping complex shapes

We will now use the simple unwrapping methods that we learned about to unwrap some more complex 3D models. For practice, we will unwrap the low-poly Tiger Tank turret, which can be downloaded using the link in the *Technical requirements* section of this book. You can see what it looks like in *Figure 7.14*.

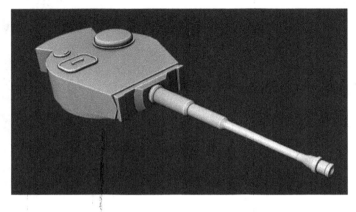

Figure 7.14 – A Tiger Tank turret

This exercise will teach us all the most important principles necessary for UV-unwrapping, which will allow us to correctly UV-unwrap almost any other object:

1.  First, let's create a new image with an **Image Texture** node, in the material on the object, and set **Generated Type** to **UV Grid**.

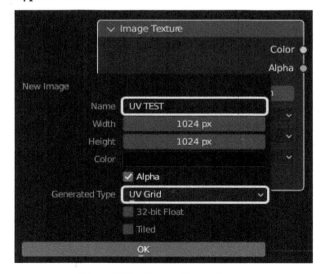

Figure 7.15 – Generating an image

Applying the UV Grid texture to the object without any mapping will probably create a messy result, as shown in *Figure 7.16*. There is a lot of visible stretching, compression, and bending in the pattern, so the texture is not mapped correctly.

Figure 7.16 – A poorly mapped texture

2.  Let's begin by focusing on the main shape at the center of the turret. If we isolate this shape, we can see that it is similar to a cylinder, so we can unwrap it as such. In *Figure 7.17*, we are marking the edges around the top and bottom faces, as we did in the *Unwrapping a cylinder* section.

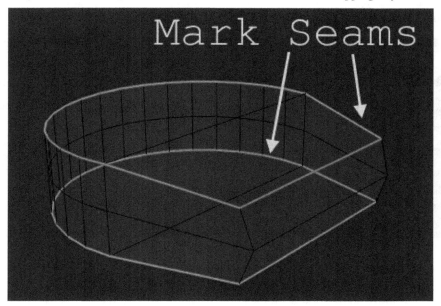

Figure 7.17 – Marking seams on the turret

3.  After unwrapping the model by pressing *U* and selecting **Unwrap**, the texture mapping becomes noticeably better, as shown in *Figure 7.18*.

Figure 7.18 – Improved texture mapping after marking seams

4.  If we mark the edges at the front, the texture will be perfectly mapped. You can see this in *Figure 7.19*.

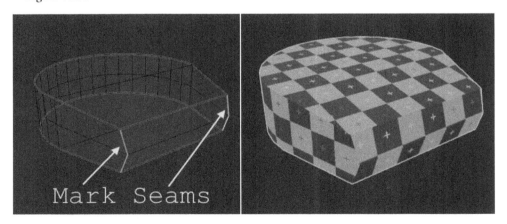

Figure 7.19 – Marking more edges as seams

5.  Next, let us move on to working on the gun. We can view the gun as two separate shapes, as shown in *Figure 7.20*.

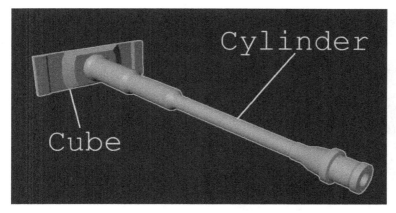

Figure 7.20 – Separating the gun into two main shapes

The base is similar to a cube, and the barrel is similar to a cylinder. The base can thus be unwrapped like a cube, as shown in *Figure 7.21*.

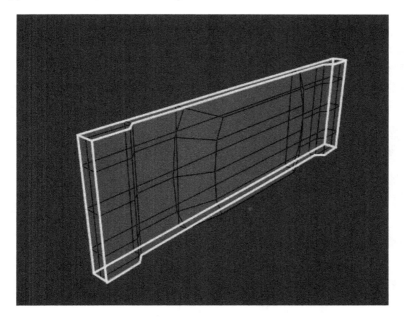

Figure 7.21 – Unwrapping the gun base

6.  If we think of this object as a cylinder, the gun can be unwrapped by marking its sides and the faces at the top of the shape. In this case, it's best to mark the edges on both sides of the gun.

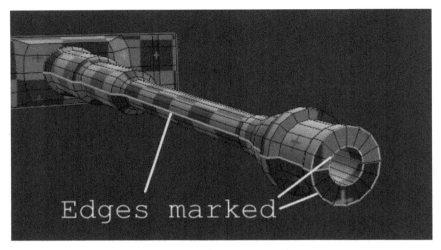

Figure 7.22 – Marking seams on the gun

7.   It is also recommended to delete the faces that aren't visible, such as the circle at the back of the gun, shown in *Figure 7.23*. This will help by freeing up more space on the UV map, which can be used by other faces.

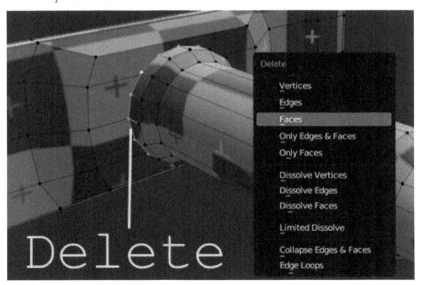

Figure 7.23 – Deleting invisible faces

8.   On this model, we have many nearly flat surfaces, such as hatches or bolts. These types of shapes do not need to be cut because they can already be unwrapped without much deformation, as shown in *Figure 7.24*. We can thus UV-unwrap these shapes by simply selecting and unwrapping them. Remember to delete the invisible face at the bottom.

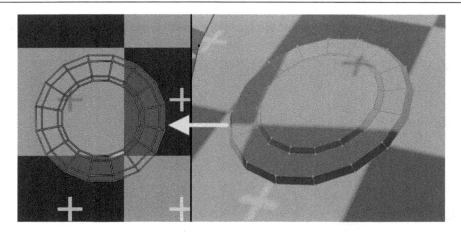

Figure 7.24 – Unwrapping flat surfaces

9.  More complex shapes, such as this hatch with a handle, can also be separated into multiple simple objects without much difficulty. The hatch is flat, so nothing needs to be marked, as discussed in *step 8*. The handle can simply be unwrapped as a set of cylinders.

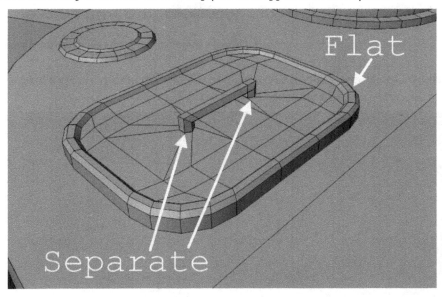

Figure 7.25 – Separating geometry on a hatch

We have now practiced unwrapping the shapes on this model, and we can use the same methods to unwrap almost any other object. Once the object is fully UV-mapped, it is ready for further texturing.

We can easily categorize almost any shape into one of the three categories that we learned about in this chapter – a cube, a flat surface, or a cylinder – as shown in *Figure 7.26*.

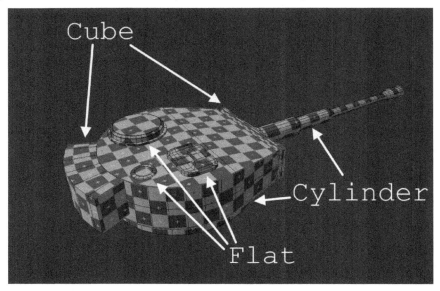

Figure 7.26 – Nearly all shapes belong to one of three categories in the context of UV-unwrapping

Alternatively, you can always go down the easy route and have Blender automatically unwrap the object. To do this, press *U* in **Edit** mode and select **Smart UV Project**.

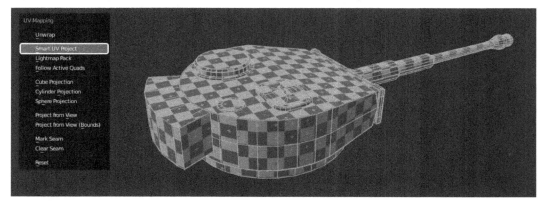

Figure 7.27 – Automatically unwrapping a 3D model

This method will generally work well but is not recommended as it often makes unnecessary seams, which can make an object look unrealistic, as shown in *Figure 7.28*.

Figure 7.28 – Bad seams caused by automatic UV-unwrapping

We have now learned a couple of ways to UV-unwrap 3D models, both manually and automatically. This will allow us to create better custom textures and give us the freedom to texture paint on our models.

## Summary

In this chapter, we introduced UV mapping as a means of applying textures to 3D models by manually or automatically unwrapping objects. We can use manual unwrapping when we need to ensure realism and are willing to invest extra time into unwrapping. We can use automatic unwrapping when realism isn't very important, and we just need a quick UV map.

In the next chapter, we will use manual UV mapping to create Ambient Occlusion maps, which will allow us to increase the level of realism of our objects by making their shading more in tune with the environment.

# 8

# Baking Ambient Occlusion Maps

In this chapter, we will introduce **Ambient Occlusion (AO)** maps and learn how to use them to improve our materials and textures. We will first study what they are and how they work, before moving on to learning how to create them and apply them to our scenes.

By the end of this chapter, you will be able to bake AO maps and use them to improve the texture quality and realism of your models.

We will cover the following topics in this chapter:

- Understanding Ambient Occlusion maps
- Baking an Ambient Occlusion map
- Applying an Ambient Occlusion map with nodes
- Mixing Diffuse and Ambient Occlusion maps in GIMP

## Technical requirements

This chapter includes an exercise that requires you to download a 3D model. You can do so with the following link: `https://github.com/PacktPublishing/Photorealistic-Materials-and-Textures-in-Blender-Cycles`.

The prepared resources can be found in the Chapter08 folder within the book's downloadable resources folder, available here: `https://packt.link/mA1OU`

# Understanding Ambient Occlusion maps

AO maps are texture maps used to simulate soft shadows on 3D models. *Figure 8.1* shows a model without an AO map (left) and a model with one (right). The left model has no shading and does not look realistic, while the right model has visible shading and looks like it is in a real environment.

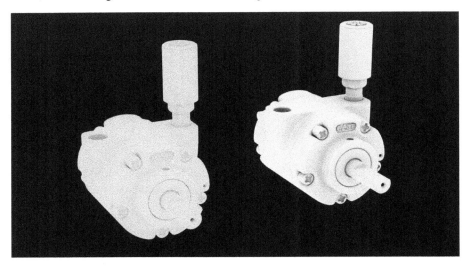

Figure 8.1 – A model before and after adding an AO map

Now let's dive into what an AO map looks like. In *Figure 8.2*, we can see the AO map used on the model from *Figure 8.1*.

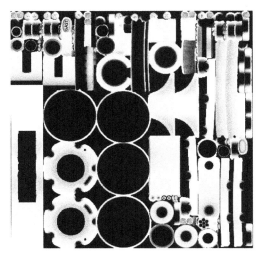

Figure 8.2 – An AO map

As you can see, it is mostly white with some gray and black areas. The purpose of this texture map is to shade the creases of the model. We can use this image texture in combination with other textures to improve their shading and shade creases to make the model look more realistic.

Now that we understand what an AO map is, we will move on to learning how to make one in Blender.

## Baking an Ambient Occlusion map

We will now use a model to create an AO map. This model can be downloaded from the *Technical requirements* section of this chapter. In the following steps, we will generate the AO map using the Cycles render engine:

1.   UV-unwrap the model, as shown in *Figure 8.3*.

     This model already has marked seams, but you are encouraged to clear the seams and mark them again manually to practice UV-unwrapping.

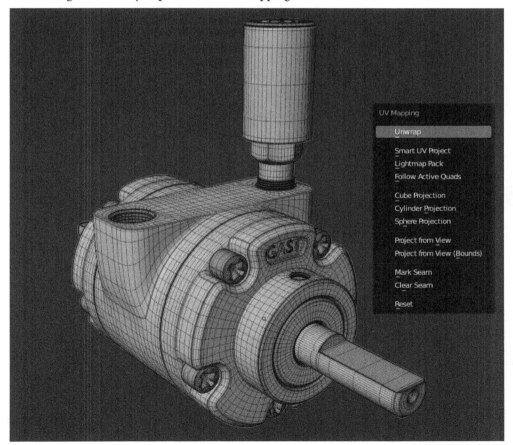

Figure 8.3 – Marking seams on a 3D model

*Figure 8.4* shows the UV map for this model.

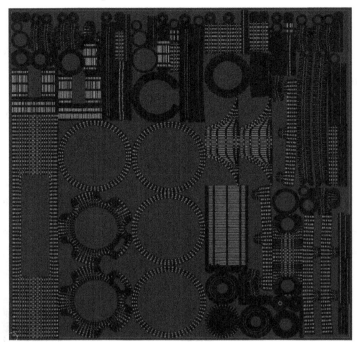

Figure 8.4 – A UV map

2.   Switch to the **Cycles** render engine, as shown in *Figure 8.5*.

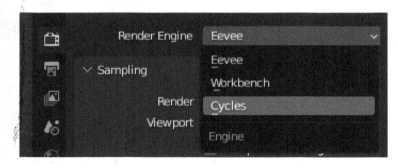

Figure 8.5 – Switching to the Cycles render engine

3.   Create a new material for the 3D model and generate a new image in an **Image Texture** node, as shown in *Figure 8.6*.

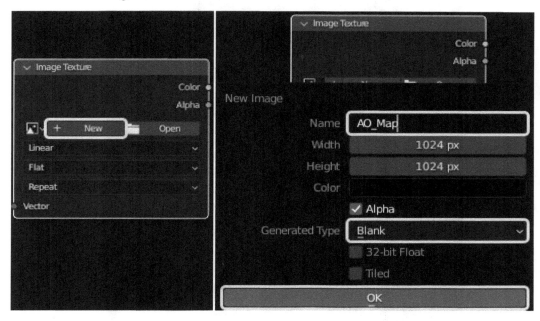

Figure 8.6 – Generating a new image

4.   In the **Bake** section of the Render Properties tab, set **Bake Type** to **Ambient Occlusion** and bake the image.

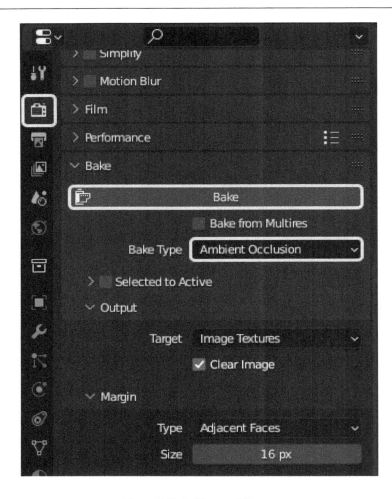

Figure 8.7 – Baking an AO map

This will create an AO map in the image editor, according to the UV map (*Figure 8.4*), as shown in *Figure 8.8*.

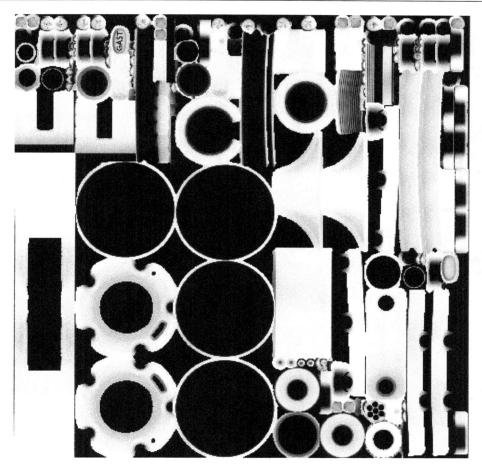

Figure 8.8 – A newly baked AO map

5.  Save the baked image to your computer with the **Save As...** option, as shown in *Figure 8.9*.

    Due to a glitch, sometimes the AO map becomes completely black for no apparent reason, so we will save the image to our computer to prevent this.

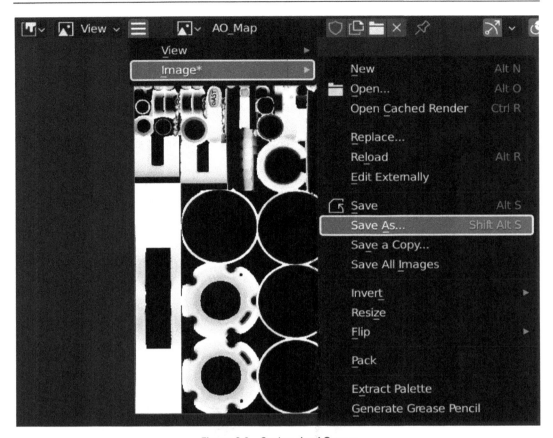

Figure 8.9 – Saving the AO map

With the help of the preceding steps, we have successfully baked our own AO map. Next, let's learn how to apply this image to our model.

## Applying the Ambient Occlusion map with nodes

We will now learn how to apply an AO map to a material and use it to improve our textures.

First, let's plug the **Image Texture** node with the AO map into the **Base Color** input of the **Principled BSDF** node, as shown in *Figure 8.10*.

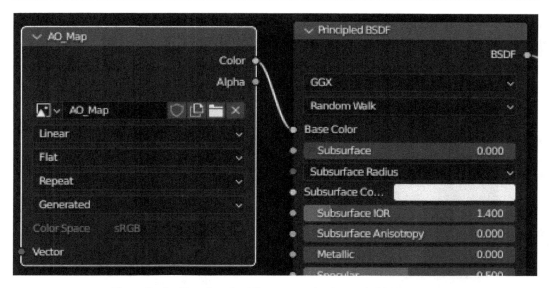

Figure 8.10 – Plugging the AO map into the Principled BSDF node

This will add some shading to the 3D model, as shown in *Figure 8.11*.

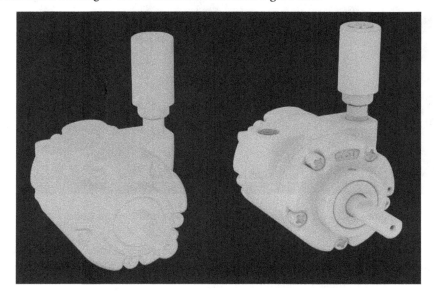

Figure 8.11 – The effect of an AO map as visible in the viewport

Currently, the shading is not very noticeable and makes a minimal difference. In the next few steps, we will add some nodes so that we can tweak the result:

1. Add a **Bright/Contrast** node and tweak the values to change the darkness and width of the shadows to your preference. This is demonstrated in *Figure 8.12*.

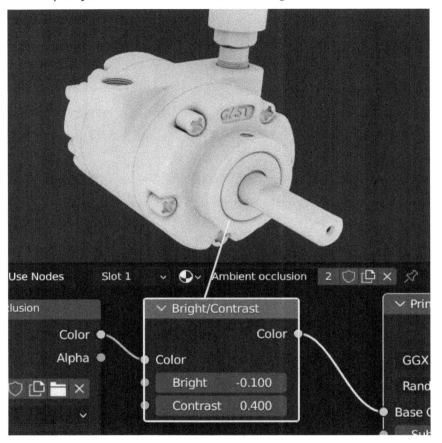

Figure 8.12 – Controlling the AO map with a Bright/Contrast node

2. Add a **ColorRamp** node between the Bright/Contrast node and the Principled BSDF node. Use the color markers to control the gradient between the dark and light shades, as shown in *Figure 8.13*. This can make the shadows sharper.

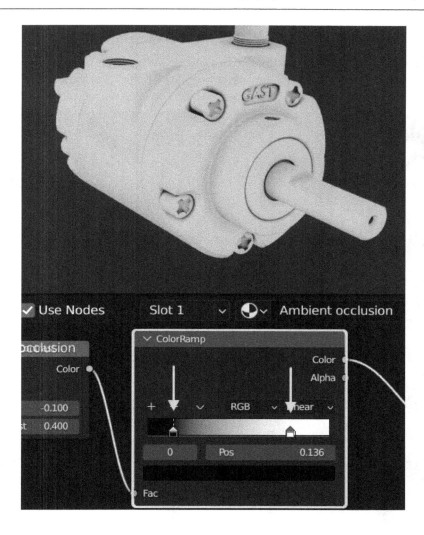

Figure 8.13 – Controlling the AO map with a ColorRamp node

These two nodes can be used to control the intensity and shape of the shadow simulated by the AO map. This is useful because it gives us the freedom to improve the final result and adjust it to our preference.

In the next few steps, we will combine the AO map with an Albedo texture:

1.  First, create a texture of your choice and complete it with texture maps, as we learned how to do in *Chapter 5, Generating Texture Maps with Cycles. Figure 8.14* shows some key texture maps added to a material.

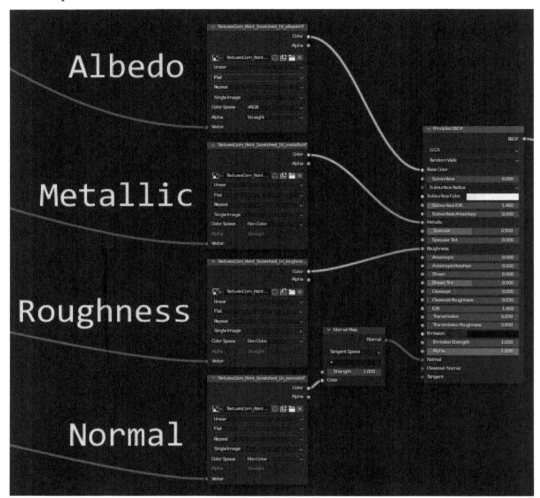

Figure 8.14 – Creating a texture with texture maps

For this example, I created a scratched metal texture, as shown in *Figure 8.15*.

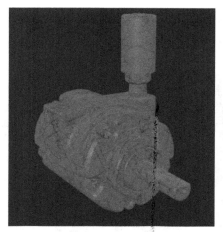

Figure 8.15 – Scratched metal texture

2.  Unplug the Diffuse texture and add a second **Image Texture** node below the Albedo Texture node, like in *Figure 8.16*.

    Load the AO map into the new Image Texture node.

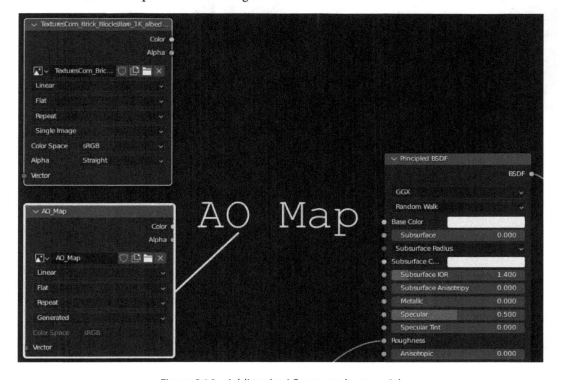

Figure 8.16 – Adding the AO map to the material

3.    Add a **Mix** node between the two image texture nodes and the **Principled BSDF** node.

In the **Mix** node, set **Type** to **Color**. This will allow us to mix the colors of two images together, as shown in *Figure 8.17*.

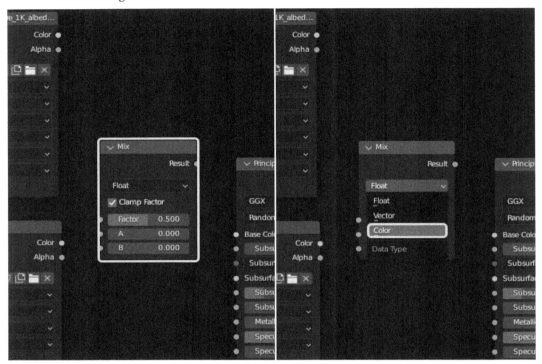

Figure 8.17 – Adding a Mix node (left), setting Type to Color (right)

4.  Plug the Albedo map into the **A** input of the **Mix** node and the AO map into the **B** input. Then, plug the **Mix** node into the **Principled BSDF** node.

We are now combining the colors of the two image textures, as shown in *Figure 8.18*.

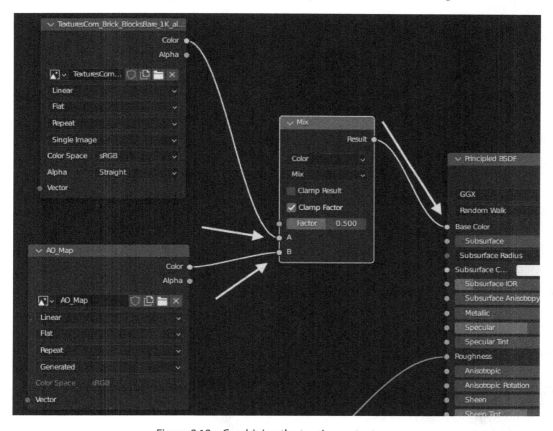

Figure 8.18 – Combining the two image textures

5.  Set **Blending Mode** to **Multiply** in the **Mix** node and increase **Factor** to **1.000**, as shown in *Figure 8.19*.

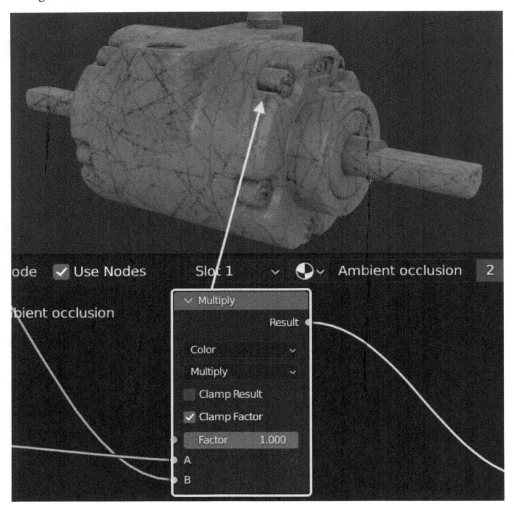

Figure 8.19 – AO impact increased by multiplication

Now, the darker colors have more impact than the lighter colors. The black-shaded parts of the AO map are mixed with the other image texture, while the white parts are not. This makes the effect of the AO map more noticeable.

6.  Add a **Bright/Contrast** node between the AO map and the **Mix** node to control the intensity of the AO map.

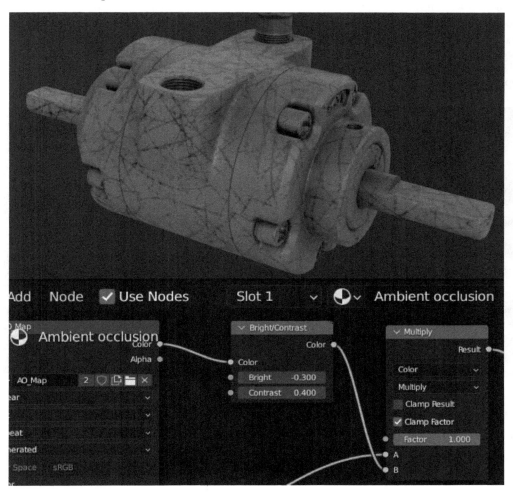

Figure 8.20 – Adding a Bright/Contrast node

We can now load an AO map into a material using some basic nodes. Next, we will learn how to apply an AO map to a texture externally in GIMP.

# Mixing Diffuse and Ambient Occlusion maps in GIMP

We will now learn how to bake a Diffuse map and mix it with an AO map with GIMP. This will allow us to store both textures in one image, which reduces the number of nodes needed. In the following steps, we will bake our texture into a Diffuse map:

Add an **Image Texture** node and generate a blank image named **Diffuse Map**, as shown in *Figure 8.21*. Keep this node disconnected from other nodes.

Figure 8.21 – Generating a blank image

1.  In the **Bake** section of the Render Properties tab, set **Bake Type** to **Diffuse**.

    For the best results, unplug all the nodes except the base color.

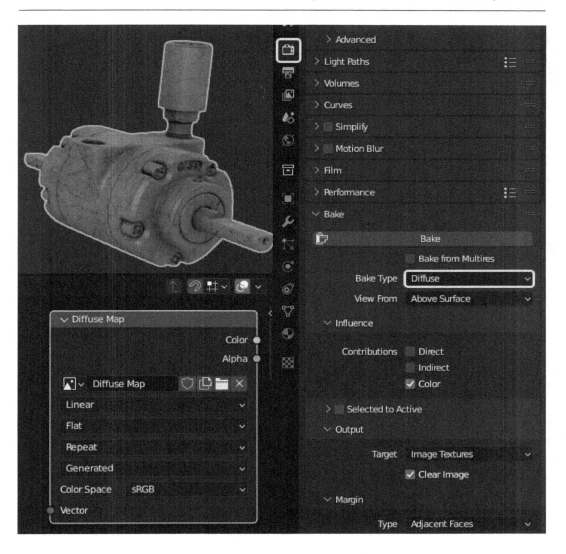

Figure 8.22 – Setting Bake Type to Diffuse

2.    Uncheck **Direct** and **Indirect** and bake the image by clicking on the **Bake** button.

Disabling direct and indirect contributions will prevent reflections of light from interfering with the color of the image. Make sure that the **Image Texture** node with the **Diffuse** map is selected in the Shader Editor, to indicate which image we want to use to bake this texture.

Figure 8.23 – Baking the Diffuse map

This will create a texture based on the UV map in the image editor, as shown in *Figure 8.24*. This image can be plugged into the base color input of the **Principled BSDF** node.

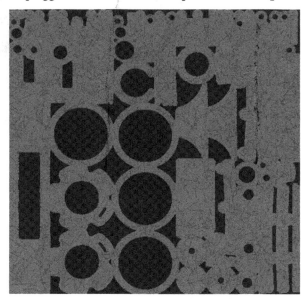

Figure 8.24 – A baked Diffuse map

3.  Save this image to your computer using the menu in the top-left corner of the image editor.

At this point, we should already have our AO map saved. If you do not have it saved, repeat the steps from the *Baking an Ambient Occlusion map* section.

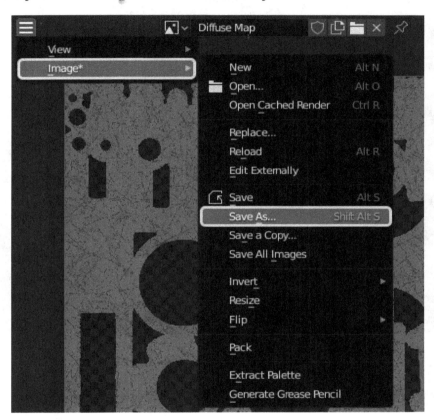

Figure 8.25 – Saving the Diffuse map

4.   Load the Diffuse map into GIMP by pressing *Ctrl + O* and locating the image.

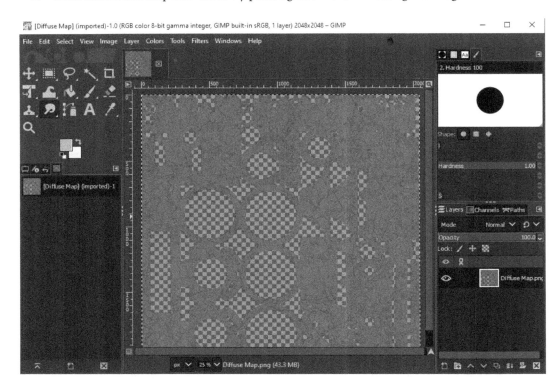

Figure 8.26 – Loading the Diffuse map into GIMP

5.   Click and drag the AO map file into the **Layers** section in the lower-left corner of the GIMP window.

This will load the AO map as a new layer. Ensure that the new layer is above the Diffuse map layer. The dark areas of the AO map will now be used to shade this texture.

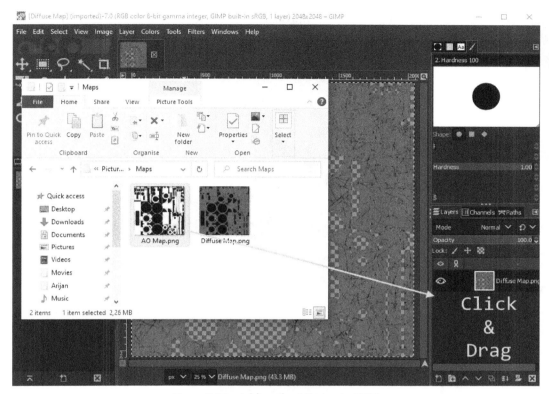

Figure 8.27 – Adding the AO map to GIMP

6.    Select the AO map layer and set **Mode** to **Multiply**.

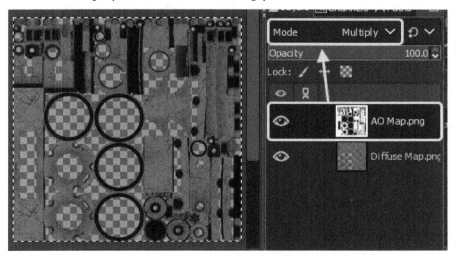

Figure 8.28 – Setting Mode to Multiply

7.    Select the AO map layer and merge it with the layer below it, as shown in *Figure 8.29*.

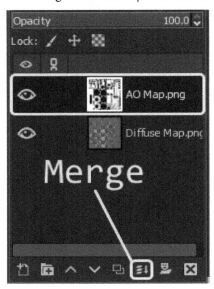

Figure 8.29 – Merging layers

8.    Save the image to your computer again with the **Export As…** option in the **File** menu.

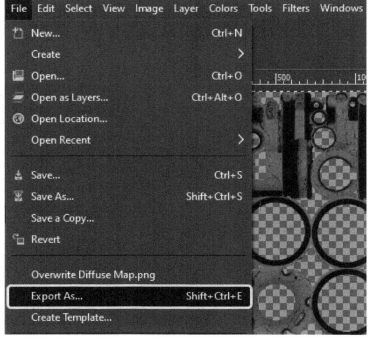

Figure 8.30 – Exporting the image

9.  Load the saved image with an **Image Texture** node and plug it into the **Principled BSDF** node.

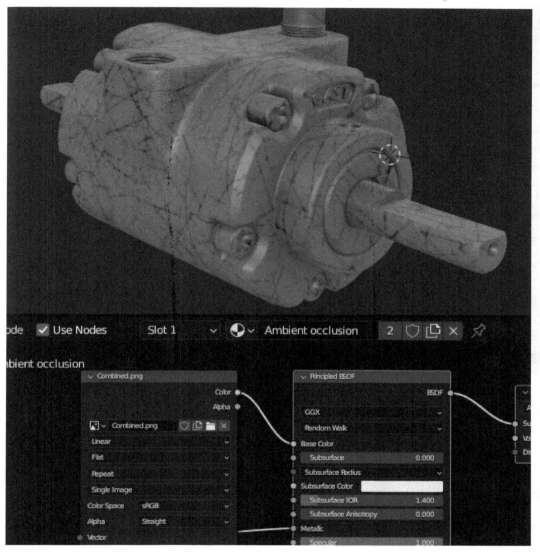

Figure 8.31 – A Diffuse map and an AO map combined into one image

*Figure 8.32* shows the final node tree that was created for this material.

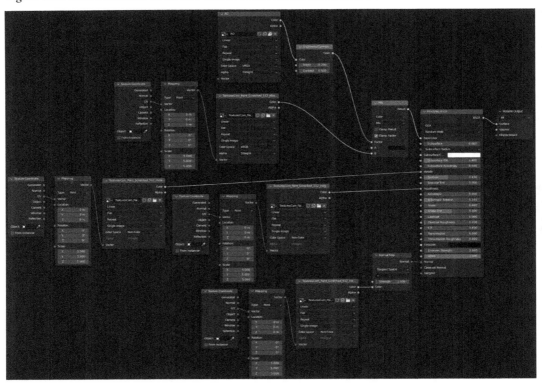

Figure 8.32 - An overview of the full node tree for this material

We now have a Diffuse map mixed with an AO map in a single image, which can easily be loaded with a single node. This makes things simpler in the Shader Editor because we don't need to use any other nodes. Our texture is now also ready for texture painting.

## Summary

In this chapter, we learned what AO maps are and how they can be used to improve the quality of our textures and materials. We then learned how to create custom AO maps and apply them to our materials with nodes or mix them with other textures in GIMP.

In the next chapter, we will learn how to add more details to our textures using Blender's powerful texture painting tools. This will allow us to add custom edges, wear, stains, decals, and other details.

# 9

# Introducing Texture Painting

In this chapter, we will introduce Blender's powerful and versatile **Texture Paint** feature. We will learn to use the texture painting workspace and tools, creating our own custom brushes and textures. By the end of this chapter, you will be ready to start texture painting independently and greatly improve your textures and materials.

The following topics will be covered in this chapter:

- Understanding the basics of texture painting
- Improving edges with texture painting
- Creating custom brushes in GIMP
- Creating a bullet hole decal
- Using stencils in Blender

## Understanding the basics of texture painting

**Texture painting** is the process of using brushes and digital painting tools to create custom textures, patterns, shapes, and details on image textures. We will now learn how to prepare a model for texture painting and how to use the basic Texture Paint interface.

First, let's select the **Texture Paint** workspace at the top of the screen:

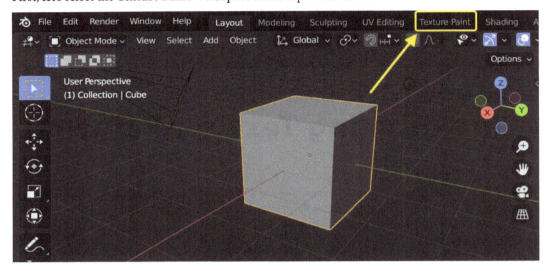

Figure 9.1 – Switching to the Texture Paint workspace

In the **Texture Paint** workspace, we have the Image Editor window on the left, and the 3D Viewport window on the right. In the Image Editor, there are some extra tools available because we are in **Paint** Mode, as shown in *Figure 9.2*. We can also see the UV map of the default cube in the Image Editor:

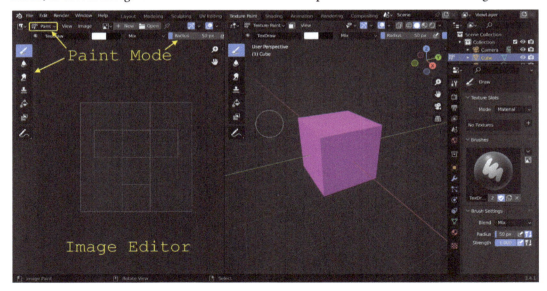

Figure 9.2 – The Texture Paint workspace

In the 3D Viewport, we also have some extra tools because we are in **Texture Paint** mode, as shown in *Figure 9.3*. We can easily switch between **Texture Paint** Mode, **Object** Mode, and **Edit** Mode in the 3D View by pressing *Ctrl + Tab*. This shortcut will allow us to quickly add or edit objects while texture painting if need be:

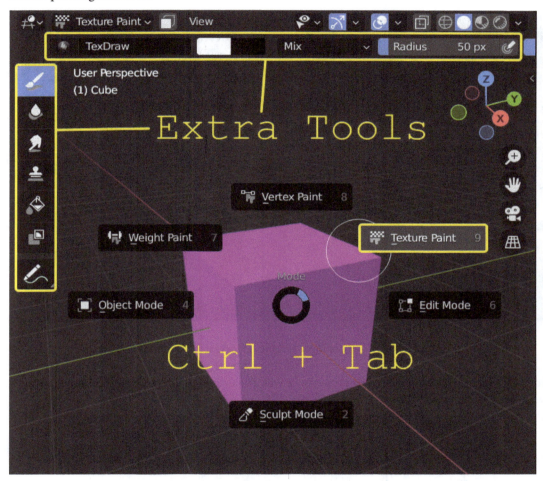

Figure 9.3 – The Texture Paint 3D View

Currently, the default cube is purple because there is no texture loaded in the Image Editor. We can easily create a new texture by clicking the **New** button at the top of the Image Editor. When creating a new image, set a name and a color, and set **Generated Type** to **Blank**. You can see this in *Figure 9.4*. In this example, we used a dark gray color.

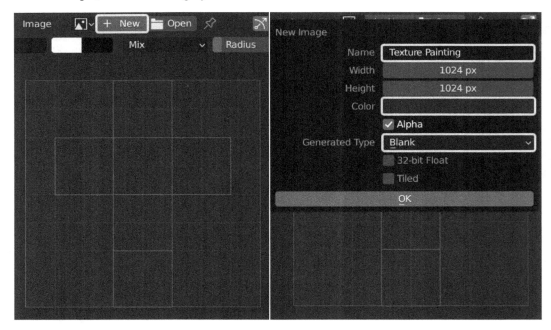

Figure 9.4 – Generating a new image for texture painting

To apply this generated image to our object, we will use an **Image Texture** node in the **Shading** workspace, as shown in *Figure 9.5*.

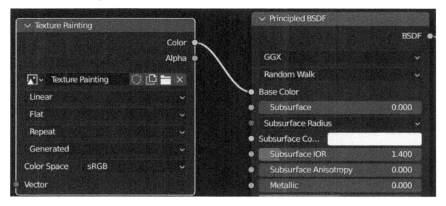

Figure 9.5 – Connecting the generated image to the Principled BSDF node

This action will turn the color of the surface of the default cube into the color of our image:

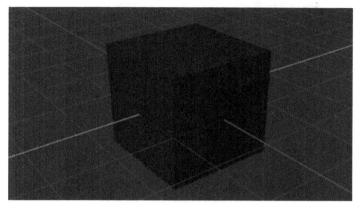

Figure 9.6 – A blank texture on the default cube

We can now paint over this image by clicking and dragging the brush over the object in **Texture Paint** mode. We are currently using the default brush, which is white and circular, as shown in *Figure 9.7*. We will learn to change this later in the *Creating custom brushes in GIMP* section.

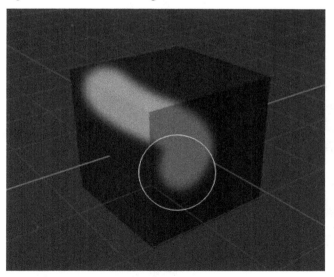

Figure 9.7 – Using the default brush

We can also paint in the Image Editor, as you can see in *Figure 9.8*. Anything we paint on the object in the 3D View will instantly appear in the image in the Image Editor, and anything we paint in the Image Editor will instantly appear on the object. Painting on the object in the 3D view is easier because it gives us a better view of our result, but painting within the Image Editor can be more precise.

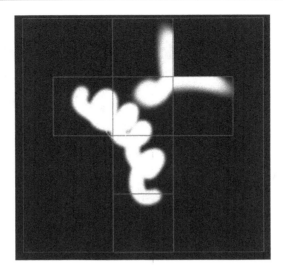

Figure 9.8 – Painting in the Image Editor

In the 3D View, we can use the **Radius** slider at the top of the screen to adjust the size of the brush and the **Strength** slider to adjust the opacity. Reducing the strength will make the brush more transparent:

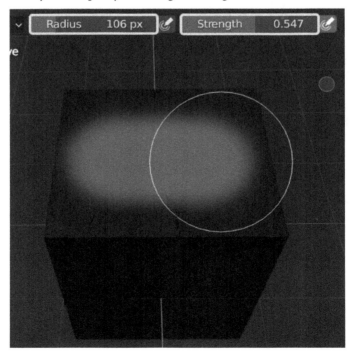

Figure 9.9 – Adjusting the brush radius and strength

We now know how texture painting works and how to prepare our object for texture painting. Next, let's go over some of the useful texture painting tools and features.

## Improving edges with texture painting

We will now learn how to use texture painting to improve our material by painting over its edges. We will use a simple cube to demonstrate this technique, but you can apply it to any model or texture. In the following steps, we will shade the edges of our cube:

1.  First, add some loop cuts near the edges and smooth shading to the cube to make the edges appear smoother, as shown in *Figure 9.10*.

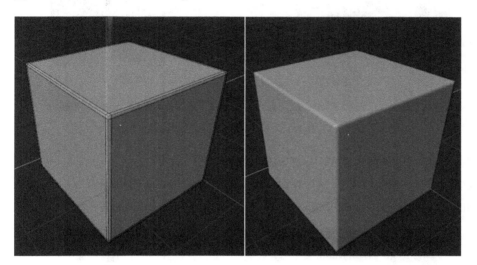

Figure 9.10 – Smoothing the edges

The loop cuts will automatically be added to the UV map.

2.   Open the **Color** menu in the Image Editor and select the Eyedropper tool, as shown in *Figure 9.11*.

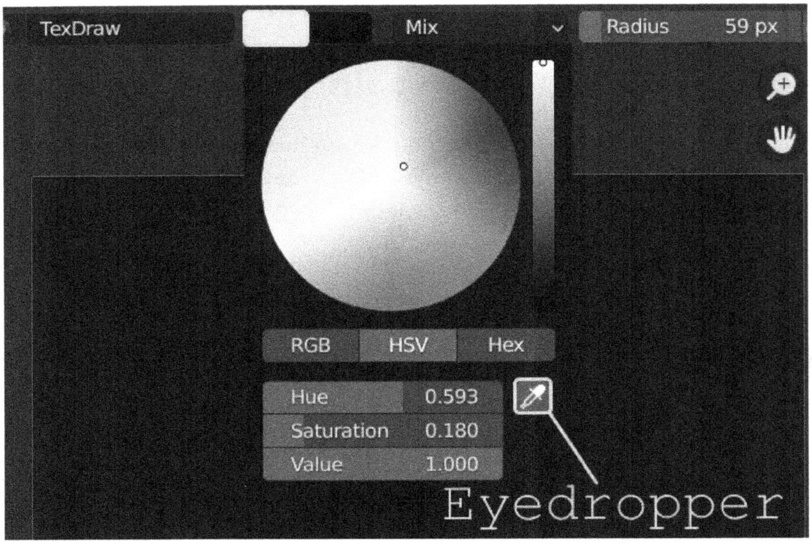

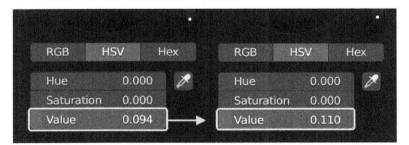

Figure 9.11 – Picking a color with the Eyedropper tool

Then, click on the dark image texture to copy its color.

3.   Increase the **Value** setting by approximately 0.015, as shown in *Figure 9.12*.

This slight increase in brightness will allow us to lightly shade the edges.

Figure 9.12 – Increasing the color value

4.  Use a small brush and ensure that **Strength** is set to 1.000. Then, color all the edges of the cube. This will make them slightly brighter.

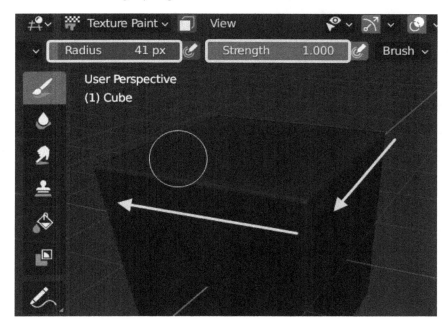

Figure 9.13 – Painting the edges with a small brush

5.  Next, make the brush even smaller and the color slightly brighter again, and paint the edges again. Repeat this a few times with smaller and brighter brushes every time.

    Note that the specific brush size and color are dependent on the situation, and it is completely up to you to decide how thin or bright the edges should be. Texture painting will work much better with a pen and a tablet, as it allows for greater control over the stroke style and intensity.

    This will greatly improve the aesthetic of the edges, especially if done carefully. *Figure 9.14* shows an example of a result that can be achieved by repeating *steps 2–5* a few times. In this example, the brush size ranged between 5 pixels and 40 pixels, with small value increments of 0.015 for every smaller brush size.

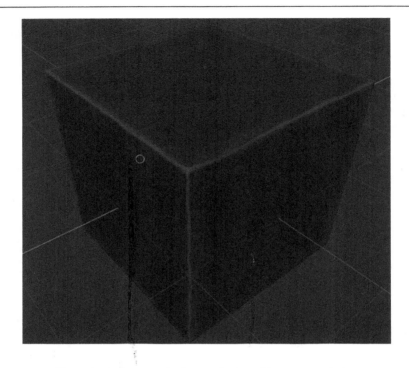

Figure 9.14 – Improved edge aesthetics with texture painting

6.  Now, let's learn how to paint the edges with straight lines. In the **Stroke** menu at the top of the screen, we can set **Stroke Method** to **Line**. This will make it much easier to draw straight lines.

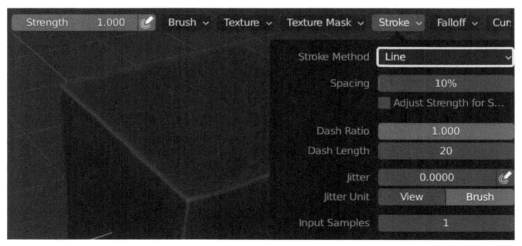

Figure 9.15 – Setting Stroke Method to line

7.  With these settings configured, we can now click and drag across the object to draw perfectly straight lines, which allows us to paint over the edges more precisely.

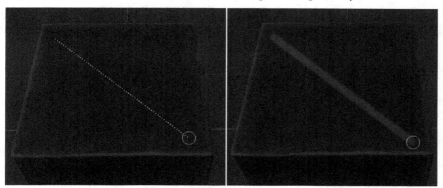

Figure 9.16 – Painting perfect lines with the line stroke method

In this section, we learned how to make the edges of an object brighter by painting a gradient over them. Shading edges lightly is a good way to improve the aesthetic of a model, and it can be applied to any 3D model. Next, we will learn how to create special brushes and stencils so that we can paint more complex details.

# Creating custom brushes in GIMP

We will now learn to create and import into Blender our own custom-made brushes and stencils. This will allow us to texture-paint more realistic and detailed shapes and patterns onto objects. In the following steps, we will draw a brush in GIMP and load it into Blender:

1.  Open GIMP and create a new image with *Ctrl + N*. Set the resolution of the new image to 256 x 256, and click **OK**.

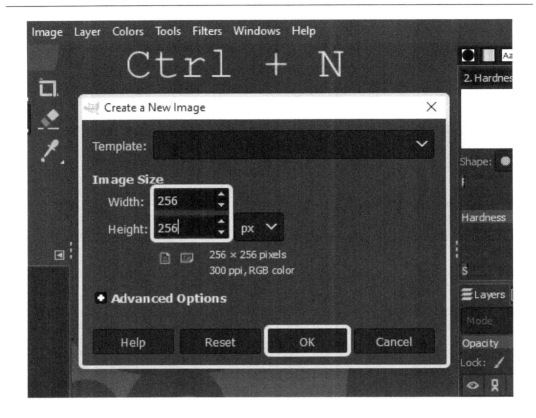

Figure 9.17 – Generating a new image in GIMP

2.  In the **Layer** menu at the top of the screen, open the **Transparency** section and click on **Add Alpha Channel**.

    This will allow us to create a transparent background for this image.

Figure 9.18 – Adding an alpha channel to the image

3.   Select the entire image with *Ctrl + A*, and press *Delete*.

This will make the entire image transparent. We now have a background for our brush. Anything we paint over this will be the shape of the brush.

Figure 9.19 – Clearing the image to make it transparent

4.  Select the brush tool, and set the color to white.

    We will use white because that is the typical color for brushes, which Blender can understand and use for texture painting. You can increase or decrease the size of the brush by pressing *Ctrl + Alt* and scrolling up or down, respectively.

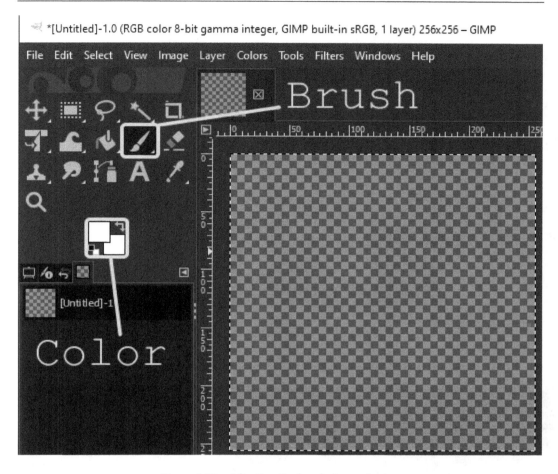

Figure 9.20 – Adjusting the brush size and color

5.  Use the white brush to paint a messy shape, as shown in *Figure 9.21*.

    We will use this shape as a brush to texture-paint edge wear and other messy patterns in Blender.

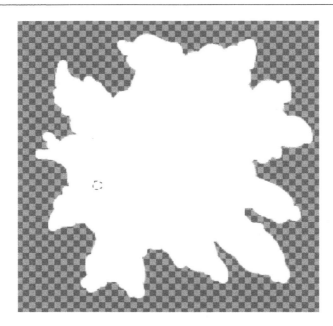

Figure 9.21 – A custom brush shape

6.   Export the image in the .png format with the **Export As...** option, as shown in *Figure 9.22*.

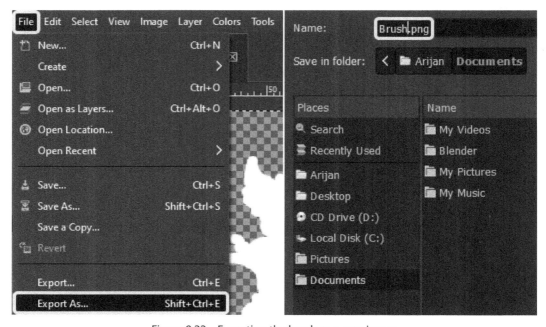

Figure 9.22 – Exporting the brush as a .png image

We now have a finished brush. In the following steps, we will load and use it in Blender:

1.  In the **Texture Properties** tab, create a new texture slot and open the brush that we just exported from GIMP. Set the **Type** dropdown to **Image or Movie,** and then use the **Open** button to load the brush.

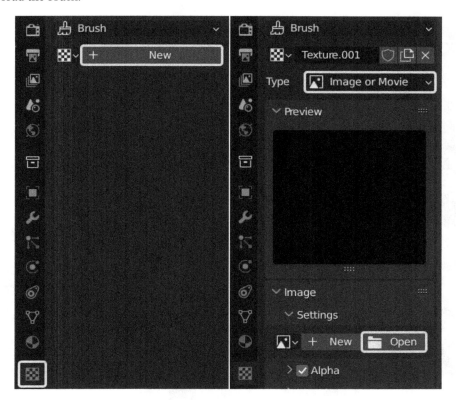

Figure 9.23 – Opening the custom brush in Blender

In the Image Editor of the Texture Paint workspace, we can now select the brush using the **Texture** section of the tool menu on the right.

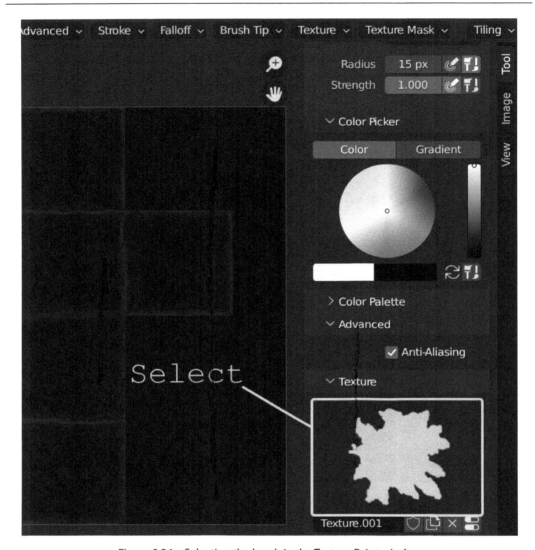

Figure 9.24 – Selecting the brush in the Texture Paint window

2. Set **Mapping** to **View Plane**, and check the **Random** box.

Checking the **Random** box will rotate each stroke of the brush, which will make the stroke look more messy and realistic.

Figure 9.25 – Adjusting the brush settings

We can now create different patterns and strokes using this new brush. *Figure 9.26* shows a comparison of the default brush and the custom brush.

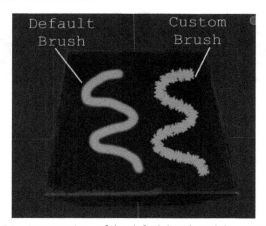

Figure 9.26 – A comparison of the default brush and the custom brush

In this section, we learned how to create custom brushes and how they can give us more flexibility and realism when texture painting. Next, let's learn how to create custom decals and stencils.

# Creating a bullet hole decal

**Decals** are images with transparent backgrounds that can be painted onto a texture to look like a sticker. When painting decals, it is useful to have a reference image of what we try to paint. This will help us accurately recreate a shape as a decal.

In the following steps, we will use GIMP to create a bullet hole decal, which we can then texture-paint on any other texture:

1.   Open GIMP and create a new image with *Shift + N*. Set the size to 512 x 512.

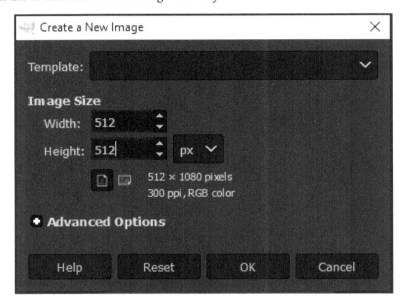

Figure 9.27 – Creating a new 512 x 512 image

2.  Add an alpha channel using the **Layer** menu.

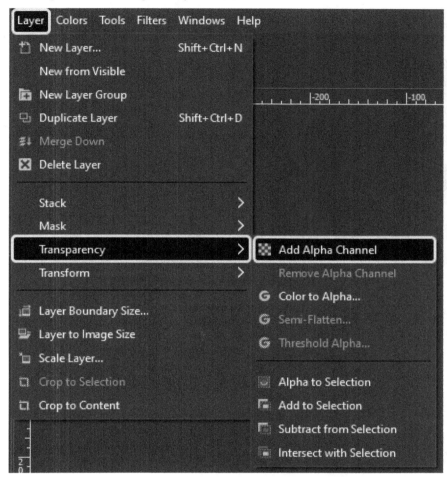

Figure 9.28 – Adding an alpha channel to the image

3.  Delete the background, set the brush color to gray, and set a large brush size with a diameter of approximately half the width of the canvas, by pressing *Ctrl + Alt* and scrolling up. This brush will be used to create the shape of the bullet hole.

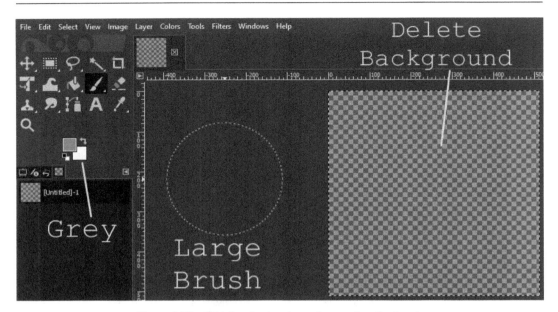

Figure 9.29 – Clearing the image and preparing the brush

4.  Click once in the middle of the transparent image to create a large gray circle, as shown in *Figure 9.30*.

Figure 9.30 – Creating a circle with a large brush

5.  Use a smaller brush to paint a few variously sized spikes coming out of the circle, as shown in *Figure 9.31*.

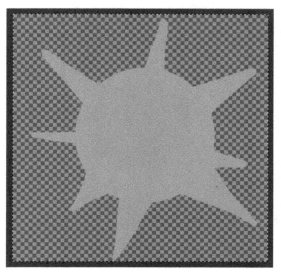

Figure 9.31 – Adding spikes around the circle with a smaller brush

6.  Use an even smaller brush, about half the size of the previous one, to create some smaller bumps in between the large gray spikes.

Figure 9.32 – Adding smaller bumps around the shape

7.    Next, use a black brush to create a blob in the middle of the gray shape, as shown in *Figure 9.33.*

Figure 9.33 – Adding a black blob in the middle of the shape

8.    Finally, add a thin white outline with a small brush on one side of the black blob, as shown in *Figure 9.34.*

Figure 9.34 – Adding a white outline to the black shape

9.  Export the image, and remember to save it in the `.png` format because it has a transparent background.

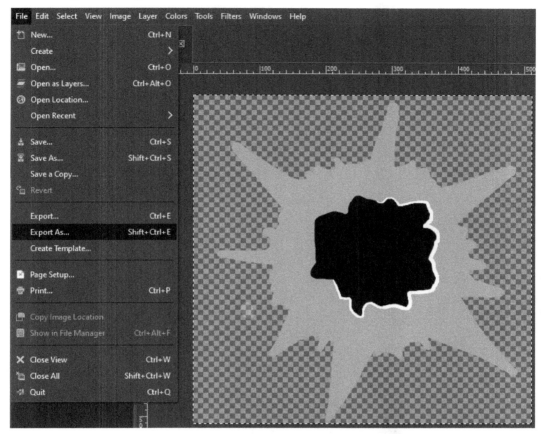

Figure 9.35 – Saving the decal

We now have a bullet hole decal, which we can paint over a texture on a 3D model. Next, we will learn to use this decal as a stencil to paint it onto surfaces.

## Using stencils in Blender

We will now learn how to use the stencil texture painting feature in Blender. This allows us to add custom decals to our textures. In the following steps, we will use the bullet hole decal as a stencil in Blender, by importing from the bullet hole decal that we just created in GIMP:

1.    In Blender, create a new texture slot and load the bullet hole decal, as shown in *Figure 9.36*.

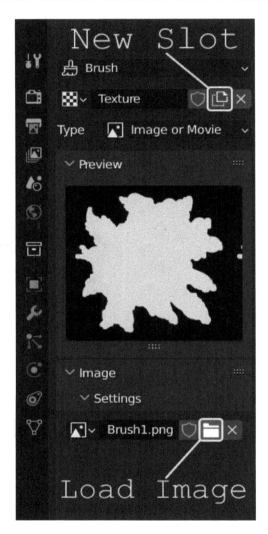

Figure 9.36 – Loading the bullet hole decal in Blender

2.   Next, select the bullet hole decal in the **Texture** section of the Image Editor toolbar, and set **Mapping** to **Stencil**.

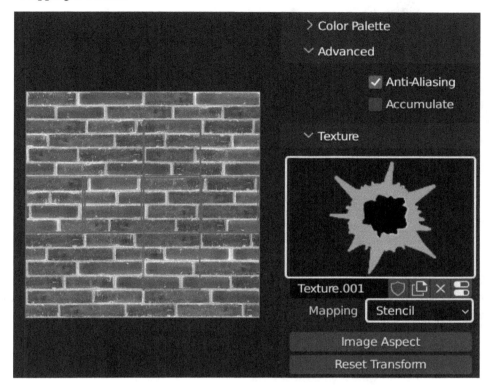

Figure 9.37 – Using the bullet hole as a stencil

This will load the bullet hole decal in the lower-left corner of the 3D View. We can move this image around by right-clicking on it and dragging it.

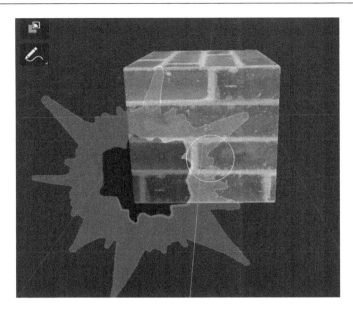

Figure 9.38 – The stencil visible in 3D View

If you hold *Shift* and then click and drag the **Right Mouse Button** (**RMB**), you can change the size of the stencil before painting over it, as shown in *Figure 9.39*.

Figure 9.39 – Adjusting the stencil size

Additionally, holding *Ctrl* and clicking and dragging the RMB will rotate the stencil.

Figure 9.40 – Rotating the stencil

We can now place this custom-made image anywhere on an object, as shown in *Figure 9.41*. We can also do this with any other image with a transparent background.

Figure 9.41 – Painting over the stencil to create bullet holes

We have now learned how to create custom decals and use them as stencils to paint them over a texture on a 3D model. This allows us to easily place any logo, decal, symbol, or other detail on top of an existing texture.

## Summary

In this chapter, we learned how to use the fundamental texture painting functions and how to create custom brushes and custom decals. This allows us to create custom texture details and improve the look of our models. We also learned how to paint decals onto a surface using the stencil painting feature, which will give us the freedom to add lots of custom details to our models and textures.

In the next chapter, we will exercise the texturing skills that we have learned so far by creating and applying multiple textures to a model, turning it from a plain clay object into a photorealistic asset.

# 10

# Creating Photorealistic Textures on a 3D Model

In this chapter, we will apply all the skills that we've learned so far in a project working with a 3D model. We will first download a steering wheel model and add some materials to it, before adding some unique, custom-made details.

By adding high-quality textures, we prepare our 3D models for impressive animations and renders. Models that appear realistic are highly sought after in advertising, product visualization, interior design, and other fields where aesthetics are important. By the end of this chapter, you will be able to apply photorealistic textures finished with high-quality texture maps to your models and create custom texture-painted details and features.

The following topics will be covered in this chapter:

- Adding basic materials to the steering wheel
- Baking a custom Normal map
- Applying a logo to the steering wheel
- Painting buttons with stencils

## Technical requirements

This chapter includes exercises that require you to download some content. You will have to download a 3D model of a steering wheel, to which we will apply some textures created throughout this chapter, among other resources:

- Steering wheel 3D model
- Custom Normal map
- Logo texture and Normal map
- Dashboard icons stencil

Each of these files can be found in the `Chapter10` folder within the book's downloadable resources folder, available here: `https://packt.link/mA1OU`

# Adding basic materials to the steering wheel

In this section, we will add some simple materials and texture maps to the steering wheel model. First, we will create two separate leather materials for the handles and the center pad, and then a carbon fiber material for the connectors.

## Adding texture to handles

In the following steps, we will take a downloaded leather texture and its texture maps and apply them to the steering wheel's handles:

1.  First, download a leather material of your choice from `textures.com`.

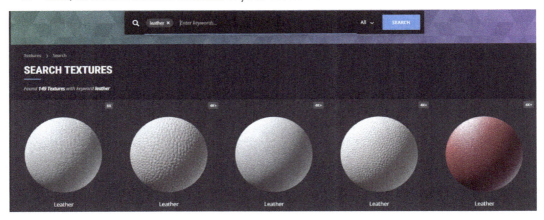

Figure 10.1 – Downloading a leather material from textures.com

2.  Add a new black material to the steering wheel handles, as shown in *Figure 10.2*.

Figure 10.2 – Adding a black material

We will use texture maps to turn this material into leather.

3.  Add a Node Wrangler with *Ctrl + T* and load the downloaded leather Normal map into the **Image Texture** node. Set **Texture Coordinate** to **Object**, **Mapping** to **Box**, and **Color Space** to **Non-Color**.

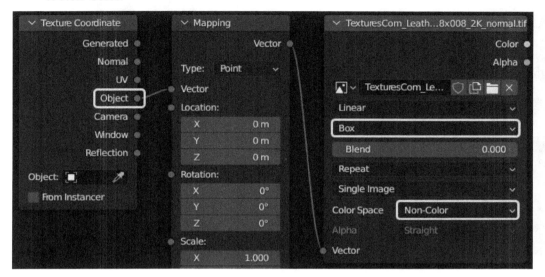

Figure 10.3 – Mapping the leather texture with a Node Wrangler

4.  Add the leather **Normal Map** node between the **Image Texture** node and the **Principled BSDF** node.

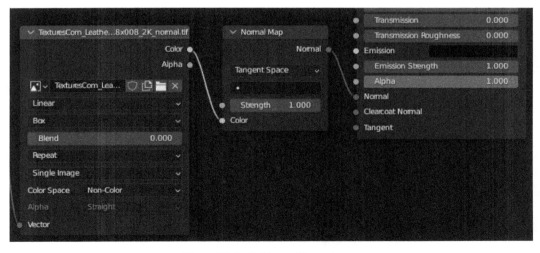

Figure 10.4 – Adding a Normal map

5.    Set **Scale** to 3.000 on all three axes in the **Mapping** node.

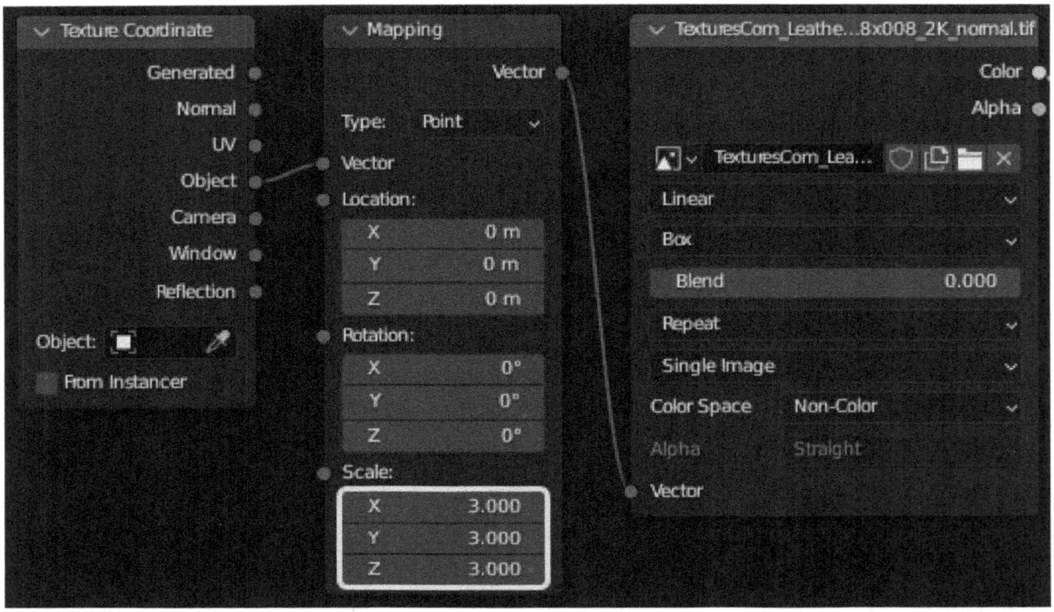

Figure 10.5 – Increasing the texture scale

This will create a fine leather texture on the handles. Adding the other texture maps such as roughness to this material is optional since it will make only a minimal difference here. *Figure 10.6* shows the material created by simply setting a black base color and using a leather Normal map.

Figure 10.6 – A fine leather texture on the steering wheel

Our first leather texture is now ready. Next, let's take a few steps to generate our own slightly different leather texture for the center pad.

## Adding texture to the center pad

In the following steps, we will add a procedural leather texture to our steering wheel's center pad:

1.  Add a new black material to the center pad.

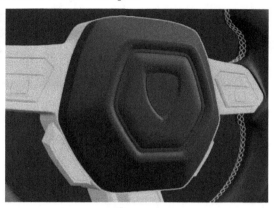

Figure 10.7 – Creating a second black material

2.  Add a **Noise Texture** node to this material. Set **Scale** to 170.000, **Detail** to 1.000, and **Roughness** to 0.020. This will generate a good pattern for a procedural leather texture.

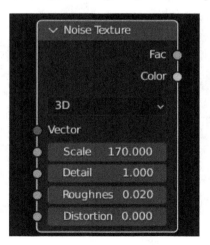

Figure 10.8 – Configuring a Noise Texture node

3. Next, add a **ColorRamp** node and a **Bump** node, with settings as shown in *Figure 10.9*.

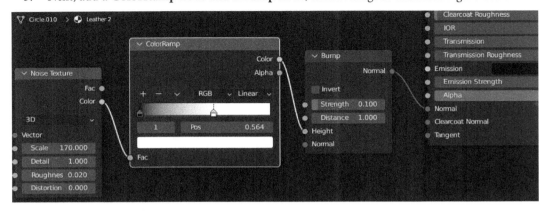

Figure 10.9 – Adding more nodes to control the material

This will turn the noise texture into a bump simulation for our surface.

4. Add a Node Wrangler to the **Noise Texture** node with *Ctrl + T* and set the **Texture Coordinate** node to **Object**.

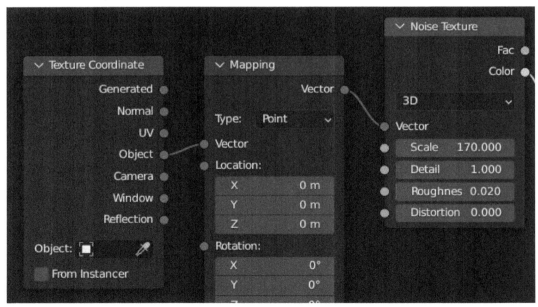

Figure 10.10 – Adding a Node Wrangler to the Noise Texture node

This creates a procedural leather material on our object, as shown in *Figure 10.11*.

Figure 10.11 – The steering wheel center pad with our procedural leather material

Next, we will add a carbon fiber material to the lower part of the steering wheel. By doing so we will increase the material variety on the object to make it look more complex and complete.

## Adding carbon fiber to the steering wheel

In the following steps, we will learn how to add a carbon fiber material to our steering wheel:

1. Create a new black material named Carbon Fiber and apply it to the object as shown in *Figure 10.12*.

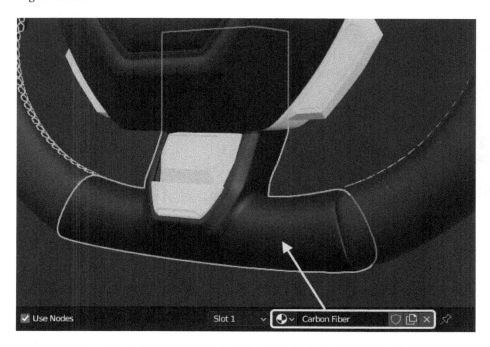

Figure 10.12 – Creating and applying the Carbon Fiber material

2.  Apply a carbon fiber Normal map downloaded from `textures.com` to the material. Here, it is best to add another Node Wrangler with *Ctrl + T* to quickly map the texture.

Figure 10.13 – Adding a Node Wrangler to the carbon fiber map

3.  In the **Principled BSDF** node, set the **Metallic** and **Clearcoat** values to 1.000. These properties are key for making carbon fiber look realistic.

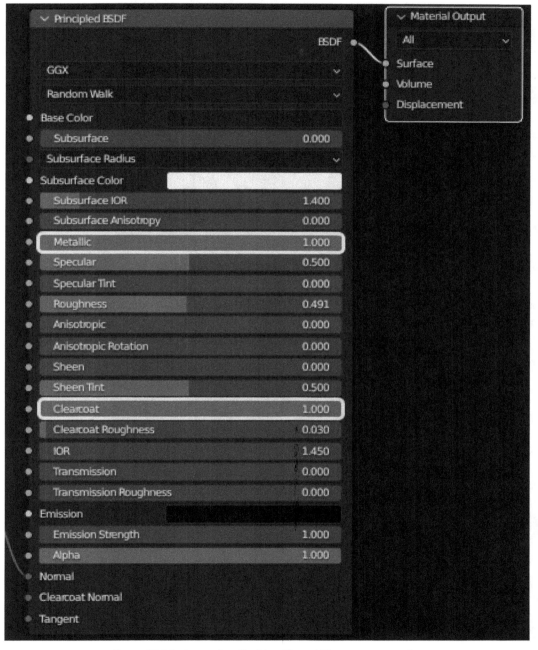

Figure 10.14 – Increasing the Metallic and Clearcoat properties

We can now use this material on other parts of the model, as shown in *Figure 10.15*.

Figure 10.15 – Assigning the carbon fiber material

Lastly, let's add a simple black material to the button frames in the middle of the steering wheel, and a metallic red to the button at the bottom of the steering wheel, as shown in *Figure 10.16*.

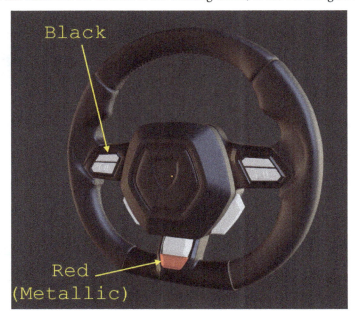

Figure 10.16 – Adding more basic materials

We now have enough basic materials for our steering wheel. Next, let's bake a custom pattern into a Normal map so that we can use it in on the center pad.

## Baking a custom Normal map

We will now learn how to create a custom Normal map pattern. Although these textures can be downloaded as at the beginning of this chapter, you are encouraged to bake the pattern yourself to learn how to create custom Normal maps. In the following steps, we will model and bake the custom pattern as a Normal map:

1.  Shape a simple hexagon using a plane, as shown in *Figure 10.17*. Make sure to copy the exact measurements.

    It is important to use the same measurements because otherwise the texture will not be seamless, and there will be inconsistencies in the pattern.

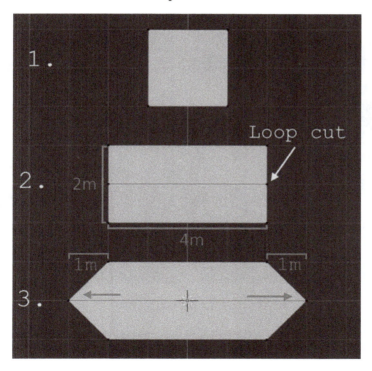

Figure 10.17 – Modeling a hexagon

2.    Inset the faces and push them down as shown in *Figure 10.18*.

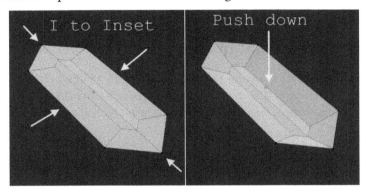

Figure 10.18 – Insetting faces in the hexagon

3.    Add an **Array** modifier with a **Constant Offset** value of 2m on the *Y* axis.

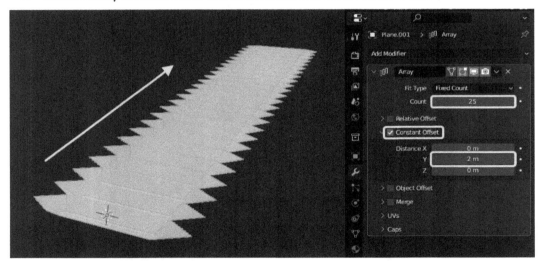

Figure 10.19 – Adding an Array modifier

4.    Add a second **Array** modifier to the object with a constant offset of 5   m on the *X* axis and 1 m on the **Y** axis. Leave the **Z** axis value at the default value, **0 m**.

This will turn the object into a large plane using the hexagonal pattern that we shaped in *steps 1* and *2*. Apply both modifiers with *Ctrl + A*.

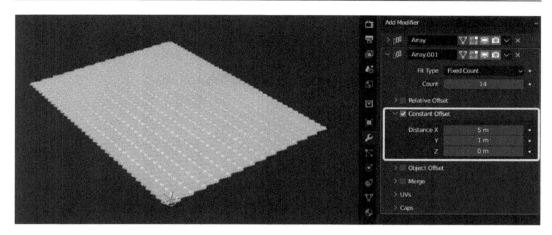

Figure 10.20 – Adding a second Array modifier

5.  Add a plane just above the surface and scale it by a factor of 5. We will use this plane to bake a Normal map, as we learned in *Chapter 5*, *Generating Texture Maps with Cycles*. It is important to copy the exact measurements, otherwise the texture will not be seamless.

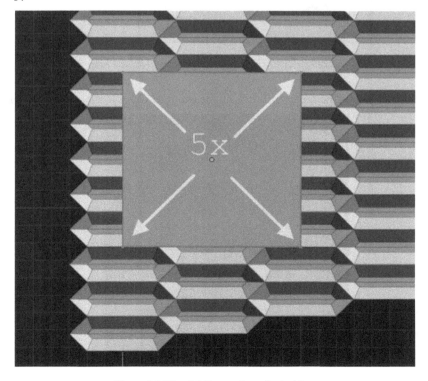

Figure 10.21 – Adding a plane for baking

The resulting image will look like Figure *10.22*.

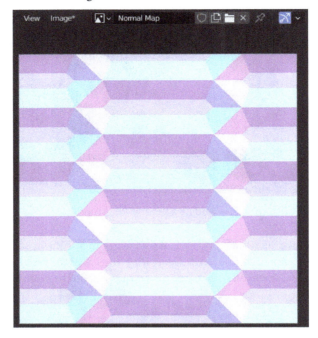

Figure 10.22 – Custom pattern baked into a Normal map

Applying this Normal map to the center pad with a node wrangler will give a result like in *Figure 10.23*.

Figure 10.23 – Custom Normal map applied to the center pad

Now that we've added a pattern to the center pad, we need to add a logo. Let's learn how to download and apply a logo to the model.

## Applying a logo to the steering wheel

We will now learn how to apply a logo to the center of the steering wheel. To do this, we must first download the logo texture from the *Technical requirements* section. Additionally, you can find and download any logo online by searching for " [any supercar] logo" online.

In the following steps, we will apply a logo to the center of the steering wheel:

1.  Create a new material and assign it to the logo in the middle.

Figure 10.24 – Assigning a new material to the logo shape

2.  Use an **Image Texture** to load the logo into the material. By default, the image will probably not be mapped correctly. We will fix that in the upcoming steps.

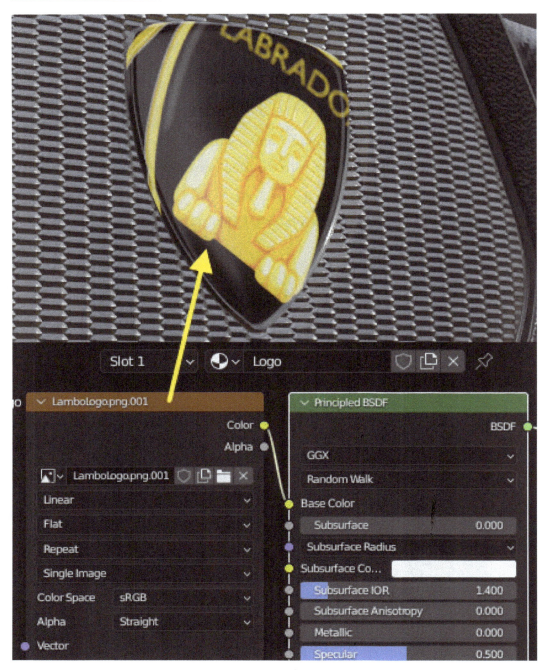

Figure 10.25 – Incorrectly mapped logo

3.  Unwrap the surface in **Edit Mode** by pressing *U*.

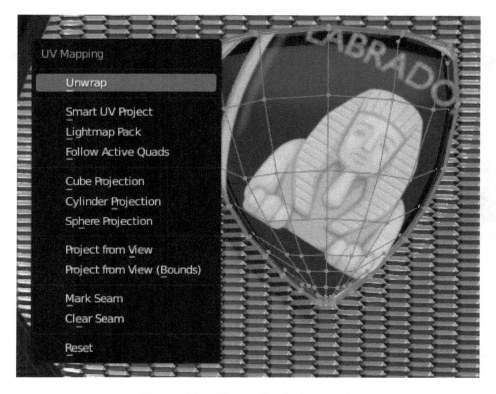

Figure 10.26 – Unwrapping the logo mesh

4.  Switch to the **UV Editing** workspace.

Figure 10.27 – Switching to the UV Editing workspace

5.  Adjust the UV map in the UV Editor by rotating it, moving it, and rescaling it.

    You might need to reshape the UV map manually. If so, you can use many of the same tools as you would when editing a mesh (such as vertex select, proportional editing, and 2D cursor).

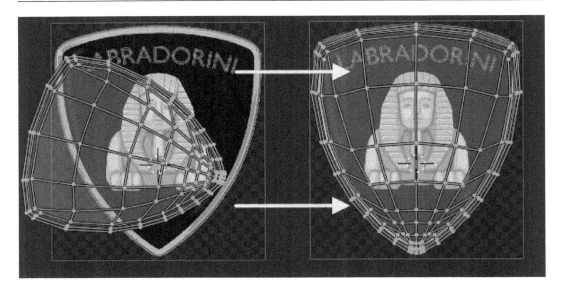

Figure 10.28 – Manually mapping the image

If done correctly, the logo image should be displayed on the model as in *Figure 10.29*.

> **Tip**
>
> Set the **Metallic** value to 1.000 on this material to make it look as if is made of metal, adding some extra realism.

Figure 10.29 – Logo correctly displayed on the object

Using the techniques we learned in the *Generating Normal maps in GIMP* section of *Chapter 5, Generating Texture Maps with Cycles*, it is also possible to generate a Normal map for this image and apply it to the logo. This will greatly improve the material, as shown in *Figure 10.30*.

Figure 10.30 – Logo with a Normal map

We have now finished texturing the logo and we are left only with the buttons. Next, we will create some stencils and paint them onto the buttons to finish them.

## Painting buttons with stencils

We will now use a custom stencil to texture-paint some icons onto the buttons on the steering wheel. Lots of icons can be found online by searching for `dashboard icons`, but you can download a pre-made icon stencil from the link provided in the *Technical requirements* section of this chapter to save time.

In the following steps, we will prepare the buttons for texture painting so that we can use the stencil:

1.  Add a new material to the buttons and name the material `Buttons`.

    In the material, add an **Image Texture** node.

Figure 10.31 – Creating a new material for the buttons

2.  In the **Image Texture** node, generate a new black image named Button Icons and set the resolution to 2048x2048.

Figure 10.32 – Generating a new image for the buttons

3.  With the buttons selected in **object mode**, switch to the **Texture Paint** workspace. The object has already been UV-unwrapped.

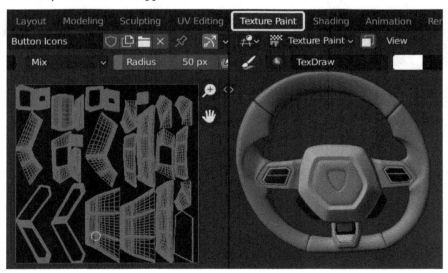

Figure 10.33 – Preparing the workspace

4.  In the **Texture Properties** tab, load the icon stencil using the **Open** option.

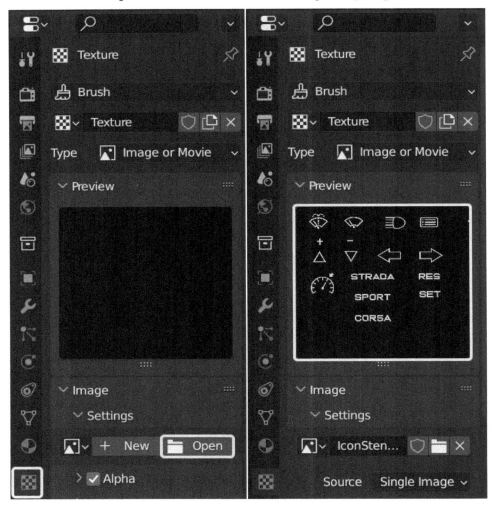

Figure 10.34 – Opening the stencil

5.  In the image editor, load the stencil in the **Texture** menu and set the **Mapping** dropdown to **Stencil**.

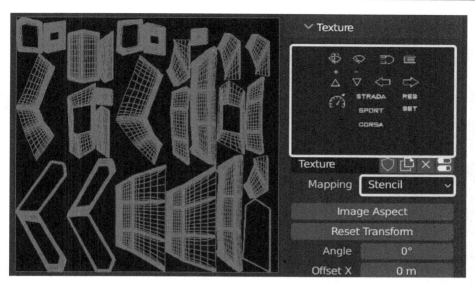

Figure 10.35 – Preparing the stencil for texture painting

6.  Move the stencil by clicking and dragging it with the right mouse button. Then paint over it to place the icons on the buttons.

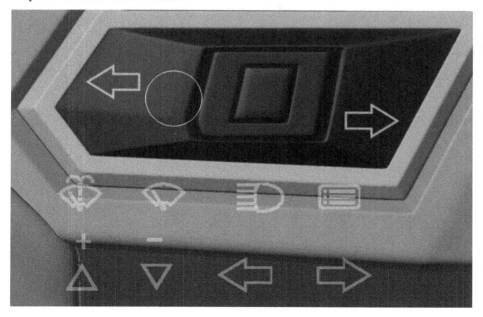

Figure 10.36 – Painting with the stencil

*Figure 10.37* is a reference for how the icons should be placed on the buttons.

Figure 10.37 – Painted buttons on the steering wheel

*Figure 10.38* shows the finished steering wheel, as displayed in viewport shading.

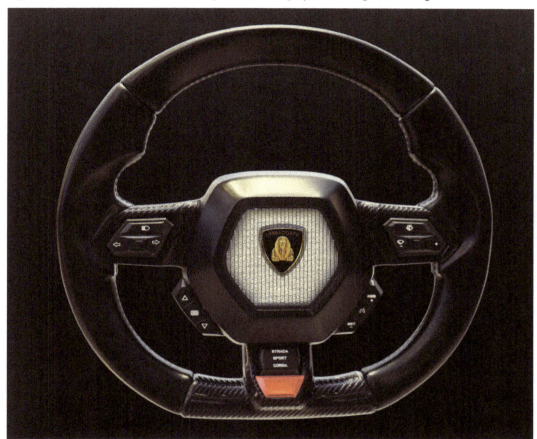

Figure 10.38 – Fully textured steering wheel

We added materials to all parts of the steering wheel, and the model is now complete.

## Summary

In this chapter, we took a 3D model of a steering wheel and completed it with realistic materials and textures. We learned how to create leather, carbon fiber, custom Normal maps, and buttons with custom texture-painted icons.

In the next chapter, we will explore the different types of lights available for use to light a scene. This will allow us to finalize our work and render it for an impressive portfolio item.

# Part 4:
# Lighting and Rendering

In *Part 4*, we will learn how to finalize our projects by turning our scenes into beautifully rendered artwork. To do so, we must master lighting, creating custom world environments, setting camera controls and properties, and optimizing render settings in the Cycles render engine.

This part has the following chapters:

- *Chapter 11, Lighting a Scene in Cycles*
- *Chapter 12, Creating Photorealistic Environments with HDRIs*
- *Chapter 13, Preparing the Camera for Rendering*
- *Chapter 14, Rendering with Cycles*

# 11
# Lighting a Scene in Cycles

In this chapter, we will learn how to correctly add lights to a scene and create a realistic environment for our 3D models. We will first explore the different lighting options available in Blender and then learn how to simulate natural, environmental lighting, which will allow us to create photorealistic scenes. Finally, we will learn about some lighting techniques for simulating artificially lit environments.

By the end of this chapter, you will have a great understanding of how lights work in Blender, what contributes to realistic lighting, and how to create high-quality lighting environments. Creating good lighting is a key element in the presentation of a 3D model or scene, and it will allow us to greatly increase the impressiveness of our work.

The following topics will be covered in this chapter:

- Generating light in Blender
- Simulating realistic lighting
- Generating studio lighting

## Technical requirements

The prepared resources can be found in the Chapter11 folder within the book's downloadable resources folder, available here: `https://packt.link/mA1OU`

## Generating light in Blender

In Blender, there are several different methods for generating light. We will sort these methods into three categories: light objects, emission lighting, and environmental lighting. We will now go over them one by one to find out how they work and what they can be used for. This will give us a lot of options for creating the perfect lighting for many different scenarios.

## Using light objects

**Light objects** are a special type of object intended for adding individual sources of light into a scene. They are easy to use and allow us to manually create any type of lighting environment we want. There are four different types of lights: point, sun, spot, and area. To understand how they work, we will study them individually.

### Point light

A **point light** is an object that generates light from a single point. It emits light evenly in all directions from where it is located. The best way to understand how it works is to create one and try to use it yourself, so let's do that.

To add a point light, press *Shift + A* in **Object** mode and, in the **Light** section, select **Point**.

Figure 11.1 – Adding a point light

*Figure 11.2* shows a point light in a simple scene. As you can see, a point light serves as a great light source for a scene with a small light bulb. The point light can be used to simulate small light sources such as light bulbs or candles, since it emits light equally in all directions from a single point.

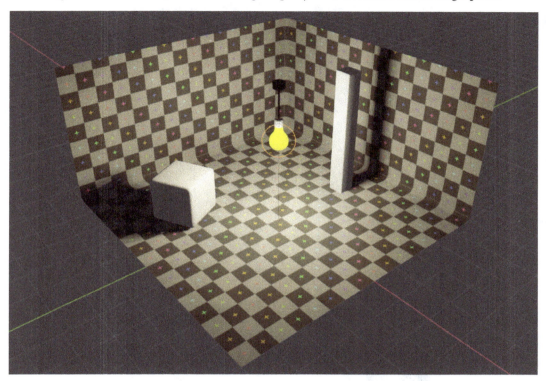

Figure 11.2 – A point light in a 3D space

The point light has lots of properties, which can be controlled in the **Object Data Properties** tab. We will mostly only control **Color**, **Power**, and **Radius**, which we can do using the controls shown in *Figure 11.3*.

Figure 11.3 – Light properties

Here's some more information about these three fields:

- **Color**: This property, quite obviously, controls the color of the light emitted and can be adjusted the same as the base color of a material, using a color wheel.

- **Power**: This property controls the intensity of the light produced by the object.

- **Radius**: This property determines the size of the space in which the light is distributed. A bigger radius will cause softer shadows and a less intense shine.

## Sun light

The sun light emits light in the entire world in the same direction, which is the direction of the line coming from the object's center. Much like shadows cast by objects sitting in real sunlight, the **sun light** in Blender ensures that the shadows are all pointing in the same direction. Because of this feature, the position of a sun light in a scene is completely irrelevant as the shadows and light are only determined by its direction, not location. The sun light is more powerful and has a longer range than other light sources. Regardless of how far away it is from a surface, the light projected by a sun light does not get any weaker. This is useful for lighting large scenes, especially outdoor ones.

To add a sun light, press *Shift + A* in **Object** mode and, in the **Light** section, select **Sun**. This light can be used to imitate real sunlight, as shown in *Figure 11.4*.

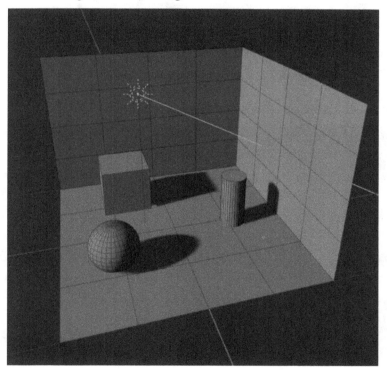

Figure 11.4 – A sun light

The sun light has almost the same properties as the point light, but instead of the radius, we can control its angle. Increasing **Angle**, as in *Figure 11.5*, will cause the shadows to become softer. Reducing **Angle** will make the shadows sharper instead.

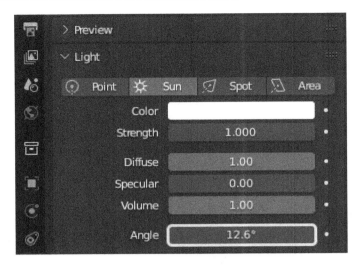

Figure 11.5 – Adjusting the sun light angle

*Figure 11.6* shows us the difference between soft shadows and sharp shadows.

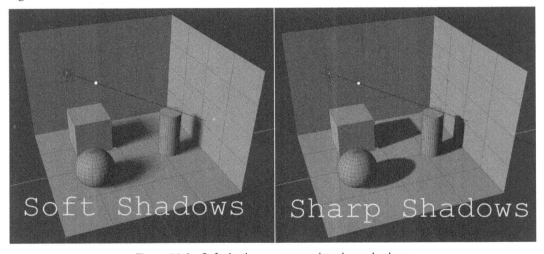

Figure 11.6 – Soft shadows compared to sharp shadows

## Spot light

A **spot light** produces a beam of light that is strictly contained by a cone expanding from the object. To add a spot light, press *Shift + A* in **Object** mode and, in the **Light** section, select **Spot**.

Apart from the basic properties such as color and strength, the spot light has two important controls:

- **Size**: The size determines the size of the circle of light produced by the object
- **Blend**: The blend determines the softness of the circle's edges

*Figure 11.7* shows the **Size** and **Blend** properties of a spot light.

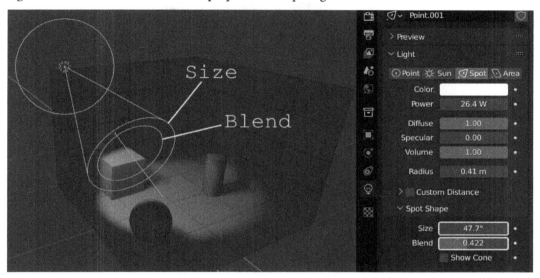

Figure 11.7 – Size and Blend of a spot light

The spot light lights a specific area without adding any light to the surroundings, which can be useful for simulating museum-like exhibitions or casting custom shadows. Let's look at an example.

*Figure 11.8* shows how a spot light can be used to create a custom shadow, defined by an object blocking the light. The object acts as a stencil for the light.

Figure 11.8 – Shadows created by a spot light

To create such sharp and precise shadows, we must reduce the **Radius** value, as shown in *Figure 11.9*. The radius does not have to be 0, but a lower radius value will result in a sharper shadow.

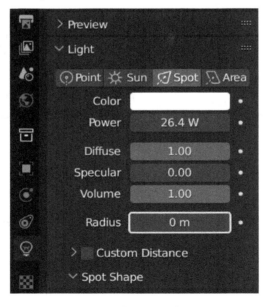

Figure 11.9 – Setting Radius to 0

## *Area light*

An **area light** produces light from a rectangular shape, and only in the direction in which it is facing. Since it produces light from a bigger surface, it creates soft shadows and can be used to simulate the light produced by a screen or a window. The shape of the light can be changed by scaling the object. When creating natural lighting, area lights are the most used type of light.

To add an area light, press *Shift + A* in **Object** mode, and in the **Light** section, select **Area**. You can see how this light looks in *Figure 11.10*.

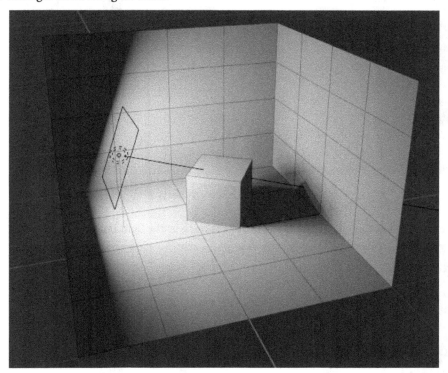

Figure 11.10 – An area light in a scene

So far, we have learned how to use light objects in Blender. Now, let's dive into emission lighting, which is another method for generating light.

## Emission lighting

**Emission lights** are lights created from the material of an object, turning the object into a lamp. They are created by increasing the **Emission** value in the **Material Properties** of an object, as we learned in *Chapter 1*, *Creating Materials in Blender*, in the *Tweaking material properties* section. Emission materials will not work well in Eevee, so it is recommended to use this method in Cycles for the best results.

Emission lighting is useful because it can be added to any mesh or object in the form of a material. This means that the light source can have any shape, which can be used to create lights with distinct shapes, such as car headlights.

*Figure 11.11* shows a plane and a sphere that have materials assigned to them with an **Emission** value higher than 0.

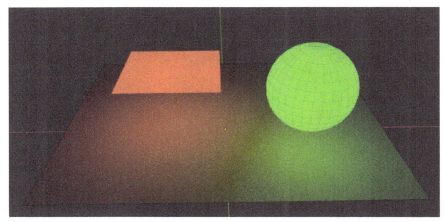

Figure 11.11 – Emission objects

We can use emission lighting to create glowing objects, such as the light bulbs in *Figure 11.12*.

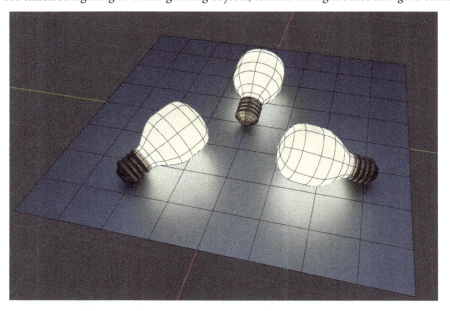

Figure 11.12 – Light bulbs created with emission lighting

To create a glowing material like this, we must set the emission color and increase the emission strength to 2, as shown in *Figure 11.13*.

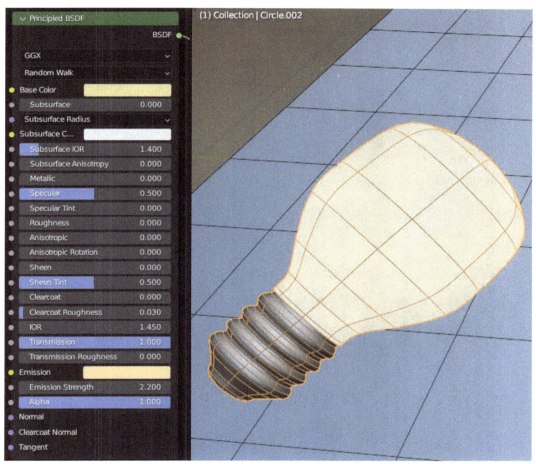

Figure 11.13 – Creating an emission material

We can also use images to control the emission color, which can be used to create a screen or another type of glowing image. *Figure 11.14* shows how we can use an Image Texture node to apply an image as the emission color.

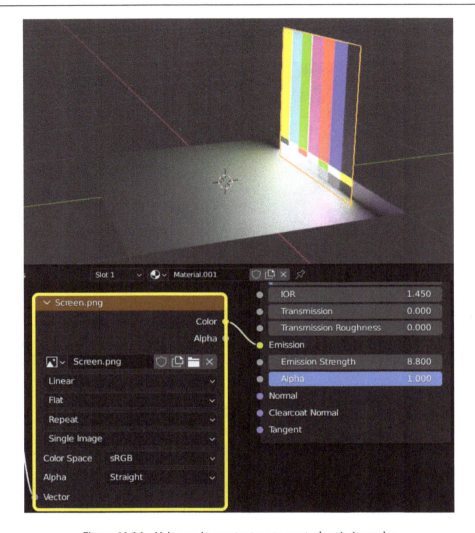

Figure 11.14 – Using an image texture to control emission color

As you can see, the screen consists of multiple colors and thus emits various kinds of light into the scene. We will further explore using images as light sources in *Chapter 12, Creating Photorealistic Environments with HDRIs*, where we will use images as background light sources.

## Environmental lighting

Environmental lighting is produced by the environment of a scene. This light is constant everywhere in the 3D world and it is generated based on the color of the scene background. Learning how to control environmental lighting is important because every scene and object will have a different environment that produces different lighting, and this is a key factor in achieving photorealism.

*Figure 11.15* shows a default cube rendered in a scene with no light objects, where the only light is that which comes from the gray background. As you can see, the scene is not completely dark when all lights are removed, as there is still some light coming from the environment.

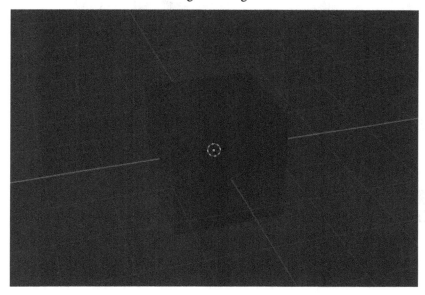

Figure 11.15 – Environmental lighting on a default cube

We can control the color and strength of the environmental lighting the same way we can control the color and strength of the light emitted by an object, as we learned previously. To do this, we must switch to editing **World** nodes in the Shader Editor window, as shown in *Figure 11.16*.

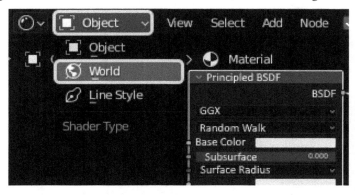

Figure 11.16 – Switching to World nodes in the Shader Editor

Here, we will find the **Background** node, which can be used to control the color and strength of the environmental lighting.

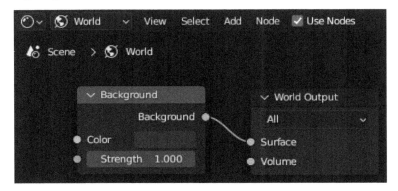

Figure 11.17 – Background node

In *Figure 11.18*, we can see the effects of having a different color in our environment.

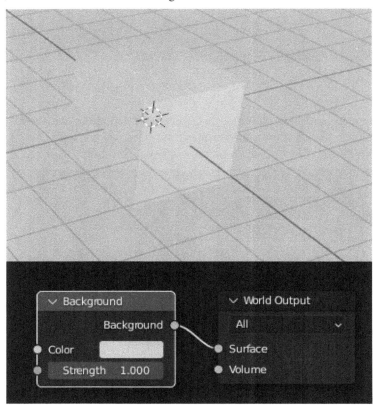

Figure 11.18 – Changing the environmental lighting color

We will further explore this feature and learn how to use it to create high-quality, realistic environments in *Chapter 12*.

We have now learned how the different types of lights work in Blender. Next, let's learn how we can use these lights to create a realistic lighting environment for an object or scene.

## Simulating realistic lighting

We will now learn how to use lights in Blender to create a realistic environment. To understand how realistic lighting can be created, we will introduce the hot/cold lighting principle.

The **hot/cold lighting principle** is simply a method of lighting a scene by using both warm- and cold-colored lights simultaneously to create a universally applicable lighting environment. Red, orange, and yellow are warm colors, while green, blue, and purple are cold colors. *Figure 11.19* shows a simple scene with a warm-colored area light on the left and a cold-colored area light on the right.

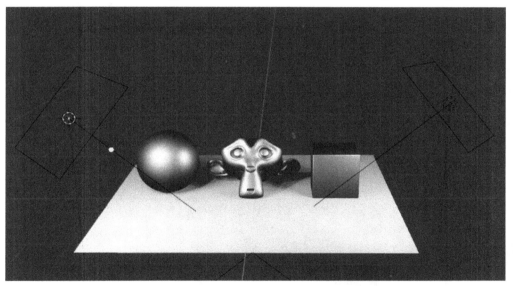

Figure 11.19 – Hot/cold lighting principle

The reason that this is effective is because, in real life, there are typically multiple light sources in a scene. For example, there can be direct, orange-colored sunlight shining into a room, as well as indirect blue or white light being reflected from buildings or the sky through a window. Adding multiple light sources of any kind with slight color variations will further increase the level of realism for the same reason. *Figure 11.20* shows another simple scene with multiple warm and cold light sources. As you can see, the warm light sources are scattered on one side of the scene, while the cold light sources are scattered on the other side.

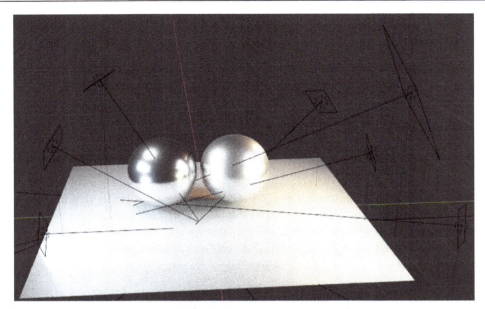

Figure 11.20 – Multiple lights with varying colors

This method works well because, as in real life, there is light coming from several different directions in various colors. In *Figure 11.21*, we can see how having multiple light sources can improve the reflections on surfaces. This improves the overall aesthetic and level of realism of a material or scene, making it look more convincing.

Figure 11.21 – Reflections in materials

We can use this lighting technique to create simple but effective and aesthetic lighting environments for nearly any scene or object.

In this section, we learned how to simulate realistic lighting. Next, let's look at how we can generate studio lighting.

## Generating studio lighting

We will now learn how to create lighting that simulates a studio environment. This will allow us to create renders that are suitable for advertising, product presentations, and other visualizations. In the following steps, we will use Emission lighting to simulate a studio environment:

1.  Create a simple scene consisting of a surface and an object, as shown in *Figure 11.22*.

    For this demonstration, we will use a sphere because reflections are best visible on round, smooth surfaces.

Figure 11.22 – Creating a simple scene

2.  Create a new material for the sphere, with a **Metallic** value of 1.000 and a **Roughness** value of 0.25 or less.

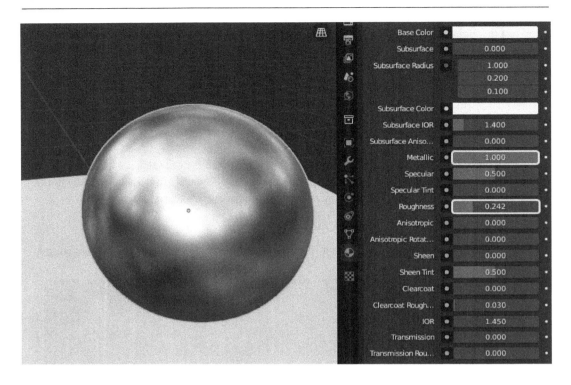

Figure 11.23 – Creating a new material

3.　Create another plane above the scene and use an **Array** modifier to create multiple instances of the shape, as shown in *Figure 11.24*.

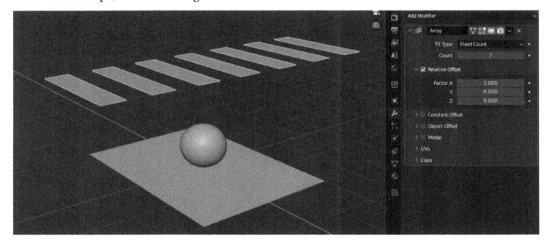

Figure 11.24 – Adding a plane with an array modifier

4.    Create a new material for this object.

In the new material, set the **Emission** color to white and **Emission Strength** to 5.000.

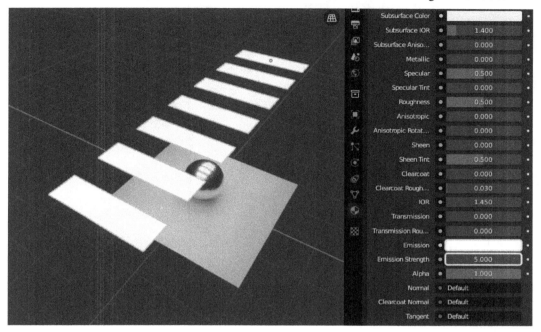

Figure 11.25 – Adding Emission to the plane

5.    Repeat *steps 3-4*, but with a different color, shape, and placement, as shown in *Figure 11.26*.

This will give us the same effect as the warm-cold lighting principle, but with a light shape that is clearly artificial and suitable for a studio. Feel free to adjust the shape and color of the lights to your preference.

Figure 11.26 – Adding a second set of lights

6.   Set the **Viewport Shading** method to **Render** in the top-right corner of the screen.

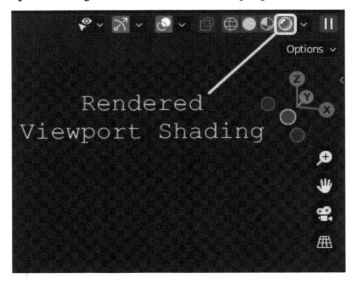

Figure 11.27 – Rendered Viewport Shading

This will give us a preview of our rendered scene.

With multiple shapes and colors, we can create a perfect setting for presenting objects in studio-like lighting, as shown in *Figure 11.28*.

Figure 11.28 – Studio lighting

By combining the lighting methods that we've learned so far, we can create compelling results, as shown in *Figure 11.29*.

Figure 11.29 – An object with colored studio lighting

This is the same steering wheel model that we worked on in *Chapter 10, Creating Photorealistic Textures on a 3D Model,* but with studio lighting. We have now learned some of the fundamental lighting principles in Blender. Keep in mind that controlling the light positions, colors, intensity, shadows, and saturation can greatly impact the mood or ambiance in a scene. This is completely subjective and it is the artist's job to leverage different lighting tools and techniques to create a specific and unique image.

## Summary

In this chapter, we learned about the different types of lights available in Blender and how they can be used to create compelling scenes that present a 3D model in a better light. With the help of these lighting techniques, we can quickly and easily make our scenes and 3D models much more attractive. This will help us create compelling renders and artwork. If you would like to explore some more lighting techniques and concepts, I encourage you to investigate three-point lighting, IES lighting profiles, compositing with light passes, or color temperatures.

In the next chapter, we will learn how to apply custom environment images known as HDRIs to simulate real-life lighting and improve our scenes.

# 12

# Creating Photorealistic Environments with HDRIs

In this chapter, we will learn to create photorealistic environments using custom environment textures known as **High Dynamic Range Images** (**HDRIs**). We will first discuss what HDRIs are and how they work, before diving into how to acquire them and apply them in Blender.

By the end of this chapter, you will be able to download and apply a custom background to create more realistic scenes in Blender. This will allow you to complete your scene with lighting and backgrounds effortlessly.

The following topics will be covered in this chapter:

- What are HDRIs?
- Downloading HDRIs
- Applying HDRIs in Blender

## What are HDRIs?

HDRIs are special images that contain a higher range of brightness values than regular images. This allows them to capture the lighting of a real-life environment, which makes them ideal to simulate environments in a 3D scene in Blender. An HDRI will create a background in our world and project light into our scene, which allows us to complete our projects with better lighting and backgrounds.

*Figure 12.1* shows a simple scene that has an HDRI applied as an environment texture.

Figure 12.1 – A simple scene with an HDRI environment

As you can see, the metal sphere looks photorealistic simply because of the lighting and shading cast onto the object from the environment.

*Figure 12.2.* shows what an HDRI looks like when viewed as a regular image. HDRIs are 360-degree images that can be imported into Blender as a spherical light source.

Figure 12.2 – An HDRI image

To understand how HDRIs work, imagine a large, bright TV showing an image of an alley in a simple 3D scene, as shown in *Figure 12.3*. The screen emits light into the scene in various colors and brightness levels.

Figure 12.3 – A flat HDRI in a scene

Now, imagine an enormous spherical screen wrapped around the 3D world, showing the same image. The result would be identical to placing the scene in a real-life alley, as shown in *Figure 12.4*.

Figure 12.4 – An HDRI wrapped around a scene

We now understand what HDRIs are, how they work, and what they can be used for. Next, we will learn how to find and download some new HDRIs.

## Downloading HDRIs

We will now explore some online libraries for HDRI images. This will allow us to download HDRIs with a wide variety of environments.

The following platforms offer free HDRI images:

- `https://polyhaven.com/hdris`
- `https://hdrmaps.com/freebies/free-hdri-maps/`
- `https://www.openfootage.net/`

*Figure 12.5* shows the HDRI section at `polyhaven.com`. Here, we can get a preview of the 2D image as well as a demonstration of how some common materials would look in these environments.

Figure 12.5 – HDRIs available on polyhaven.com

To download an HDRI from Poly Haven, simply click on an image, and then click on the **Download** button in the top-right corner.

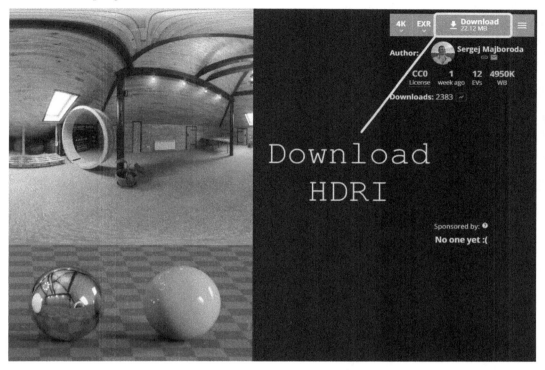

Figure 12.6 – Downloading an HDRI

The other HDRI libraries work the same, and images can be downloaded by simply clicking on them and using the download button.

We will now have the HDRI saved to our computer in either the `.EXR` or `.hdr` format. The key difference between the two formats is that `.EXR` files store more types of data than `.hrd` files, making them superior. For example, an `.EXR` file, unlike an `.hrd` file, supports transparency because it stores an additional set of data that determines the transparency of pixels. An `.EXR` file can also store Z-depth data, which is data that determines the apparent distance of objects in an image. This can interfere with the depth of field effect, which we will explore further in *Chapter 13*, *Preparing the Camera for Rendering*.

Next, let's apply this image to our scene.

## Applying HDRIs in Blender

We will now learn to apply the downloaded HDRI image in Blender. This technique will allow us to load custom textures as world backgrounds. In the following steps, we will load the `.EXR` file in Blender using nodes:

1.  In the **Shading** workspace, switch the Shader Editor mode to **World**, as shown in *Figure 12.7*.

    This will load a separate node space where we can create materials for the world instead of an object.

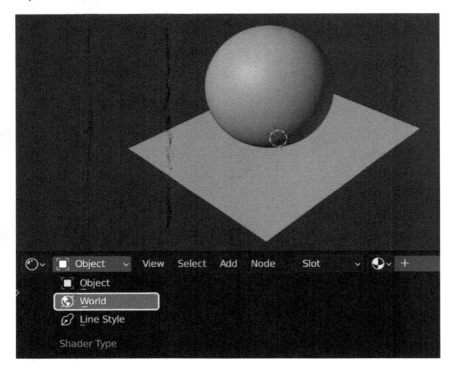

Figure 12.7 – Switching to world shading

Here, we will find the **Background** node, which defines the color and brightness of the environment. This is where we will apply our HDRI background. By default, the environment is dark gray and emits some light, as we can see in *Figure 12.8*.

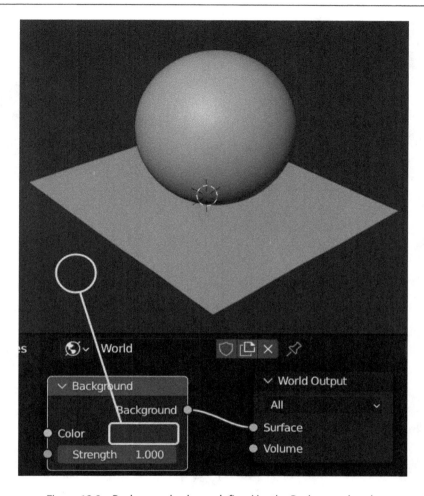

Figure 12.8 – Background color as defined by the Background node

We can change this color the same way we change the base color of a material in a **Principled BSDF** node, as we learned in the *Creating materials* section of *Chapter 1, Creating Materials in Blender*. In *Figure 12.9*, we can see the same scene with a red background color and increased strength to make the effect more obvious. This is only visible in rendered viewport shading.

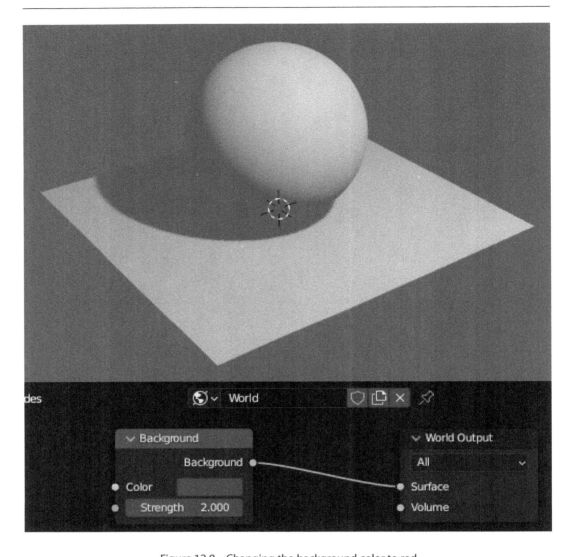

Figure 12.9 – Changing the background color to red

*Figure 12.10* shows how the background can be replaced with an image or a custom texture. For example, we can create a procedural environment texture with a Noise Texture node and a ColorRamp node.

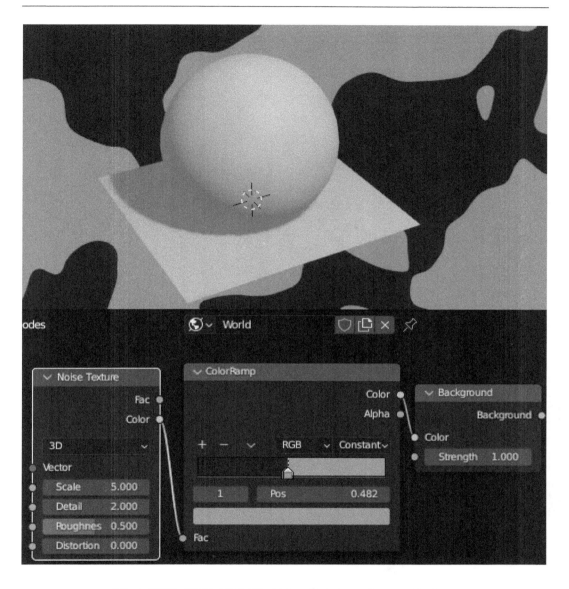

Figure 12.10 – Using a Noise Texture node as an environment texture

However, in this chapter, we are focused on applying HDRIs as backgrounds, so let's see how to do this.

2.  Add an **Environment Texture** node, and connect it to the color input of the **Background** node, as shown in *Figure 12.11*.

Using the **Open** button, load the downloaded HDRI.

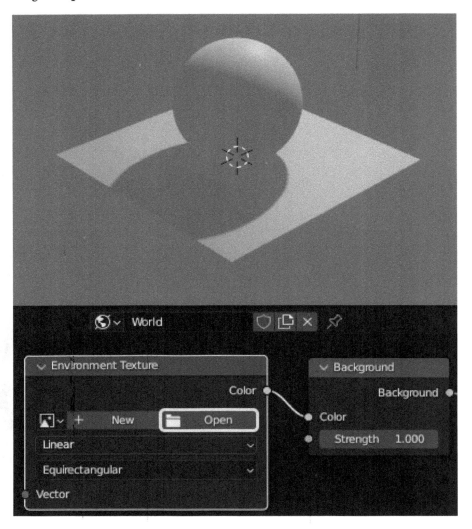

Figure 12.11 – Adding an Environment Texture node

This will automatically display the HDRI as a background image, as shown in *Figure 12.12*.

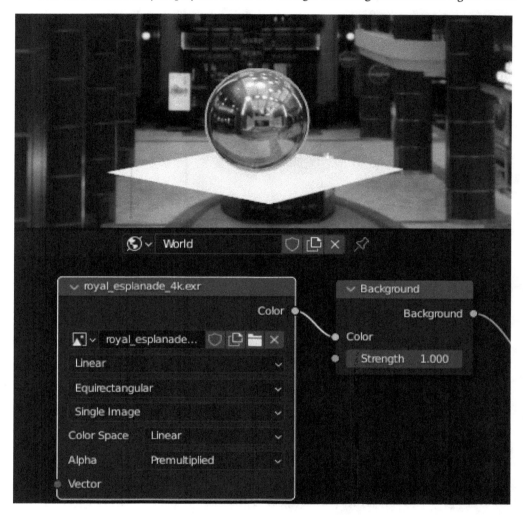

Figure 12.12 – Loading an HDRI into the Environment Texture node

3.    Adjust the **Strength** value to control how much light is emitted by the environment.

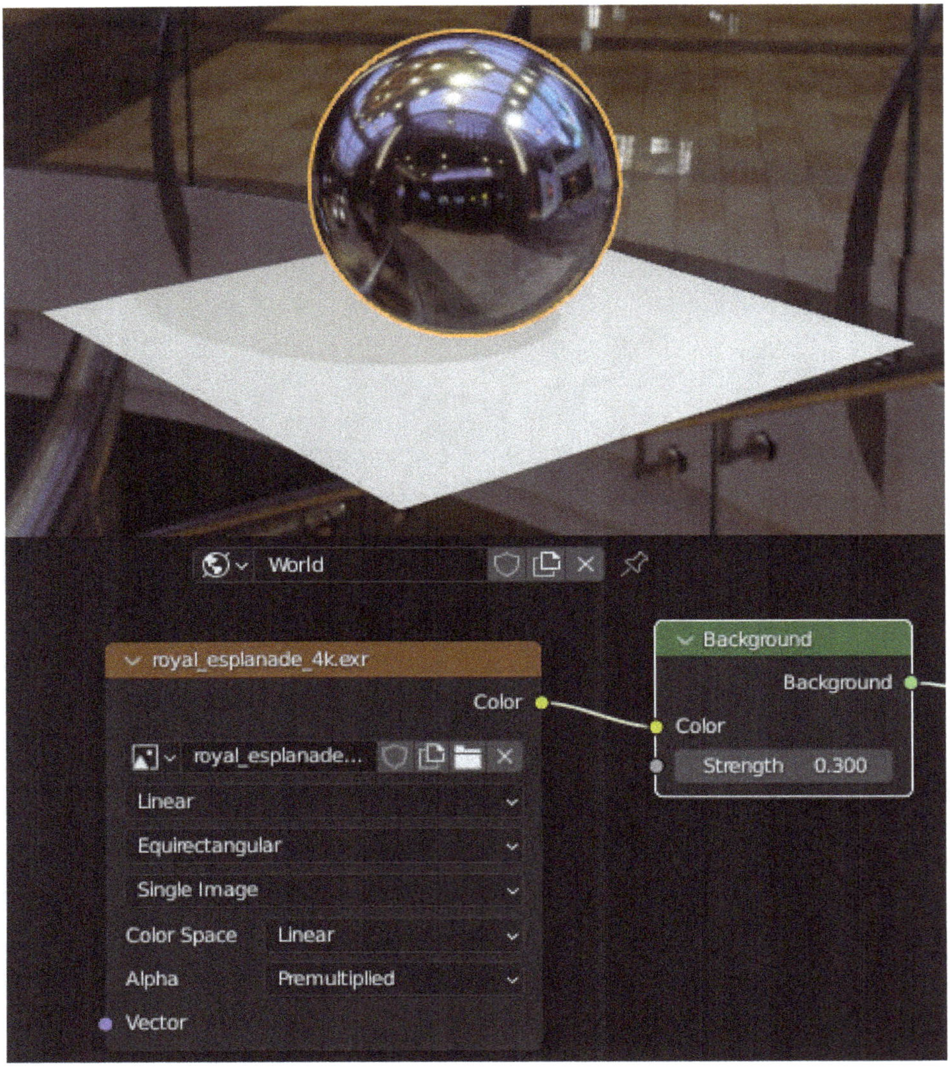

Figure 12.13 – Adjusting the background strength

4.    Add some more nodes to control the colors of the HDRI, as we learned in the *Adding more material nodes* section of *Chapter 2*, *Introducing Material Nodes*.

5.    This can produce colorful lighting without manually adding multiple light sources, as shown in *Figure 12.14*.

Figure 12.14 – Adding color control nodes

We can also manually control the placement of the background image using a node wrangler. If we select the **Environment Texture** node and press *Ctrl + T* to add a node wrangler, as shown in *Figure 12.15*, we will gain some more control over the HDRI background.

Figure 12.15 – Adding a Node Wrangler

We can now rotate the background by changing the *Z* **Rotation** value in the **Mapping** node, as shown in *Figure 12.16*. This feature can be used to control which part of the HDRI is visible in the background, as well as how the lighting affects the scene.

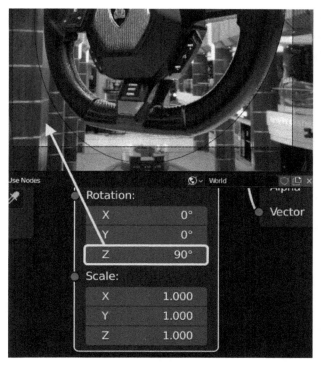

Figure 12.16 – Rotating the HDRI environment

Rotating the HDRI texture around the *Z* axis is the equivalent of rotating an object, as shown in *Figure 12.17*.

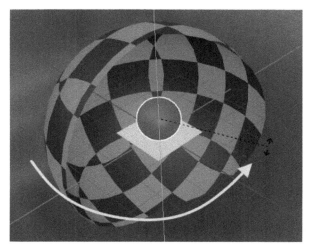

Figure 12.17 – Rotating a dome on the Z axis

We have learned how to use HDRIs as background images by loading them with an **Environment Texture** node. We also learned some techniques to modify and adjust the HDRI in Blender using color control and mapping nodes.

## Summary

In this chapter, we learned how to download HDRIs, import them into Blender, and modify them with some nodes. We can now use HDRIs to create custom backgrounds and realistic environmental lighting. This can help us create beautiful renders with our 3D models and scenes in Blender.

In the next chapter, we will learn to use, set up, and tweak the camera and its settings to create a good foundation to render high-quality images.

# 13

# Preparing the Camera for Rendering

In this chapter, we will learn how to use the camera in Blender to prepare a scene for rendering. We will explore how the camera works and how we can control it, as well as some key parameters and best practices for producing high-quality results.

Learning how to control the camera allows you to set up renders and animations that show your works in a more attractive and professional manner, and it is crucial to master this in nearly any branch of 3D design.

The following topics will be covered in this chapter:

- Getting to know Blender's camera
- Snapping and moving the camera
- Controlling camera settings and parameters
- Animating the camera with keyframes

## Getting to know Blender's camera

The camera is an object in Blender that allows us to turn a 3D scene into a rendered image. It can be moved and placed like a regular 3D object, but it has many more properties that can be controlled to achieve different results. *Figure 13.1* shows the camera in a default Blender scene.

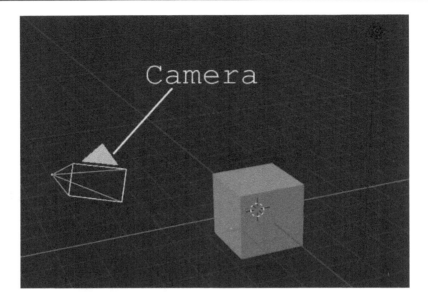

Figure 13.1 – Camera in a default Blender scene

At the back of the camera, there is a point that represents the observer location. This is where the image is viewed from when we render an image. In *Figure 13.2*, we can also see the frame of the camera, which defines the borders of the image.

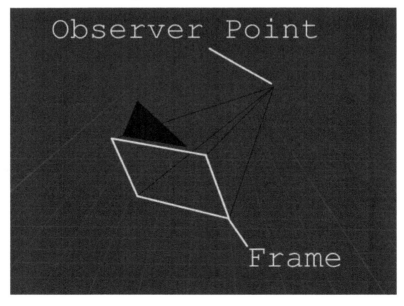

Figure 13.2 – Parts of a camera

In a default scene, we can render an image by pressing *F12*, or by clicking the **Render Image** button in the **Render** menu in the top pane of the screen, as shown in *Figure 13.3*.

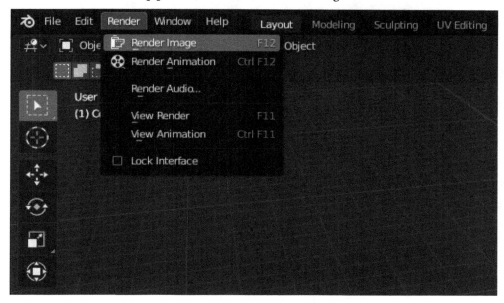

Figure 13.3 – Rendering an image

Now that we have a basic understanding of what the camera is and how it works, let's explore how to control it better.

## Snapping and moving the camera

In this section, we will study some ways to snap and move the camera. Snapping the camera means instantaneously bringing it to a certain point in space. Moving the camera means smoothly panning, shifting, and sliding it as, for instance, a cameraman would on a movie set. We will begin by snapping it so that we can set a starting point for the camera.

### Snapping the camera

There are two ways of snapping the camera in Blender. One way is to snap it to the 3D view, and another is to snap it to the 3D cursor. The best way to place a camera is to align it with your 3D view. This is because we can get a preview of what the camera will see before placing it there. To do so, place your 3D view in a way that you can see what you would like the camera to see. For example, we can place our 3D view so that we are looking at the scene from above, like in *Figure 13.4*.

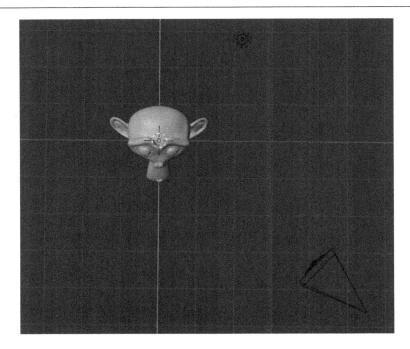

Figure 13.4 – Top view of the scene

We can now align the camera with our view by pressing *Ctrl + Alt + Num0*. This will snap the camera to our 3D view, as shown in *Figure 13.5*.

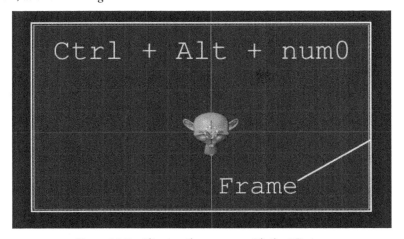

Figure 13.5 – Aligning the camera with the 3D view

The camera is now moved above the scene, as shown in *Figure 13.6*. We can enter the camera view at any time by pressing *Num0*.

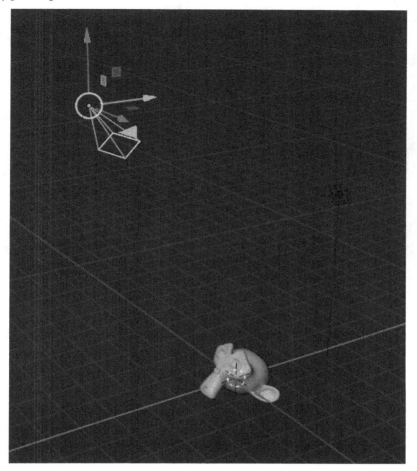

Figure 13.6 – The camera placed above the scene

The camera can also be snapped into different places using the 3D cursor. We must first place the 3D cursor somewhere, either by clicking the left mouse button somewhere in the 3D view or by snapping it to a selected object with *Shift + S*. Then, we must select the camera and snap it to the 3D cursor by pressing *Shift + S* and selecting the **Selection to Cursor** option, as shown in *Figure 13.7*.

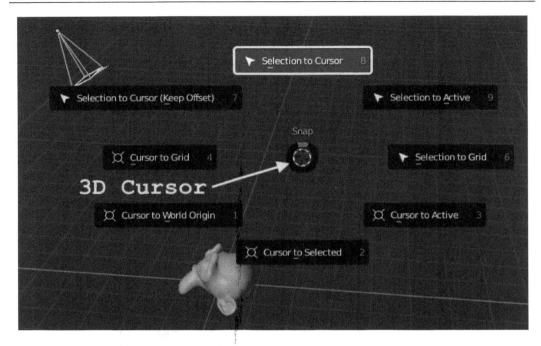

Figure 13.7 – Snapping the selected camera to the 3D cursor

Snapping the camera is a great way to set its location to a point in space, but it is difficult to make minor adjustments to the location by snapping. To make smaller changes, we will move the camera using other methods.

## Moving the camera

We will now learn some methods of moving the camera that will give us more control over what exactly the camera can see. The camera can be moved, scaled, and rotated the same way as any other object in Blender, as shown in *Figure 13.8*.

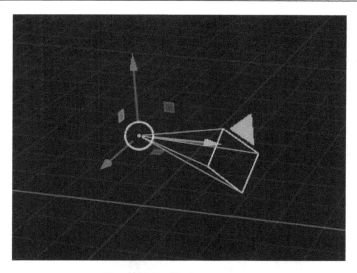

Figure 13.8 – Moving a camera

We can, however, move the camera more precisely by transforming it on its local axes. For example, we can select the camera, press *G* to move it, and then double-press *Z* to move it along the local *Z* axis, as shown in *Figure 13.9*. Likewise, you can double-press *X* or *Y* to move it along other local axes as well. This will move the camera toward or away from the direction in which it is facing.

Figure 13.9 – Moving the camera on its local Z axis

We can also make this movement after entering the camera view with *Num0*. This will give us better control because we can see exactly what the camera sees. This movement will result in bringing the camera closer to or further away from the objective, as shown in *Figure 13.10*.

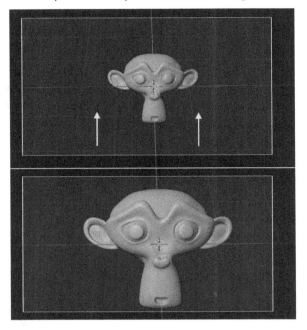

Figure 13.10 – Moving the camera closer to the object

Similarly, we can rotate the camera around a particular axis, or a local axis, as shown in *Figure 13.11*.

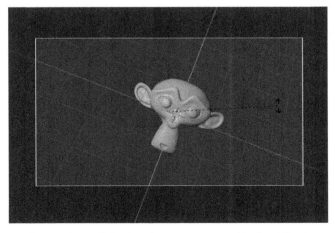

Figure 13.11 – Spinning the camera around its local Z axis

When snapping the camera, it is important to keep in mind that it is difficult to know what the camera will see without looking through it by pressing *Num0*. Because of this, it is best to use a combination of the two methods of snapping to get the best result. For instance, we might snap the camera onto the face of the character to align it with the character's eyesight, but we must also move it around to make minor adjustments to its position.

We have now learned the basic controls for moving and placing the camera. Next, we will introduce some important camera settings that will allow us to produce better results.

## Controlling camera settings and parameters

We will now learn about the most important camera settings and parameters offered by Blender. This will allow us to get better renders by adjusting the zoom level and focus blur.

To exercise these functions, let's prepare a simple scene with randomly scattered basic shapes, as shown in *Figure 13.12*.

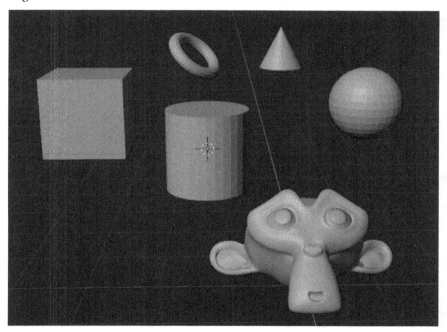

Figure 13.12 – A simple scene with scattered shapes

Using the *Ctrl + Alt + Num0* shortcut, we can align the camera so that it includes all the objects in the frame. As you can see in *Figure 13.13*, some objects are closer and others are farther away.

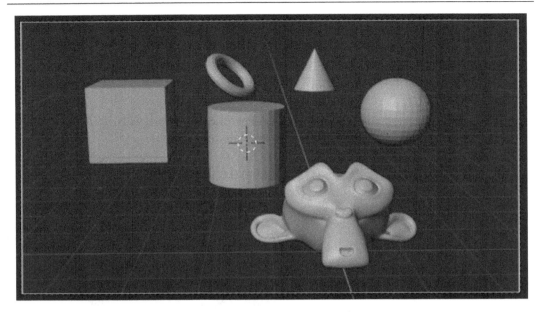

Figure 13.13 – Placing the camera into the scene

When we select the camera, a new **Camera Properties** tab appears on the right side of the screen, as shown in *Figure 13.14*. Here, we can control the camera settings.

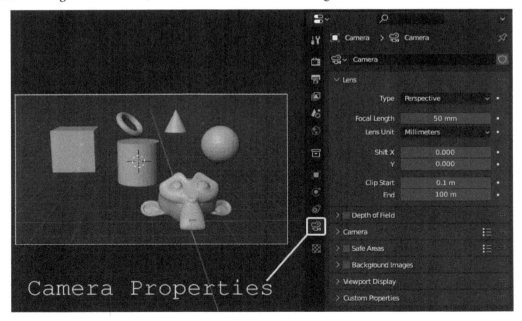

Figure 13.14 – The Camera Properties tab

Let us now look at some of these settings and their uses in more detail:

- **Focal Length**: In the **Camera Properties** tab, we can adjust **Focal Length**, as shown in *Figure 13.15*. Increasing the focal length will reduce the field of vision, which causes the camera to zoom in. Decreasing the focal length increases the field of vision, which causes the camera to zoom out.

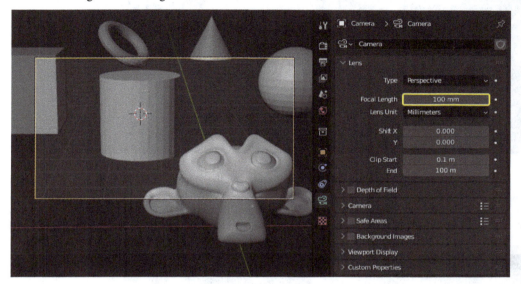

Figure 13.15 – Increasing the Focal Length value

It is important to understand that increasing the focal length to zoom in is not the same as moving the camera closer. In *Figure 13.16*, we can see the difference between having a close-up camera with a low focal length (left) and having a far-away camera with a high focal length (right).

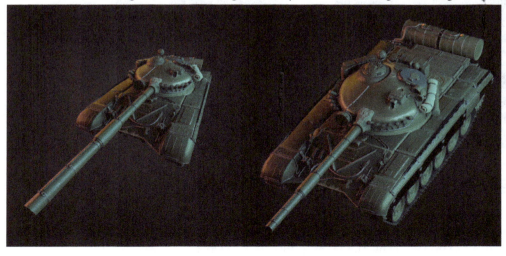

Figure 13.16 – Close camera with low focal length (left) and far away camera with high focal length (right)

- **Depth of Field**: We can also enable **Depth of Field** by checking the box highlighted in *Figure 13.17*. This will allow us to focus the camera on a specific area while blurring out everything else.

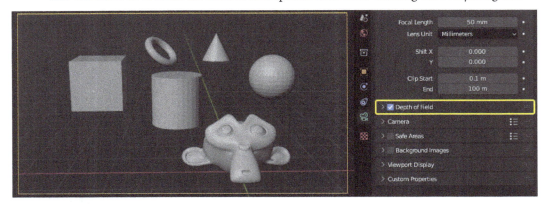

Figure 13.17 – Activating Depth of Field

*Figure 13.18* shows the **Depth of Field** effect on the turret of a T-72 tank. In the left image, there is no **Depth of Field** effect, and the image is sharp. In the right image, the **Depth of Field** effect makes it so that one part of the object is in focus while everything else is severely blurred.

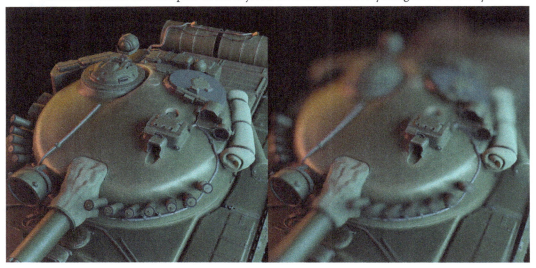

Figure 13.18 – An image without depth of field (left) compared to an image with depth of field (right)

- **F-Stop ratio**: To view the **Depth of Field** effect, we must switch to **Material Viewport Shading** mode and set the **F-Stop** ratio to a low value, such as 0.1. Setting a low **F-Stop** ratio value will increase the level of blur on the areas that are out of focus, as visible in *Figure 13.19*.

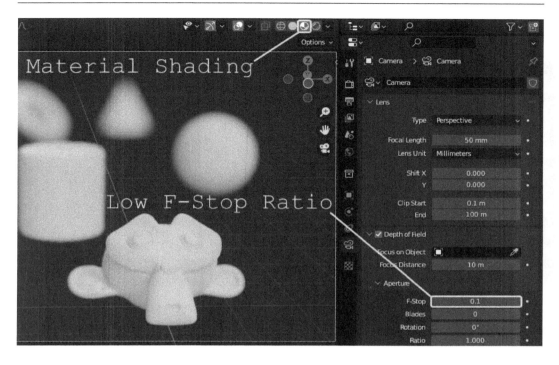

Figure 13.19 – Depth of field in a scene

*Figure 13.20* shows the difference between a low **F-Stop** value (left) and a higher **F-Stop** value (right). As you can see, a lower **F-Stop** value makes the out-of-focus areas very blurry, while a higher **F-Stop** value makes them less blurry.

Figure 13.20 – Low F-Stop (left) versus high F-Stop (right)

- **Focus Distance**: We can now control **Focus Distance** to change the area of focus. By increasing the distance to 3 0  m, we can focus on the objects in the background, as shown in *Figure 13.21*.

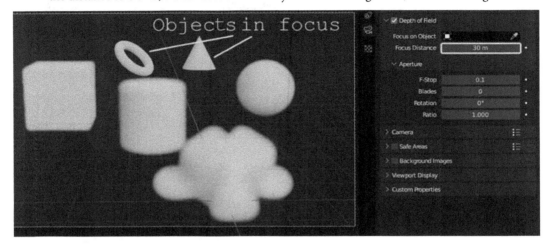

Figure 13.21 – Changing the area of focus by adjusting Focus Distance

- **Focus on Object**: We can also focus on a specific object by loading it in the **Focus on Object** menu, as shown in *Figure 13.22*. This will make the camera always focus on this specific object, regardless of whether the camera or the object moves.

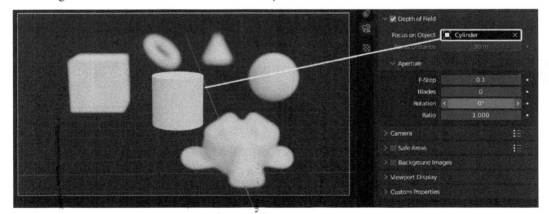

Figure 13.22 – Focusing on a targeted object

This can be useful for scenes with objects of varying distances, as it is easier to simply target a single object than to manually adjust the focus distance every time the object moves. *Figure 13.23* shows an image where the nearby object is in focus on the left, and then shows the same image with the distant object in focus on the right.

Figure 13.23 – Setting the focus to different objects in the scene

We have now learned how to control some important camera properties, which will allow us to create higher-quality renders. Next, let's learn how to animate the camera with keyframes.

## Animating the camera with keyframes

We will now learn how to create animations for the camera by utilizing keyframes. This will help us create more compelling renders because we will be able to render animated scenes as opposed to just still images. These animation concepts are universal to all forms of keyframe-based animation, so this knowledge will carry over to other animation skills beyond camera movement.

Before learning how to animate the camera, we must understand what keyframes are and how they work.

**Keyframes** are frames that represent a specific point in time where properties such as position, rotation, or scale are defined. For example, when animating with keyframes, we set the location of an object to point A on the first keyframe and point B on the second keyframe two seconds later. Blender will then automatically make the object move from point A to point B within those two seconds.

There are many different things that can be controlled with keyframes, beyond just the movement and rotation of objects. For example, it is also possible to animate the focal length of the camera, so that it has a low focal length at one point in time and a high focal length at another point in time.

We will now learn how to use keyframes to create useful camera animations.

## Animating the camera

To start animating the camera, we must first switch to the **Animation** workspace. This will load three windows, **3D View**, **Camera View**, and **Timeline**, as shown in *Figure 13.24*.

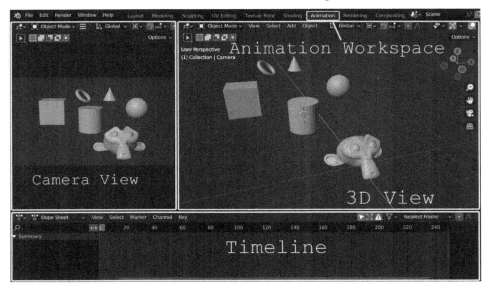

Figure 13.24 – The Animation workspace

We will now use the timeline to create our first keyframes and animate the camera. In the following steps, we will animate the camera so that it slowly orbits around the scene:

1.  With *Ctrl + Alt + Num0*, place the camera so that it can see the entire scene, while sitting slightly to the side, like in *Figure 13.25*.

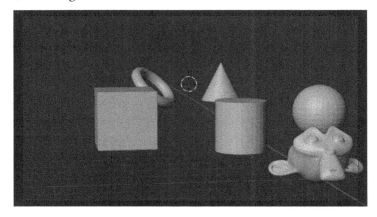

Figure 13.25 – Placing the camera into the starting position

2.  With *Shift + A*, create a new sphere using the **Empty** menu, and place it in between the background objects of the scene.

    We will use this object to define the point around which the camera will orbit.

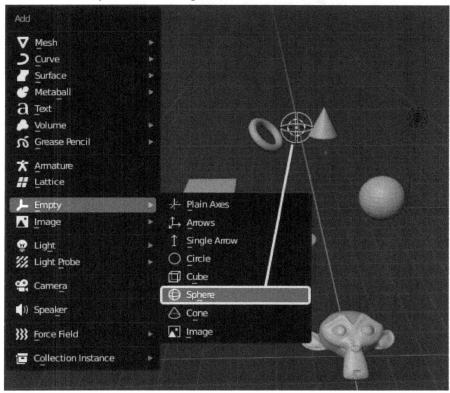

Figure 13.26 – Adding an empty sphere

3.  Select the camera first and the empty sphere second. Then, press *Ctrl + P* and select **Object (Keep Transform)**.

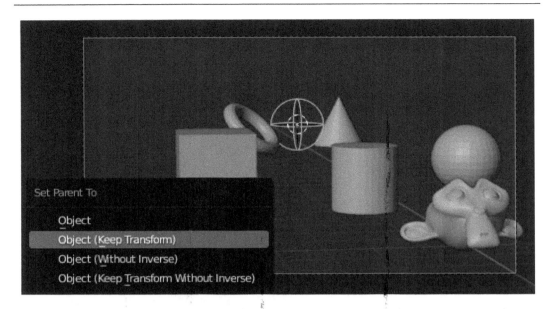

Figure 13.27 – Parenting the camera to the empty sphere

Parenting will make the camera follow the empty sphere while retaining its relative position to the sphere. Try moving or rotating the empty sphere to see how the camera reacts.

4.    Select the empty sphere and set the timeline marker to frame 1.

This is the beginning of the timeline; it is where our animation starts.

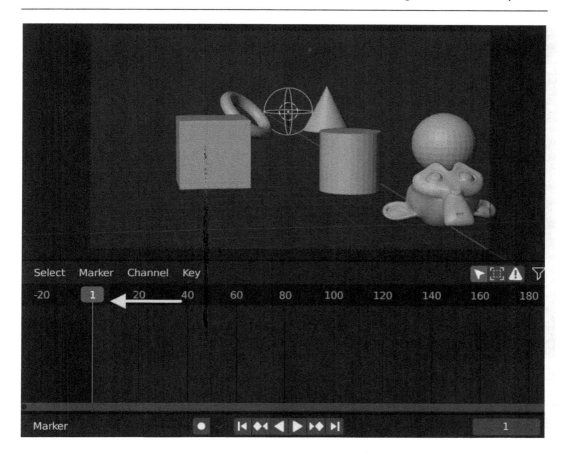

Figure 13.28 – Moving the timeline marker to frame 1

5.   With the sphere selected, press *I* and select **Location & Rotation**.

This tells Blender that we want to have the sphere placed and rotated in this way on the first frame.

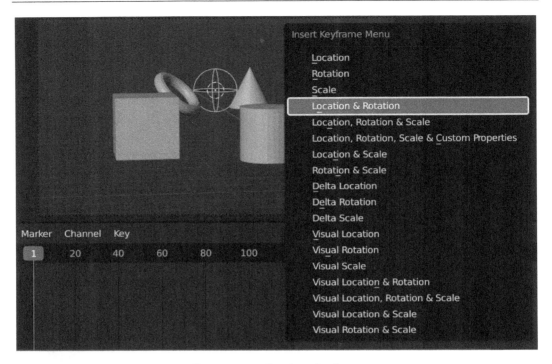

Figure 13.29 – Creating a keyframe

6.   Next, move the marker to frame *80* and rotate the sphere so that the camera moves into a different position.

You are free to use any other frame, but the more frames we have between different positions and keyframes, the slower the animation will be.

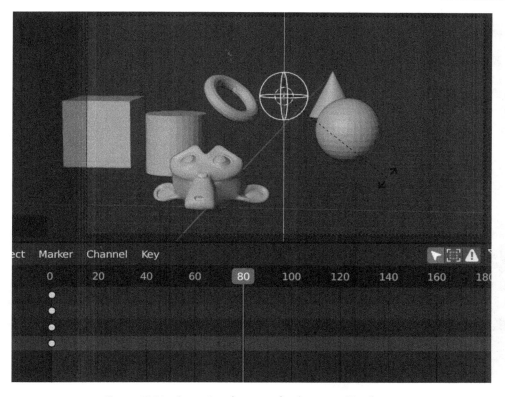

Figure 13.30 – Preparing the scene for the second keyframe

7.    Press *I* with the sphere selected and click **Location & Rotation** to define the second keyframe.

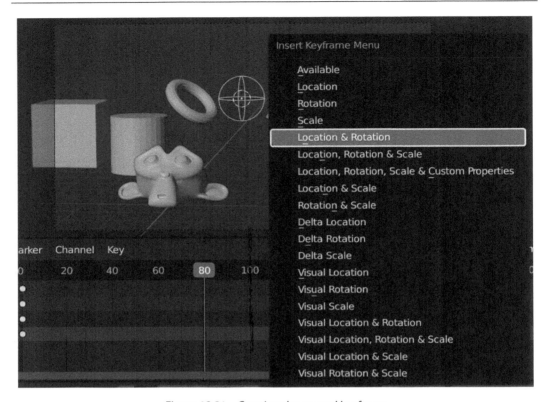

Figure 13.31 – Creating the second keyframe

8.  Slide the marker to frame 1 and play the animation.

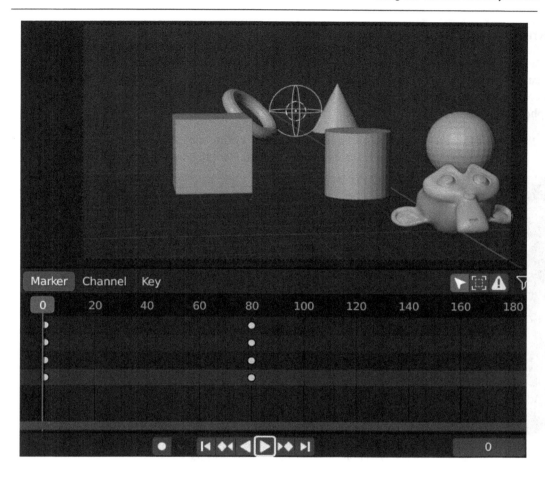

Figure 13.32 – Playing the animation

We now have a simple animation for our camera. Next, let's animate the focus distance.

## Animating the focus distance

We will now learn how to animate the focus distance. The purpose of this exercise is to demonstrate that we can keyframe and animate effects and values such as the focus distance. In the following steps, we will adjust and keyframe this effect much like we keyframed the rotation properties of the sphere previously:

1.  With the camera selected, set **Focus Distance** to a value such that the nearby objects are in focus while the distant objects are out of focus, and place the marker on frame 1.

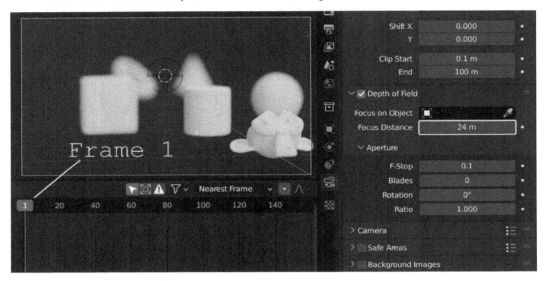

Figure 13.33 – Adjusting the focus distance for the first frame

2.  Click on the icon next to the **Focus Distance** slider to create a keyframe with this distance.

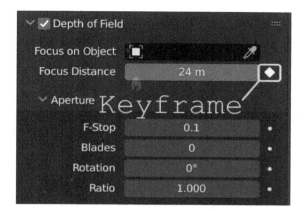

Figure 13.34 – Keyframing the focus distance

3.  Move the marker to frame 80 and create a second keyframe with a higher focus distance, such that the distant objects are in focus while the nearby objects are out of focus.

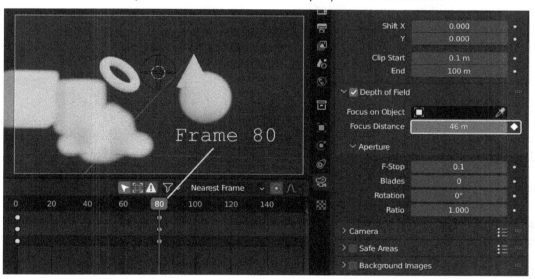

Figure 13.35 – Creating the second focus distance keyframe

4.  Play the animation.

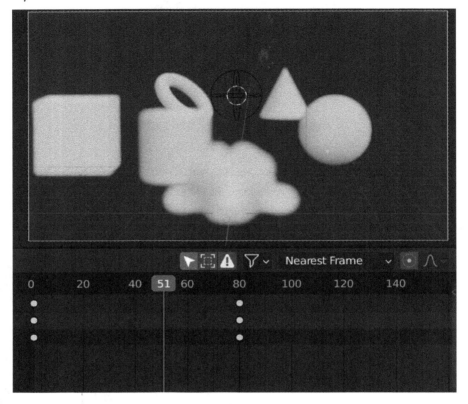

Figure 13.36 – Playing the final animation

We will now have an animation where the camera is slowly shifting its position while changing its focus from the nearby objects to the distant objects. The skills we learned in doing so allow us to create animated scenes and dynamic rendered clips.

We now know how to use keyframes to animate the movements and properties of different objects. The same function can be applied to nearly all other objects and properties, including modifiers, material properties, constraints, and physics simulations.

## Summary

In this chapter, we learned how the camera works and what it can be used for. We learned how to control some of its basic properties, as well as how to animate it to create dynamic scenes.

In the next chapter, we will learn how to control the render properties to turn our scenes into beautiful final images or videos. This is the final step of a 3D project.

# 14

# Rendering with Cycles

In this chapter, we will learn how to utilize control key render properties and tools to allow us to turn our 3D scenes into beautiful artworks. By the end of this chapter, we will be able to export any 3D artwork as a final 2D image or video.

We will discuss the differences between Eevee and Cycles renders; however, the focus in this chapter is on the Cycles render engine as it creates much more realistic results. We will then explore the various rendering and export settings and how to optimize them to get the best renders.

The following topics will be covered in this chapter:

- How does rendering work in Blender?
- Configuring render properties
- Exporting images and videos

## How does rendering work in Blender?

**Rendering** is the process of turning a 3D scene into a finished image or video. To render a scene, Blender needs to perform various calculations to visualize all materials, light rays, reflections, shadows, and more. To get a preview of what a scene would look like with its current lighting, materials, and shadows, we can use rendered viewport shading. *Figure 14.1* shows the same image with solid viewport shading and rendered viewport shading.

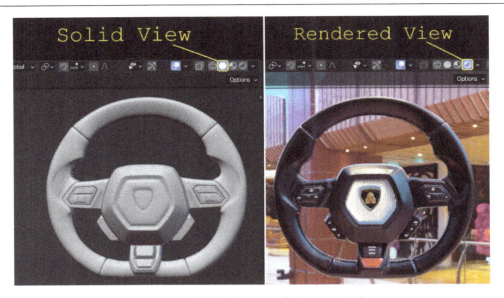

Figure 14.1 – Solid and rendered viewport shading

Note that using rendered viewport shading gives us only a preview of the rendered scene and will not allow us to export a final image in any quality higher than that of a screenshot. To render a scene, we must press *F12* or use the **Render** menu in the top pane of the screen, as shown in *Figure 14.2*.

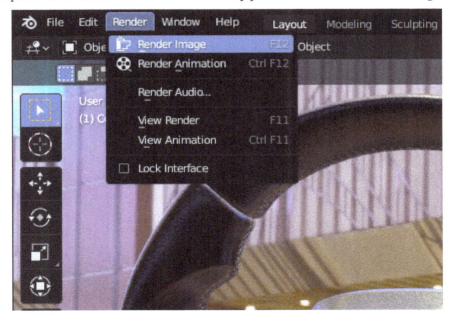

Figure 14.2 – Rendering an image

This will produce a result likely very similar to the render preview. We will now learn how to improve the result and get a more appealing render using Blender's engines.

# Configuring render properties

We will now learn how to control some render properties to get the result that we want. First, we must understand the difference between the two render engines available in Blender: Eevee and Cycles.

## Eevee versus Cycles

**Eevee** is the default render engine, and it is used to make faster, less complex renders. It serves well for previewing renders or producing low-realism scenes such as medical or industrial animations.

**Cycles** is the more powerful and advanced counterpart to Eevee, and is used for creating more sophisticated, photorealistic renders. It uses a different mechanism to produce high-quality renders, but it takes a much longer time to do so. *Figure 14.3* shows a comparison of the same scene rendered by Eevee and Cycles respectively.

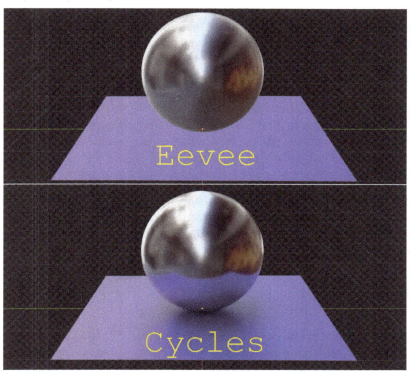

Figure 14.3 – Eevee versus Cycles render

As you can see, Cycles produces better reflections and shading than Eevee. However, *Figure 14.4* shows the differences in render times for the two scenes. As you can see, Eevee only took 2.97 seconds to render this scene, while Cycles took 9.76 seconds to render the same scene. This value can be found in the top-left corner of the **Render** window that opens when we render a scene.

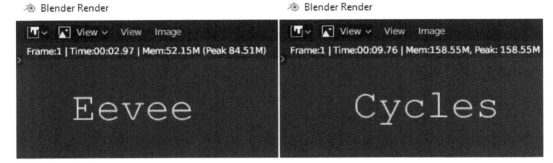

Figure 14.4 – Eevee render time (left), Cycles render time (right)

Because of the significant difference in quality, we will use Cycles to achieve the best results, but you are encouraged to explore both render engines. Next, let's discuss one of the first and most important render properties, sampling. This will allow us to control the quality of our rendered images.

## Sampling

**Sampling** is the process in which a render engine sends multiple virtual light rays from the camera into the scene to calculate how each pixel should appear in the final image. The more light rays are sent, the better the result will be. The number of samples per pixel is thus one of the key parameters that must be defined for a render, and one of the most important factors that contribute to the render time required for an image. Having more samples results in longer render times.

The number of samples can be separately controlled for viewport rendering and for final rendering. Generally, the number of samples for viewport rendering is kept relatively low because it is just a preview, so we do not need the highest quality. For the final render, the number of samples should be kept considerably higher.

The number of samples can be controlled in the **Render Properties** tab, as shown in *Figure 14.5*. By default, the **Viewport** and **Render** samples are set to 1024 and 4096 respectively, but this value can be adjusted according to the purpose.

For example, it may be better to reduce the number of render samples to 128 or 256 for a simple scene or just to get a quick render. It is generally sufficient to render scenes with up to 1,024 samples, which is much lower than the default value.

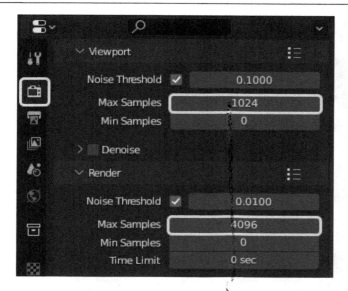

Figure 14.5 – Adjusting the number of samples

It is also recommended to enable denoising, using the checkbox shown in *Figure 14.6*. This will reduce the amount of noise visible in the final render with an automatic post-processing procedure.

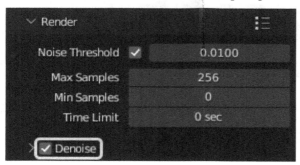

Figure 14.6 – Enabling Denoise

*Figure 14.5* shows a low-sample render with and without denoising. Even with high samples, there will usually still be visible noise, which is why it is always recommended to use a denoiser.

Figure 14.7 – A render without denoising (top), and a render with denoising (bottom)

We now know how to manually control the number of samples in our renders. Next, we will activate background transparency, which will allow us to create custom backgrounds and layer the image in post-processing.

## Adding background transparency

Background transparency is useful for integrating rendered scenes into other images. For example, we can easily add custom backgrounds such as gradients behind images with transparent backgrounds. *Figure 14.8 (left)* shows an example of an image with a transparent background, and *Figure 14.8 (right)* shows the same image combined with a custom gradient background in an image editing program.

Figure 14.8 – Transparent background (left), custom gradient background (right)

To activate background transparency, we must find the **Film** menu in the **Render Properties** tab. Here, we can simply check the **Transparent** box, as shown in *Figure 14.9*.

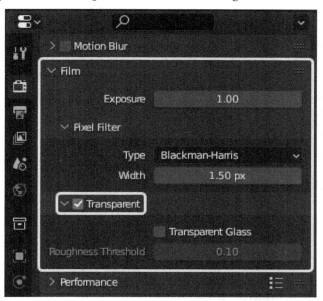

Figure 14.9 – Adding background transparency

Activating transparency will make it so that our rendered image will only contain the objects in the scene, while the background is transparent. This allows us to create custom backgrounds in external image editing programs, or to layer multiple images. *Figure 14.10* shows two renders, one with a visible background (left), and another with a transparent background (right).

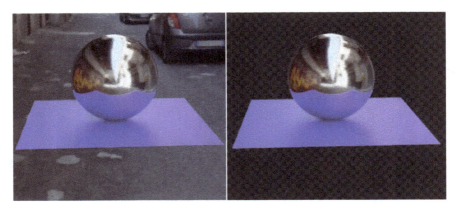

Figure 14.10 – A render with a visible background (left) and a render with a transparent background (right)

> **Note**
> Rendering with a transparent background still allows HDRIs to cast light onto scenes.

Transparent backgrounds also work in rendered viewport shading. We can save a viewport image by opening the **View** menu and clicking on **Viewport Render Image**, as shown in *Figure 14.11*.

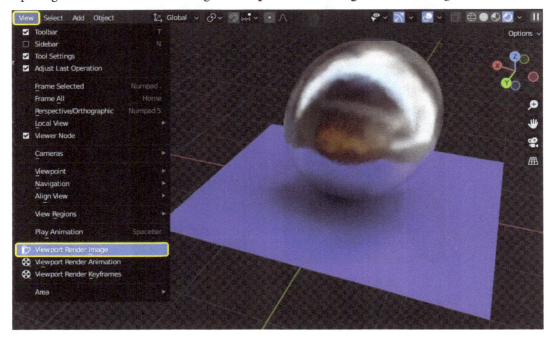

Figure 14.11 – Rendering the viewport image

Rendering the viewport image allows us to keep special features such as the grid floor, axes, wireframes, and selection outlines, but the quality is considerably lower than that of conventionally rendered images. Next, let's dive into exporting images.

## Exporting images and videos

Regardless of the engine you choose to work in, there are many settings that can be configured when exporting images. These settings define the resolution of your image, which keyframes will be rendered, which format you are exporting as, the frame rate used, and more. These settings can be found in the **Output Properties** tab, as shown in *Figure 14.12*.

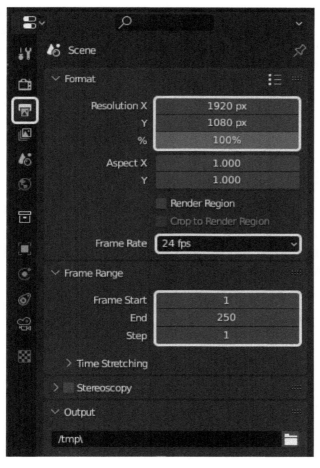

Figure 14.12 – Export settings in the Output Properties tab

Let us look at them in more detail:

- **Resolution**: Firstly, it is important to define the **Resolution** values. By default, it is set to 1920x1080 (full HD). For quick renders or previews, it is recommended to set the resolution to 1280x720 to reduce render time. Naturally, final renders should be created in higher resolutions.

- **Frame Range**: When exporting animations, such as the animation we created in *Chapter 13, Preparing the Camera for Rendering*, it is important to define which frames should be rendered in **Frame Range**. This can also be done in the **Output Properties** tab, as we can see in *Figure 14.12*. By default, Blender will render only the first 250 frames of an animation. Since our animation only lasted for 80 frames, when rendering this animation, the **End** value should be set to 80.

- **Output**: Finally, the **Output** menu is where we define the export settings such as file types, destination files, encoding method, and more. Before exporting an image, we must tell Blender where we want this file to be saved. We can do so using the button highlighted in *Figure 14.13*.

Figure 14.13 – Selecting the destination file

After selecting a destination file, we must choose a file format. By default, the format is set to **PNG**, which also allows us to save transparent images.

For rendering animations, **Fmpeg Video** is the recommended format for animations as it creates the smoothest videos. The file format can be changed in the **File Format** drop-down menu, as shown in *Figure 14.14*. By using different settings, it is also possible to render animations with transparent backgrounds, which can be useful for motion graphics.

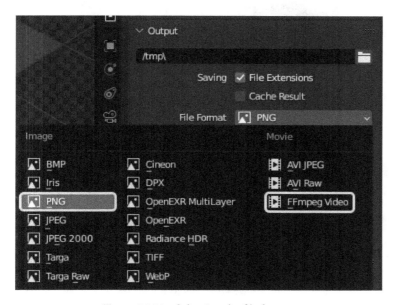

Figure 14.14 – Selecting the file format

When rendering animations in the FFmpeg format, it is recommended to copy the following settings to ensure that your video will produce smooth, good-quality playback, as shown in *Figure 14.15*.

Figure 14.15 – Adjusting the export properties

Once all our output settings are configured, we are ready to render our scene. We can do so by opening the **Render** menu in the top pane of the screen and selecting **Render Image** or **Render Animation**, depending on which output type you have selected.

Figure 14.16 – Rendering an image or animation

When rendering single images, once the render is complete, we must save it manually using the **Image** menu in the top pane of the **Render** window, as shown in *Figure 14.17*.

Figure 14.17 – Saving a rendered image

We can now prepare, configure, and render images and animations using either Cycles or Eevee.

## Summary

In this chapter, we learned how rendering works in Blender, how to configure render properties, and how to correctly export images and animations. You now have all the fundamental skills needed to render images and videos, but you are encouraged to explore more advanced rendering techniques such as path tracing, subsurface scattering, compositing, and render passing. These techniques are useful for specific situations and can help you further improve your artwork.

This is the last step of a project in Blender, and it allows you to present your works outside of Blender and continue with post-processing in an external image editing program. With all the tools, techniques, and concepts learned so far, you are now ready to create your own materials, textures, texture maps, decals, stencils, light scenes, HDRIs, animations, and renders. This allows you to turn any 3D model into a beautiful, finalized artwork in Blender and start building an impressive portfolio.

# Index

# U

**UV mapping  186**
   functioning  186, 187

# V

**Vornoi Texture node  55**

# W

**workspaces  4**

www.packtpub.com

Subscribe to our online digital library for full access to over 7,000 books and videos, as well as industry leading tools to help you plan your personal development and advance your career. For more information, please visit our website.

## Why subscribe?

- Spend less time learning and more time coding with practical eBooks and Videos from over 4,000 industry professionals

- Improve your learning with Skill Plans built especially for you

- Get a free eBook or video every month

- Fully searchable for easy access to vital information

- Copy and paste, print, and bookmark content

Did you know that Packt offers eBook versions of every book published, with PDF and ePub files available? You can upgrade to the eBook version at www.packtpub.com and as a print book customer, you are entitled to a discount on the eBook copy. Get in touch with us at customercare@packtpub.com for more details.

At www.packtpub.com, you can also read a collection of free technical articles, sign up for a range of free newsletters, and receive exclusive discounts and offers on Packt books and eBooks.

# Other Books You May Enjoy

If you enjoyed this book, you may be interested in these other books by Packt:

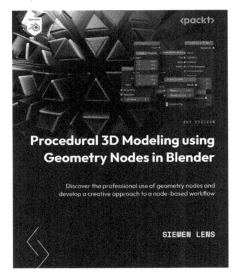

**Procedural 3D Modeling Using Geometry Nodes in Blender**

Siemen Lens

ISBN: 978-1-80461-255-2

- Discover the different node inputs and outputs that geometry nodes have to offer
- Get the hang of the flow of the geometry node system
- Understand the common nodes you'll be using along with their functions in the geometry node editor
- Modify basic mesh primitives using the node system inside Blender
- Scatter and modify objects aligned onto a curve
- Become familiar with the more advanced nodes in the geometry nodes system
- Link geometry and material nodes editors using named attributes
- Implement your new-found knowledge of nodes in real-world projects

**Learn Blender Simulations the Right Way**

Stephen Pearson

ISBN: 978-1-80323-415-1

- Discover what Mantaflow is and how to use it effectively
- Understand domains, flows, and effectors, and why they are important
- Create realistic fire, smoke, and fluid simulations
- Produce satisfying soft and rigid body simulations with ease
- Use the cloth simulation to bring animated fabric to life
- Explore canvas and brush objects in Dynamic Paint to create eye-catching animations

## Packt is searching for authors like you

If you're interested in becoming an author for Packt, please visit authors.packtpub.com and apply today. We have worked with thousands of developers and tech professionals, just like you, to help them share their insight with the global tech community. You can make a general application, apply for a specific hot topic that we are recruiting an author for, or submit your own idea.

## Share Your Thoughts

Now you've finished *Photorealistic Materials and Textures in Blender Cycles*, we'd love to hear your thoughts! Scan the QR code below to go straight to the Amazon review page for this book and share your feedback or leave a review on the site that you purchased it from.

https://packt.link/r/1-805-12963-5

Your review is important to us and the tech community and will help us make sure we're delivering excellent quality content.

# Download a free PDF copy of this book

Thanks for purchasing this book!

Do you like to read on the go but are unable to carry your print books everywhere? Is your eBook purchase not compatible with the device of your choice?

Don't worry, now with every Packt book you get a DRM-free PDF version of that book at no cost.

Read anywhere, any place, on any device. Search, copy, and paste code from your favorite technical books directly into your application.

The perks don't stop there, you can get exclusive access to discounts, newsletters, and great free content in your inbox daily

Follow these simple steps to get the benefits:

1.  Scan the QR code or visit the link below

https://packt.link/free-ebook/9781805129639

2.  Submit your proof of purchase
3.  That's it! We'll send your free PDF and other benefits to your email directly

www.ingramcontent.com/pod-product-compliance
Lightning Source LLC
Chambersburg PA
CBHW080609060326
40690CB00021B/4629